Religion and the Creation
of Race and Ethnicity

RACE, RELIGION, AND ETHNICITY
General Editor: Peter J. Paris

Public Religion and Urban Transformation:
Faith in the City
Edited by Lowell W. Livezey

Down by the Riverside:
Readings in African American Religion
Edited by Larry G. Murphy

New York Glory:
Religions in the City
Edited by Tony Carnes and Anna Karpathakis

Religion and the Creation of Race and Ethnicity
An Introduction
Edited by Craig R. Prentiss

Religion and the Creation of Race and Ethnicity

An Introduction

EDITED BY

Craig R. Prentiss

New York University Press

NEW YORK AND LONDON

NEW YORK UNIVERSITY PRESS
New York and London

Library of Congress Cataloging-in-Publication Data

Religion and the creation of race and ethnicity : an introduction /
edited by Craig R. Prentiss.
p. cm. — (Religion, race, and ethnicity)
Includes bibliographical references.
ISBN 0-8147-6700-1 (cloth : alk. paper) — ISBN 0-8147-6701-X (pbk. : alk. paper)
1. Ethnicity—Religious aspects.   I. Prentiss, Craig R.   II. Series.
BL65.E75 R47 2003
291.1'78348—dc21   2002152479

New York University Press books are printed on acid-free paper,
and their binding materials are chosen for strength and durability.

Manufactured in the United States of America
10 9 8 7 6 5 4 3 2 1

To Benjamin

Contents

Acknowledgments

This book is intended to help fill what I believe was a significant gap in the scholarship on the interplay among religion, race, and ethnicity. While much good work had been done on theories of racial and ethnic identity, and to a lesser extent on the role of religion in the formation of those identities, the vast majority of it had been written for graduate students and professional scholars in a language that was not accessible to most eighteen-year-old college students. The social construction of race and ethnicity, not to mention the role of religious mythology in that construction, struck me as something that undergraduates needed to learn. As such, this book was conceived with the intention of presenting a cross-cultural introduction to this topic with essays as free from academic jargon as possible. I think this book succeeds in helping to fill this gap.

First and foremost, thanks for this anthology must go to the contributors who took the time to write original essays addressing our topic. I am confident that the reader will agree that the results of their efforts are impressive. The one hundred or so students who have participated in my "Religion, Ethnicity and Race" course over the past three years have been essential in helping me conceive of this project. A special thanks to John Nelson and Jean Molesky-Poz for pulling me through a small crisis, and to Nimachia Hernandez and Doug Cowan for their heroic efforts in the late innings. Renee McGautha and my assistant, Trayce Cox, contributed greatly to the ultimate success of this collection. Thanks also to Kate Nicolai and Michael McDonald who critiqued the project at its earliest stage. My gratitude extends to the library staff and my department at Rockhurst University, especially Bill Stancil, who has been a constant source of good editing and good advice. Dan Martin and Pete Bicak's editing and suggestions were also quite helpful. A summer grant from

Rockhurst freed up precious time to put this book together. The anonymous readers of my proposal made excellent suggestions that have improved this anthology immensely. I will always be grateful to New York University Press, especially Jennifer Hammer and Peter Paris, for seeing the value of this project and taking a chance on me in this early stage of my career. Were it not for the encouragement of Russell McCutcheon, this book might never have come to fruition, and his advice throughout was invaluable. My mother and father, as well as my sister, Laura, were subjected to frequent frustrated rantings as it was all coming together, and they listened patiently. Finally, thanks to Shana who keeps me sane, and Ben who reminds me daily what a lucky person I am.

Introduction

Craig R. Prentiss

The essays in this anthology are intended to provide students, scholars, and anyone interested in our topic with an introduction to the role that religion has played in the creation and shaping of those categories called "races" and "ethnicities." While the interplay between religion, race, and ethnicity is not a new area of study, this collection is distinctive in its approach to the field. By far, the most common way of dealing with this topic is to explore the manner in which particular "racial" and "ethnic" communities approach religion. Scholars and teachers have tended to focus, for instance, on how "African American" subcultures have adopted, adapted, and expressed various strands of Christianity, or on understanding how Japanese or Mexicans have lived "religiously." And with good reason, since there is much to say about these topics and others like them. The academic study of religion is, after all, the study of human expression that is shaped by the particular social and temporal status of those giving life to distinctive religious traditions. The essays in this book, however, are primarily concerned with a different question: How has religion played a role in making and preserving those very social boundaries that we call "races" and "ethnicities"? So, among the questions addressed in these pages are: What part did religion have in the making of "blackness" and "whiteness"? To what extent was Japanese or Mexican identity itself the product of religious life?

Underlying these questions is the presumption that human beings are constantly engaged in making sense of their world in the context of their social environment. The way we order our lives, categorize the things we encounter daily, and make judgments about those categories all take place in the field of our encounters with other human beings. To a great extent, our self-identities, our values, and our manner of giving meaning to experiences are developed in relationship to others. Our parents, our friends, our government and religious leaders, journalists, teachers, media personalities, and countless other people have helped to make each of us who we are by exposing us to their own distinctive worldviews. This is not to say that we are *only* products of our environment, but it would be foolish to deny that we are shaped in some measure by our encounters with other human beings. The fruits of those social encounters, including shared cultural biases, shared rituals, shared value systems, shared tastes, and shared approaches to the problems of everyday life are in the continuous process of being constructed as we adapt to new circumstances. Scholars refer to these processes as "social construction." While debates over "nature versus nurture" will continue to rage, nearly all can agree that we inherit a great deal through our interaction with other individuals. Among those conceptions that are developed and shaped through social encounter are racial and ethnic categories.

We are very aware that the social construction of racial and ethnic categories involves much more than the mythologies and rituals of religious traditions. In many, if not all cases, these social boundaries grew out of profoundly complex economic, political, technological, and educational circumstances. But among those circumstances, religion has often been a vital factor, and nearly all the essays included here make this claim. At the very least, this book helps make the case that any account of the social construction of race and ethnicity will be incomplete if it fails to consider the influence of religious traditions and narratives.

For the student who is new to this area of study, one of the most difficult challenges is likely to be coming to terms with the idea that "racial" and "ethnic" categories are products of the human imagination. In countries like the United States of America, where talk of race and ethnicity is an ever-present element of public dialogue, this claim seems counterintuitive. "What do you mean that 'races' aren't real?" is a common response to this claim. "After all, there's clearly a difference in the way blacks and whites are treated. Americans even fought a Civil War that liberated one class of people, blacks, from enslavement to another class of people, whites. So how can you tell me that this is just a part of my imagination?"

Answering these questions requires that we make an important distinction: while races and ethnicities are not "real" biologically or divinely ordained categories, they are, in fact, social and political realities. In other words, these categories produce real effects in the world. One's racial or ethnic classification can impact that person's access to material, intellectual, and social resources. To parrot the title from a recent work of the prominent African American studies scholar, Cornel West, "race matters" (and so does ethnicity). They matter because our lives are impacted by our own perceptions and the perceptions of others.

One way to make sense of the distinction between an imagined category and a real effect comes from a sports analogy I have heard some people use. Are "touchdowns," "home-runs," and "goals" real? In other words, do these things exist in nature? The answer, of course, is no. Human beings created the games that employ "touchdowns," "home-runs," and "goals." These things are products of our imagination, our labor, and our creativity. Yet, at the same time, these three things *are* real in the sense that they produce real effects. People are paid, sometimes millions of dollars, to make "touchdowns" and score "goals." In fact, for that small number of people we call professional athletes, failure to engage in these activities that the human mind has created can sometimes lead to their being out of work, suffering humiliation, and having drastically altered lives. So while we can all acknowledge that "touchdowns," "home-runs," and "goals" are only the products of human creativity—not even the *replication* of something that does occur in nature—it is clear that these three categories of behavior make a difference in the lives of some of us.

Though racial and ethnic categories produce real effects, they do not spring from a divine cookie cutter but rather from the complex interplay of human consciousness. Ethnic or racial categories have not been in existence from the beginning of time, and all have undergone changes as to how they have been conceived, as most of these essays will show. Even a cursory overview of the history of the U.S. Census since 1790 illustrates that the standards for racial classification have changed with nearly every decade. Classifications that have long since lost their social import in this country such as "mulatto," "quadroon," and "octoroon" began being used in the second half of the 1800s and continued to appear on census forms until the end of that century ("mulatto" was used through the 1920 census).[1] The changes in census categories reflected cultural currents that shaped the way racial and ethnic divisions were conceived. Furthermore, each reconception served some political purpose, just as all ways of identifying and articulating social boundaries serve purposes and reflect particular ideological perspectives (for a more thorough discussion of "ideology," see Eddie Glaude, Jr.'s essay). Indeed, it should not escape our notice that this very book has been written and prepared during an age of rapid globalization, unprecedented technological advances facilitating cross-cultural communication, genomic discovery, and profound transformations in the workforce, all of which has, in turn, accelerated awareness of and attention to pluralism and diversity.

Defining Terms

In order to prepare the reader to get the most out of these essays, it is necessary that we define a few key terms used throughout this book. This is especially true for the terms "myth," "race," and "ethnicity," because each of the words has been subject to a variety of understandings. Let's begin by looking at the term "myth." Stories become myths in the context of a social group. It's important to point out that social groupings can develop through the combination of a potentially infinite number of circumstances. A professor at the University of Chicago, Bruce Lincoln— who was particularly influential to me as I formulated this project—has emphasized the importance of *discourse* in the creation of social groups.[2] Discourse, a term commonly understood to mean simply "talking," can also be defined as the use of both spoken and symbolic communication to create meaning and produce effects. Discourse is something we all engage in. We can see discourse in pronounced spoken ways, such as in the form of political speeches or church sermons, or in more subtle and symbolic ways, such as in the use of mood lighting and soft music on a date, or in the kinds of clothes we wear (for a good example of the symbolic communication of clothing, see Joel Martin's essay). In all cases, specific effects are the intended outcome, whether it be promoting policy, getting elected, promoting a faith, communicating the desire for intimacy, or expressing one's social status, comfort level, and style.

There are many forms of discourse, and the form that these essays explore most thoroughly is called *myth*. Few terms in the field of religious studies are saddled with more baggage than the word "myth." Dating all the way back to Plato, "myth" has been used to distinguish false stories from true ones. In its popular usage today, the word "myth" is frequently associated with lies and uninformed beliefs. As such, labeling a particular story a myth is often understood as a way of discounting its legitimacy or value.

In the field of religious studies, "myth" has also been a contested term, but only rarely has it been used synonymously with falsehood. For a time, scholars tended to assign the term "myth" only to those stories that told of miraculous events and superhuman beings. Later, myths were thought of as stories that revealed the deepest truths of a particular culture, while dressing those truths up in a fantastic narrative framework.[3] But some scholars have noted the problems that come with defining a myth by the characteristics of a narrative (which forces us to make arbitrary distinctions between what counts as "myth" and what does not), or by a narrative's expression of profound truths (which forces us to divine what those supposed "truths" are). An alternative to focusing upon the details of the narrative itself is to instead focus upon the way the narrative is used by a community.

This anthology utilizes a working definition of myth developed by Bruce Lincoln in his 1989 study, *Discourse and the Construction of Society: Comparative Studies of Myth, Ritual, and Classification* (Oxford University Press, 1989). With an emphasis upon the way stories are used in society, we are defining as myth a narrative that not only claims truth for itself but is also seen by a community as credible and authoritative. To hold that a narrative is credible means to understand it as being true, either literally, as is often the case, or in some sense, metaphorically. When a community sees a story as authoritative, the story is understood as setting a paradigm for human behavior. In other words, human beings point to the story to authorize (give authority to) their preferences, to justify or re-create their social patterns, or to guide their decision making.[4] So, according to this definition, stories achieve the status of myth among a given people by the way they are *used*. These stories bind groups of people, providing common reference points from which they may negotiate various facets of their lives. It's worth noting that this kind of negotiation becomes more complicated when it is engaged by two or more individuals who do not share the same myths (i.e., do not accept the credibility and authority of the same stories).

Defining terms is never an innocent task. As essays in this volume by Nimachia Hernandez and Azzam Tamimi illustrate, imposing the term "myth," however defined, from outside of a community as a way to talk about the narratives that bind that community can cause community members significant discomfort and may even be seen as offensive or, at the very least, misguided. The working definition of myth that we are using for this book is the fruit of largely Western assumptions, growing out of the "post-Enlightenment" era and arising from the social sciences, which have sought to describe and explain human behavior dispassionately, analytically, and with what we might call a "critical distance." While there is no need to apologize for this attempt, there is every need to make the reader aware of its problematic nature.

The other key terms in this book, "race" and "ethnicity," are no less complicated than "myth." In fact, scholars have been arguing for decades regarding the way these terms fit together. Many have even suggested scrapping the word "race" from our vocabulary entirely. Ironically, the scholarly field in which the term "race" had been most vital from its beginnings, anthropology, has seen its virtual elimination as a category of analysis from the pages of its books and articles since the early 1970s.[5] In the biological sciences, most scholars have long recognized that the classifications that are popularly referred to as "races" are rendered almost meaningless in light of genetic discoveries relating to human DNA. Thus, these days we often hear geneticists saying "race is not a *scientific* category, it's a cultural one." This is not to say that certain groups, segregated over time, do not come to share some genetic traits. But those genetic traits overlap very loosely (at best) with our culturally defined social boundaries, and, moreover, these variations represent only a tiny fraction of our total genetic makeup, the rest of which is shared by all humans. A genetically unique individual is created with the birth of each new person. There is not a "black" gene, a "white" gene, or an "Asian" gene, and the genetic variation between any two people classified as "white," or any two people classified as "black," may be just as great or greater than the variation between a "white" and a "black" person.[6]

The changes taking place in the terminology of anthropologists and biologists stem from the realization that where once "races" were imagined to be *natural* categories that distinguished groups of human beings, they are instead seen by an increasing number of people as the fictive products of human imagination. In fact, the use of the term "ethnicity" itself sprung from discomfort with the term "race." Not surprisingly, the word "race" began to take on a negative connotation when it became associated with the ideology of fascism during World War II. The term "ethnicity" was first used in a 1941 sociological study undertaken by two scholars, W. Lloyd Warner and Paul S. Lunt. "Ethnicity" served Warner and Lunt as an alternative to "race" in their attempt to describe social groups that came from different national backgrounds but shared cultural similarities.[7] The trend has continued, and the popularity of the term "ethnicity" seems to grow as the popularity of the term "race" declines (for more on the etymology of the term "ethnicity," see Azzam Tamimi's essay).

Since it is precisely this process of manufacturing "races" and "ethnicities" through the complexities of social imagining that this book seeks to address, it was vital that the authors of these chapters be able to use either term when necessary. Like myth, we also have a working definition for both race and ethnicity. We are defining a *race* as a social grouping or form of peoplehood that is marked by traits that are perceived to be biologically inherited. *Ethnicity*, in turn, is defined as a social grouping or form of peoplehood that is marked by traits that are perceived to be culturally inherited. We are using these definitions not because they conform to static social barriers that exist in nature but because they conform largely to the way that these terms have been commonly understood in the second half of the twentieth century and up to the present. Thus, to try and discuss, say, the development of categories like "blackness" and "whiteness" as they have occurred in an American context without using the term "race" with its biological connotations would be difficult if not impossible. In this format and for these purposes, at least, "race" remains a valuable term.

What the contributions to this anthology are likely to illustrate to the interested reader is that, while some maintain that race and ethnicity refer to two clearly distinguishable categories, both categories are ultimately the fruit of the same vine: the apparent tendency of human beings to mark boundaries that distinguish one individual from another. Admittedly, the consequences to the individual of being marked as belonging to a "race" due to physical features that societies become conditioned to identify are different from the consequences to an individual of being marked by cultural traits, such as language, diet, dress, or custom, since the latter can (in theory) be modified, while the former (presumably) cannot. Yet the process of assigning these markers that distinguish people is not, I would argue, fundamentally different in either case. After all, we could list so many differences between *any* two people that they would be impossible to count (as easily as we could list similarities). So, why do we impart significance to one difference or set of differences and not to another? This is the $64,000 question. Both ethnic and racial categories grow out of complex social dynamics taking place often over substantial periods of time, and both are shaped by particular circumstances that make the creation of a social boundary seem "reasonable" and sometimes "natural" to a significant portion of the population in question. In many cases, myths that have developed within religious traditions have played a key role in "naturalizing" those boundaries.

The Essays

Each of the contributors to this anthology responds to four questions in his or her chapter:

1. What is the "racial" or "ethnic" category/boundary being created? (There may be more than one, of course, since whenever we create an identity for any social group, that identity is set off as being distinctive from those who are not included in that group—hence, the creation of another social group on the "outside." In the American context, no more vivid example of this dynamic can be seen than the symbiotic relationship between the categories of "whiteness" and "blackness," for each category has served to define the other).

2. What mythological resources are being used to invoke these boundaries? Because the focus of this volume is the role of myth in the context of various religious traditions, this question is at the core of each chapter, as our authors grapple with myth's role in forming identity.

3. What are the sociohistorical circumstances that make these identity boundaries possible? In other words, what allowed for or caused a given myth to resonate with a people at one point in time and perhaps not at another?

4. Finally, how have the myths in question been contested and reappropriated over time to challenge boundaries or consolidate boundaries?

With this final question, it is vital that the reader be conscious of the fact that just as racial and ethnic identities are continuously in the process of change, so too is the manner in which myths are used. Myths are not static, perennial realities in the life of a community. While textual myths may remain unchanged in their written form, the way that words are understood, interpreted, and valued is in constant flux. These variations are conditioned by ever-changing circumstances that demand new readings of these binding cultural narratives if communities are to be able to respond to changes while still maintaining the centrality of their mythologies. Sometimes mythic narratives give way to new narratives better suited to making sense of a new world, while at other times old narratives are given dramatically new readings, readings that focus upon reinterpretation or upon highlighting certain elements at the expense of devaluing others. And, needless to say, these transformations usually play out in the form of conflict as a range of players within a community bound by a shared myth contest one another's readings. In fact, one's access to power, resources, status, and authority in a society often depends upon whose reading of a myth holds sway in the life of a community.

Our anthology begins with an essay by Paul Harvey, who guides us through a range of Euro-American uses for the Judeo-Christian mythology in the effort to distinguish "blackness" from "whiteness." In making this distinction, figures throughout American history assured the privileged status of "whiteness" by employing biblical stories, especially the narrative of the curse of Ham's children, to authorize and explain social boundaries marked by color schemes. If one were to doubt the range of uses to which myths can be put, Eddie Glaude Jr.'s essay explores how African Americans employed the Bible, in some cases the very same stories noted by Harvey, for very different purposes than Euro-Americans had done. While so many Euro-Americans had read the Bible as a prooftext for enforcing "black" subjugation, Glaude describes many ways that scripture was used to uplift African Americans, make sense of their sufferings, and point them toward a shared destiny.

In a close reading of the conversions of a Cherokee woman and man to Christianity at a mission school in Tennessee during the early nineteenth century, Joel Martin uncovers the extent to which Western cultural elements and preconceptions were inextricably attached to conversion in the minds of missionaries. Focusing primarily upon differences in dress (a dress code, for the Euro-Americans, shaped by their reading of Christian scripture), Martin illustrates the "ambivalent" embrace of new Native American converts by their "white" siblings-in-Christ, an embrace tempered by dynamics of racial hierarchy. At the heart of Native American identity are stories, argues Nimachia Hernandez. The stories of indigenous peoples employ the land and the cosmos to situate not only their identity, but knowledge itself. Hernandez contends that the land is inseparable from Native American self-conceptions, and illustrates the damage done to those conceptions when people are forcibly removed from that land.

Jacob Neusner provides us with an overview of the complicated constructions of "Jewishness" as both a religious and an ethnic identification. Neusner deftly develops the argument that Jewish religiosity and ethnicity are shaped by their own distinct narratives. Aminah Beverly McCloud explains the myth of Yakub and its role in the Nation of Islam's conception of "blackness." Like Glaude's earlier essay, McCloud tracks the manner in which socially marginalized African Americans tap the wellsprings of religious mythology in the process of resurrecting pride and purpose in the formation of "black" identity.

The Christian Identity movement, as investigated by Douglas E. Cowan, presents us with a classic case of the impact of myth upon the formation of racial categories, in this case, "whiteness." Guided by their reading of the Bible—a reading that blends the philo-Semitic British Israelist movement and the antiSemitic worldview of the Ku Klux Klan, Nazis, and other supremacist organizations—Identity Christians designate "the white race" as God's chosen people. Cowan describes the impact that this rendering of "whiteness" has had on Identity adherents as the movement has developed in the United States and Canada. My own essay explores the mythic resources of the Church of Jesus Christ of Latter-day Saints, more commonly known as the Mormons. I describe the manner that sacred Mormon texts have given shape to the way Native Americans and "blacks" have been understood in this fast-growing subculture.

Few examples of religion's role in shaping identity are as vivid as Our Lady of Guadalupe and her importance to the creation of Mexican identity. Roberto S. Goizueta analyzes the mythic narrative and assesses its impact on what it has meant to identify oneself as "Mexican." With our next chapter, we cross the Pacific as John K. Nelson explains the role of myths connected to the deities celebrated in the shrines and festivals that make up the Japanese institution of "Shinto," an institution that has become almost inseparable from Japanese identity. In his lively essay, we see that Shinto is infused in Japanese daily life at even the most mundane levels and gives shape to the Japanese self-conception.

Azzam Tamimi makes clear that while an "Arab" ethnic identity preexisted the rise of Islam in the seventh century, the teachings of Islam were essential in reshaping that identity by replacing ancient tribal and familial frames of reference with a divine narrative. Laurie Patton gives several examples of Hindu myths that have been central to the cultivation of social boundaries. Patton highlights the openness to multiple readings in each of these narratives and the importance of those disparate readings for the Indian social order.

Myths, as we have said, are invoked for distinctive purposes to suit particular circumstances, and Chirevo V. Kwenda's examination of Shona identity in modern Zimbabwe illustrates this claim remarkably well. The convergence of indigenous African religious traditions coupled with the consequences of the European Christian missionary movement in Africa gave rise to a stream of narrative currents that proved valuable in Zimbabwe's struggle for independence from the British and the cultivation of a cohesive national identity. Our anthology concludes with a devastating portrait by Michael A. Sells of the central role that religious narratives played in manufacturing ethnic divisions in Bosnia-Herzegovina. Sells describes this dark cloud in our most recent history by focusing on the sacred myths that served to anchor competing ethnic imaginations and the forces that gave rise to attempts at wholesale ethnic slaughter.

While these essays reflect a cross-cultural introduction to the role of religious myth in the formation of racial and ethnic identities, it is by no means comprehensive. There are countless other stories to tell, not to mention other ways to tell the stories that appear in this volume. By including suggestions for further reading at the end of each chapter, we hope that students will pursue more specialized study into the specific areas that are of interest to them. Furthermore, we encourage our readers to be attuned to the continuous, but often subtle, transformations in the manner that social boundaries are cast. How might technological advancements and improved means of communication reshape the way social boundaries are understood? Will increased trade relations cultivate new group identities? What role will discoveries in human genetics play in breaking down old barriers or building up new ones? These are just a few of the questions worth asking about the future of racial and ethnic imagination. We are always in the process of making sense of our world, and we continue to tap into mythic resources to help us do so. As our world changes, the way that we interpret our myths changes and can sometimes lead to our taking new narratives and bringing them to the status of myth. It is our hope that these essays enable students and other interested readers to draw distinctions more sharply, critique ideologies more effectively, and engage in self-reflection more deeply.

NOTES

1. For more, see Associated Press article, "Race Question Vexed Census Takers through History," (March 27, 2001).

2. Bruce Lincoln, *Discourse and the Construction of Society: Comparative Studies of Myth, Ritual, and Classification* (New York: Oxford University Press, 1989), 3.

3. For an excellent overview of the many ways in which the term "myth" has been understood, see Russell T. McCutcheon, "Myth," *Guide to the Study of Religion*, Willi Braun, and Russell T. McCutcheon, editors (New York: Cassell, 2000), 190–208.

4. This definition paraphrases Lincoln's own in, *Discourse and the Construction of Society*, 24–26.

5. Audrey Smedley, *Race in North America: Origin and Evolution of a Worldview* (Boulder: Westview Press, 1993), 2; Smedley cites a study by Alice Littlefield, Leonard Lieberman, and Larry Reynolds, "Redefining Race: The Potential Demise of a Concept in Physical Anthropology," *Current Anthropology* 23/6 (1982): 641–656.

6. For two popular treatments of genetics, race, and current attitudes among scientists, see Natalie Angier, "Do Races Differ?: Not Really, DNA Shows," *New York Times* (August 22, 2000), and Steve Olson, "The Genetic Archaeology of Race," *Atlantic Monthly* 287 (April 2001).

7. Werner Sollors, "Foreword: Theories of American Ethnicity," in *Theories of Ethnicity: A Classical Reader*, Werner Sollors, editor (New York: NYU Press, 1996), citing W. Lloyd Warner, and Paul S. Lunt, *The Social Life of a Modern Community* (New Haven: Yale University Press, 1941).

SUGGESTIONS FOR FURTHER READING

Davis, F. James. *Who is Black? One Nation's Definition*. University Park: Pennsylvania State University Press, 1991.

Jacobson, Matthew Frye. *Whiteness of a Different Color: European Immigrants and the Alchemy of Race*. Cambridge: Harvard University Press, 1999.

Smedley, Audrey. *Race in North America: The Origin and Evolution of a Worldview*. Boulder: Westview Press, 1993.

Theories of Ethnicity: A Classical Reader, Werner Sollors, editor. New York: NYU Press, 1996.

Chapter 1

"A Servant of Servants Shall He Be"
The Construction of Race in American Religious Mythologies

Paul Harvey

Genesis 9:18–27: 18 And the sons of Noah, that went forth of the ark, were Shem, and Ham, and Japheth; and Ham is the father of Canaan. 19 These are the three sons of Noah: and of them was the whole earth overspread. 20 And Noah began to be a husbandman, and he planted a vineyard. 21 And he drank of the wine, and was drunken; and he was uncovered within his tent. 22 And Ham, the father of Canaan, saw the nakedness of his father, and told his two brethren without. 23 And Shem and Japheth took a garment, and laid it upon both their shoulders, and went backward, and covered the nakedness of their father; and their faces were backward, and they saw not their father's nakedness. 24 And Noah awoke from his wine, and knew what his younger son had done unto him. 25 And he said, "Cursed be Canaan; a servant of servants shall he be unto his brethren." 26 And he said, Blessed be the Lord God of Shem; and Canaan shall be his servant. 27 God shall enlarge Japheth, and he shall dwell in the tents of Shem; and Canaan shall be his servant.

There are no white or black people as such. The specific ways in which we understand the terms "white people" and "black people" have some roots in antiquity but, as full–blown categories, they are relatively recent inventions. Once the categories of whiteness and blackness emerged in the modern world, however, they took on lives of their own, so much so that "race" became deeply inscribed in Western thought, permeating its religious beliefs, fables, and mythologies. This chapter grapples with the complicated question of how Christianity in America has mythically grounded (and frequently regrounded and revised) modern notions of race.

A complex of historical factors (such as the gigantic global enterprise of the African slave trade) and mythic groundings (such as stories from the Old Testament) influenced the construction of modern racial categories. Christianity was hardly the sole or even primary force in this process. Yet religious myth, originating from interpretations of biblical stories as well as speculations about God's Providence, played an important role in the formation, revision, and reconstruction of racial categories in the modern world. Christianity necessarily was central to the process of *racializing* peoples—to imposing categories of racial hierarchies upon groups of humanity or other societies. But as we shall see, biblical passages were powerful but ambiguous, and arguments about God's Providence in the slave trade and slavery were contentious.

The slave trade was essential to the creation of the modern international capitalist system. Products grown through slave labor—especially sugar, tobacco, and (much later) cotton—enriched the Europeans who colonized the New World, adding to the demand for more settlements, more produce, more laborers, and more profits. African slave labor provided the final and indispensable component needed for the building of the Americas. Slavery was a common feature of human societies since ancient times, one used widely for everything from establishing status ranking to forcing others to perform undesirable labor. Colonists in the Americas hungered for laborers, and slavery was well adapted to meet that need.

But the slave trade also took off during a great age of religious ferment and expansion following the Protestant reformation (and Catholic counterreformation). Thus, while the trade was fundamentally economic, the European participants sought some religious sanction for what was obviously a coercive and brutal activity.

Judeo-Christian stories were not necessarily, immediately, or inherently amenable to providing a religious basis for modern racial slavery. The Bible was silent, for example, on the specific meaning of white Europeans forcibly transporting black Africans to colonies for the purpose of ceaseless labor for European gain. The very modernity of such a mind–boggling international enterprise—with its capitalist support team of a ship–building industry, insurance against the ravages of the sea and slave revolts, venture capitalists to raise the massive funds needed for the voyages, staple crops like sugar and tobacco so in demand in Europe that they could be profitably traded for manufactured goods and luxuries— clearly extended far beyond the tightly circumscribed biblical world. Biblical characters lived in an ancient Semitic, Mediterranean, and North African world, one in which modern understandings of "white" and "black" people would have been meaningless.

Once slavery took root in the Americas, it was easy enough for religious authorities simply to decree that if slavery existed, God must have a reason for it—and that reason must be in the Bible. But because slavery in the Americas was specifically a *racial* form of bondage (in contrast to traditional forms of slavery found throughout the world, which were not "racial" in the modern sense, although they were sometimes "ethnic"), the religious justification of slavery would have to clarify God's providence particularly in having one race of people enslave another. In this way, Euro-Americans worked out some of the meanings of "race" itself in the modern sense. They began to define what constituted "whiteness" and "blackness," categories that would long outlive slavery itself.

Colonial and Early National Era (1600–1800): The "Heathenism" Debate

Early colonizers in the Americas faced first the question of whether Christianity would apply to black slaves at all. The answer required, in part, deciding on whether Africans and African Americans were fully human—a debate that raged for several centuries, and indeed continued on into the post–Civil War era of scientific racism. If only Christians were truly human—and Christians were white—then where did that leave Negroes? English and Anglo–American theologians grappled with the problem. Was there a separate category, apart from "man," into which blackness could be fit? As one early commentator put it, Negroes were "a people of beastly living, without a God, lawe, religion, or commonwealth."[1] Heathenism thus was inextricable from barbarism and blackness, from being a non-Christian. The Virginia House of Burgesses, in 1699, noted that "the negroes born in this country are generally baptized and brought up in the Christian religion; but for negroes imported hither, the gross bestiality and rudeness of their manners, the variety and strangeness of their languages, and the weakness and shallowness of their minds, render it in a manner impossible to make any progress in their conversion." The English Christians in particular, it seemed, were relatively indifferent to Christian duty: "Most men are well satisfied without the least thoughts of using their authority and endeavors to promote the good of the souls of those poor wretches," one critic exclaimed.[2]

But at least in part, this indifference might have come about because so many white settlers remained unconvinced about whether blackness ultimately was compatible with the state of being Christian. For many, blackness conjured images of savagery even in the practice of religion itself. The Reverend Morgan Goodwin, who ministered in seventeenth-century Virginia, charged that "nothing is more barbarous and contrary to Christianity, than their ... *Idolatrous Dances*, and *Revels*."[3] Other early-day Anglo–American commentators on blackness simply threw up their hands at the inadequacy of explanations for black skin color, for which they could find no clear biblical explanation but which they nevertheless assumed must signify inferiority. "We must wholly refer it to God's peculiar will and ordinance," wrote one Englishmen, invoking exactly the same evasion generally employed to "explain" why a good God allowed evil and unjustified suffering.[4]

As some slaves converted to Christianity, however, reality once again confuted ideology and theology. Anglo–Americans faced this question: Would baptism require freedom? That is, did baptism into the Christian religion make people *white*? The early advocates of slave Christianization, accordingly, had to dissociate Christianity from whiteness—from freedom—precisely for the purpose of defining "blackness" as a state of perpetual servitude continuing beyond one's potential baptism into the Christian faith, and indeed beyond one's own life into the lives of one's children, grandchildren, to perpetuity. In 1664, the Maryland legislature worked out a law "obliging negroes to serve *durante vita* [for the duration of a lifetime]. . . for the prevencion of the damage Masters of such Slaves must susteyne by such Slaves pretending to be Christ[e]ned." Virginia's statute held out the hope "that diverse masters, freed from this doubt, may more carefully endeavor the propagation of Christianity" among slaves, but this was a stretch, given the relative indifference of many planters to Christianity.[5]

In the northern colonies, Cotton Mather, the great and prolifically published Puritan minister of the late seventeenth and early eighteenth centuries, argued for the humanity of the slave and the Negro in intensively biblical tracts such as *The Negro Christianized*. Christian slaves, he said, would know "that it is GOD who has caused them to be *Servants*, and that they serve JESUS CHRIST, while they are at work for their Masters." "Show yourselves Men," Mather wrote, "and let *Rational Arguments* have their Force upon you, to make you treat, not as *Bruits*, but as *Men*, those Rational Creatures whom God has made your *Servants*."[6]

Mather's exhortations, part of a familiar litany of arguments in favor of Christianizing the slaves, met vigorous refutation among a number of northern ministerial writings in the eighteenth century. John Saffin, a Massachusetts jurist in the early eighteenth century and a slaveholder, enunciated an argument soon to be familiar in pro-slavery circles. The Bible sanctioned slavery, he insisted. The great patriarch Abraham owned slaves, so "our Imitation of him in this his Moral Action" was warranted, for "any lawful Captives of Other Heathen Nations may be made Bond men," even if Christians could not buy and sell one another. Beyond that, God had "set different Orders and Degrees of Men in the World," including some the Divine had made "to be born Slaves, and so to remain during their lives." At the same time, and somewhat contradictorily, Saffin also articulated another point dear to the heart of pro-slavery theorists: that "it is no Evil thing to bring them [Africans] out of their own Heathenish Country, [to] where they may have the knowledge of the One True God, be Converted and Eternally saved." Saffin even composed his own piece of wretched doggerel on "the Negroes Character":

> Cowardly and Cruel are those *Blacks* Innate,
> Prone to Revenge, Imp of inveterate hate.
> He that exasperates them, soon espies
> Mischief and Murder in their very eyes.
> Libidinous, Deceitful, False and Rude,
> The Spume Issue of Ingratitude.[7]

Well before the full rise of pro-slavery thought in the mid–nineteenth-century South, then, pro-slavery ideologues in the North fleshed out many of the themes that would define the American defense of slavery and solidify the category of blackness. One popular argument was that people were indeed created by God to stay in varying degrees of freedom or subjection, and that for some to enjoy full liberty, others would have to be servants; this best served the happiness of the whole. This traditional conservative stance was a defense of social hierarchy, not especially related to racial considerations. But most expositions of this sort followed up with a defense of racial bondage in particular, explications of why the enslavement of black people contributed to God's plan for the Americas. The African slave, wrote one Massachusetts conservative, was already enslaved to "the tyrannizing power of lust and passion" (the image of overpowering sexuality already being a standard image associated with blackness), and thus "his removal to America is to be esteemed a favor," for it brought Africans "from the state of brutality, wretchedness, and misery . . . to this land of light, humanity, and Christian knowledge."[8]

Still, the ambiguity of slave Christianization remained troubling. For, if it was in the nature of the "black" to be subject to such "tyrannizing power," then how could it be safe for domesticated and pure white Christians to subject themselves to such a menace? And if the black was born with that nature, was he human? If blackness was (by definition) unfreedom, and Christianity was (by natural law) freedom, then how could the two be commingled? Christianity and whiteness were both states of freedom, making it easy for many to essentially equate the two: white = free and Christian; black/Indian/other = unfree and un-Christian. Would not the ultimate freedom promised by Christianity infect the minds of the not-free, such that they would begin to question their status, or to doubt the validity of Christianity?

A Swedish traveler in the North American colonies noted how masters feared that Christianity would incite feelings of freedom and equality among slaves:

> There are even some, who would be very ill pleased at, and would by all means hinder their negroes from being instructed in the doctrines of Christianity; to this they are partly led by the conceit of its being shameful, to have a spiritual brother or sister among so despicable a people; partly by thinking that they should not be able to keep their negroes so meanly afterwards; and partly through fear of the negroes growing too proud, on seeing themselves upon a level with their masters in religious matters.[9]

For many Christians, whiteness simply became woven into the very fabric of Christianity itself.

Yet the inescapable fact remained that white Christians somehow had to fit black people into God's Providence. Passages from the Old Testament, especially Genesis 9:18–27 (which outlined the curse on Canaan, son of Ham, who had originally espied Noah's naked drunkenness)—

once exegeted "properly"—provided at least a start at a religiomythical grounding for modern racial meanings, and a long–lived one. The passage was still cited in segregationist literature of the 1950s, and even today remains a hot topic of discussion on Internet sites with amateur biblical interpreters squaring off against one another. According to the historian Winthrop Jordan, the "curse" on Canaan, son of Ham—with Ham as a figure considered to represent black people, Shem standing in variously sometimes for Indians, other times for Jews, and Japheth supposedly being the progenitor of white people—first arose as a mode of biblical interpretation during the modern age of exploration, from the sixteenth century forward. It persisted through centuries in spite of "incessant refutation," and was "probably sustained by a feeling that blackness could scarcely be anything *but* a curse and by the common need to confirm the facts of nature by specific reference to Scripture."[10] The passage popped up repeatedly in numerous biblical discussions over the course of three hundred years or more among Western Christians, becoming especially popular in the nineteenth century. In a typical nineteenth–century explanation, John Fletchers, a Mississippi slaveholder, summarized how the curse on Ham's son could account for and justify American slavery:

> On this account all of Ham's descendants, and not merely those of Canaan, were Africans or Negroes. On the other hand, Shem and Japheth were blessed with white descendants because they had married within their own race. It was only right therefore that the degenerate black descendants of Ham were doomed to perpetual servitude to the superior white offspring of Shem and Japheth.[11]

Respectable theologians often skirted the son-of-Ham story, as it smacked more of folklore than "high" theology. The fable nevertheless deeply penetrated the consciousness of religious Southerners, who were for the most part biblical literalists. The son-of-Ham thesis served well in the sense that it seemed to explain how black people could be free Christians and unfree slaves at the same time. But the curse on Ham was at best a shaky foundation for religioracial mythologizing, for the passage invoked was simply too short, mysterious, and fable-like to bear up under the full weight of the interpretations imposed upon it. Once again, the Bible proved a powerful but somewhat troubling and unreliable guide in the formation of mythoracial ideologies.

Antebellum Era (1800–1860): Christianization and Degradation

Pro-slavery theologians worked feverishly through the antebellum era (1800–1860) to enunciate a Christian pro-slavery apologetic, one that would preserve boundaries of whiteness/blackness while also supporting their efforts to Christianize the slaves. By the nineteenth century, white Southern clergymen insisted, time and time again, that Christianization would make blacks more secure in their blackness—their enslavedness—because it would make them obedient and content in that obedience. "The Scripture," explained a Christian missionary, "far from making any Alteration in Civil Rights, expressly directs, that *every Man abide in the Condition wherein he is called, with great Indifference of Mind* concerning outward circumstances."[12] And by the 1850s, Southern Methodists acknowledged, as one of their newspapers put it, that "Everybody who believes in religion at all, admits that it is the duty of Christians to give religious instruction to the slave population of the Southern States. To deny the safety and propriety of preaching the Gospel to the negroes, is either to abandon Christianity, or to admit that slavery is condemned by it."[13]

With such reasoning at hand, white Southerners supported a substantial missionary enterprise to the slaves. While it remained controversial in some quarters through the antebellum era (until the eve of the Civil War), white Southern denominations accepted that such activity was part of spreading the word of God even to the poorest and most miserable of God's creatures. Contrary to views in the seventeenth and eighteenth centuries, which often set in dichotomous relief whiteness and Christian freedom versus blackness and un-Christian unfreedom, by the nineteenth century the missions to the slaves had been successful enough that many whites came to see "black" religion as peculiarly fervent and reassuringly orthodox. Blackness now signified a particular type of Christian fervor, one with occasional fits of menace (such as in Nat Turner's rebellion in 1831), but one largely consonant with the white Southern version of paternalism. White Americans, formerly skeptical that barbaric Negroes could understand or accept the Christian faith of whites, now reassured themselves that the Negro, in his religion, was "simple" and "orthodox," if a bit "emotional" and "frenzied" in his religious expressions.[14]

Blackness still retained an association with danger and evil, however. Blackness and religious myth appeared in a mysterious form in conjure, the broad array of practices around the supernatural that were often attributed to holdovers from African ways. The white missionary C. C. Jones wrote that slaves sometimes had been

> made to believe that while they carried about their persons some charm with which they had been furnished, they were *invulnerable* . . . they have been known to be so perfectly and fearfully under the influence of some leader or conjurer or minister, that they have not dared to disobey him in the least particular; nor to disclose their own intended or perpetrated crimes, in view of inevitable death itself.[15]

Conjurers, also known as hoodoo doctors and rootworkers, used herbs and mysterious charms to treat (or to harm) others. "While operating without sanction from the churches," one historian has explained, "most Conjurers drew from a familiar repertoire of religious symbols and beliefs, utilizing Christian talismans, bibles, and prayers for their treatment of affliction." As "spiritual pragmatists," black Americans utilized both traditions of Christianity and conjure. Both arose from their perception of a universe alive and responsive to human interventions. The lack of a sharp dichotomy between the sacred and the secular led many blacks to view the supernatural world as directly impinging upon human experience. Conjure and hoodoo served to provide personal spiritual empowerment, even as it reinforced what "blackness" represented to "whites"—superstition, mysterious powers, and irrational fears.[16]

Mythoracial Ideas in Biblical Exegesis, Scientific Thought, and Popular Culture after 1865

After the Civil War, many self-proclaimed race theologians and scientists, both crackpots and serious thinkers, challenged older religious notions of the unity of races by fantasizing instead about the separately created origins of races. They reread African Americans back out of the category of "humanity," just as many of their seventeenth–century forebears had done. By mixing biblical and scientific reasoning, they took "scientific" studies of Negro inferiority (including those from phrenology, the pseudoscience of measuring the brain skeleton and inferring intelligence from such measurements) and found in scripture explanations (such as fables in Genesis) that allegedly supported the science. Many of these writers fiddled with the curse-of-Ham legend, struggling to fit the Genesis myths with the findings of the racially biased science of that era. In the mid–nineteenth century, for example, Samuel Cartwright, a physician from Louisiana, suggested that the curse could be scientifically verified in the Negro's physical and intellectual inferiority. All races descended from God, Genesis taught, but the curse on the Negro race, he believed, resulted in demonstrably different characteristics that could be systematically measured. There was, he proclaimed triumphantly, no contradiction between science and scripture. Some years later, however, Cartwright reversed positions entirely (while losing none of his argumentative self–confidence), insisting that the biblical story supported the scientific argument of polygenesis—a word referring to the separate creation of the world's races. Negroes and other races were created before Adam, he imagined, and were part of the animal kingdom over which Adam and Eve had been given "dominion." Support for slavery and (later) segregation laws easily arose, of course, from such construings of the biblical fables.[17]

The late nineteenth century witnessed the apogee of the polygenesis theory and scientific racism pioneered by Cartwright and others, seen in full–length expositions of religioscientific racism such as *Anthropology for the People: A Refutation of the Theory of the Adamic Origin of All Races*, published in 1891 under the pseudonym "Caucasian."[18] This loathsome but popular work straddled the nineteenth-century world of close biblical exegesis and the twentieth-century reliance on science. These two perspectives produced truly miscegenated offspring, including what I will call mythoscientific racism, a blending of racism, Darwinian ideas, and biblical exegesis.

Caucasian attacked the notion that all the world's races sprang from Adam's loins, substituting for that a religioscientific mythology that led to an especially virulent form of white supremacist thought:

> From this theory, that God made the yellow and the black races inferior, physically, mentally and morally, we infer that he designed them for a subordinate and dependent position; that to impose upon them the duties, obligations and civilization of the superior race and give them the same mental and moral training, is to do violence to their nature and must result in evil; that the Creator, having made different races, intended that blood purity should be preserved, and for this purpose implanted the instinctive mutual and universal repulsiveness of races; that political and social equal-

ity is unnatural and repugnant to the best human instincts, and that miscegenation, or admixture of races, is not only an enormous sin against God,
but a degrading bestiality which can result only in unmitigated evil and
final destruction.[19]

In Caucasian's view, nonwhite peoples were not descendants of Adam
and therefore not "brothers in any proper sense of the term, but inferior
creations." This view, he argued, was entirely consistent with Scripture,
for any notion that God "would degrade, by a special act of His providence, the great majority of the human race, especially as nothing of the
sort is hinted at in the Sacred Volume, and no satisfactory cause for such
an act can be assigned," was untenable. Polygeny was thus the "only theory reconcilable with Scripture."[20]

Caucasian surmised that the biblical flood possibly was a consequence
of the union of the Adamite (white) and pre-Adamite (nonwhite) races,
the "only union we can conceive of that is reasonable and sufficient to account for the corruption of the world and the consequent judgment." In
other words, sexual unions between white and nonwhite peoples in the
ancient world, Caucasian theorized (and people took such writings seriously), compelled God to wash the world away and start over again. Noah
preached against the ultimate sin of miscegenation, that is, the sexual in-
termixture or marrying of white and black people, but the people persisted in making "unholy alliances that ended in their destruction." God
intended that the Adamic race "be kept free from admixture with any inferior blood," he explained. The pre-Adamite races belonged to the *"genus
homo"* in a "zoological sense," but the "mode of their creation concludes
them only in the highest order of animals, and subjects them to the dominion of the Adamite." Because non-Adamites (nonwhites) were not
adapted to the spiritual religion of the New Testament "whenever the
Christian influence of the superior race is withdrawn, they go back to
feticism and idolatry, which are natural to them."[21]

As Caucasian's writings suggest, the mythology drawn from race and
religion figured heavily in white fears of miscegenation. Of course, white
and black men and women engaged in "race mixing" frequently. The gradations of skin color of living people (including the substantial class of
mixed–race people in the South, called "mulattoes," and in places such as
New Orleans given finer gradations such as "quadroons" and "oc-
toroons"), as well as the inability of most slave women to take any action
against white men who demanded sexual access to them, made this point

obvious, even to the most obtuse white supremacist. Nevertheless, the fear of race mixing most particularly between white women and black men, the symbol of virginal purity encountering the "black beast rapist" so feared in Southern folklore, was used to justify the entire system of segregation that separated the races. "Race purity" was at stake—and that, ultimately, meant the honor of white women.

Nowhere was the violence enforcing white supremacy more gruesomely displayed than in the often horrific acts by which white men claimed to preserve the honor of the white woman—that is, in lynching black men. Any reality behind such incendiary rape allegations was, at best, of secondary concern. The mere mention, or rumor, generally sufficed as a call to light the home-made torches and loop the rope knots. Of the nearly five thousand lynchings in America from 1880 to 1950, many of the best known were what one historian has called "spectacle lynchings." These were purposeful, solemn events—*rituals*—in which dozens, hundreds, or even thousands engaged in acts of purification (hence the frequency with which lynching victims were *burned*, and the invocations pronounced at such events by clergymen or other religious leaders). The injustices perpetrated within the legal system simply added to the violence meted out to black Americans outside the legal system—in either case, there was no respite, no safe space, no means of real recourse. For centuries, Anglo–Americans had identified blackness with impurity and found biblical sanction for this connection. This image helped to justify slavery, and had pernicious consequences as well within the post–Civil War Bible Belt South.[22]

Against centuries of onslaught of such deeply rooted myths and religiously sanctioned degradation, black Americans stood little chance of mounting an effective defense. But they tried. In the nineteenth century, particularly, when a small but significant set of educated black Americans encountered the romantic and racialist ideas of their era, many of them responded by trying to write the black man *into* the reigning mythologies and categories. It was the destiny of black Americans, some of them believed, to bring civilization back to their home continent. It was biblically prophesied that it should be so. George Wilson Brent, a black Methodist minister, took the biblical stories as evidence for the black man's indispensable role in furthering human history. "Africa, our fatherland, the home of the Hamitic race," he wrote, "is the only country on earth whose past, present, and future so concerned the Lord." Even the son of Ham himself, Canaan, was blessed, for he "invested and built up a country and settled a nation bearing his name, whose glory . . . remains today the typical ensign of the Christian's hope, concerning Africa's future glory prophecy says 'Ethiopia shall soon stretch forth her hand to God.'" Brent dated the origin of the white man to *after* Noah's flood (specifically to the biblical verses of 2 Kings 5:20–27), meaning (in this view) that the black man could claim the more ancient pedigree than the white man, no matter what the current state of power relations between the two.[22]

Other black commentators also produced "race histories" that explained the origins and destiny of black people to African American readers. They employed the standard variety of arguments and biblical stories. These race writers, usually theologians and ministers themselves, often diverged on specific points, but they all agreed on disputing the racist notions of inferiority inherent in the Western idea of "blackness." Whether to accept the biblical mythologies but to invert the stories (as did George Wilson Brent), or to put on display entirely new mythological constructs (as did the black leader Marcus Garvey in Harlem in the 1920s), or to insist that blackness and whiteness were simply not biblical categories because "of one blood hath God made all nations," black Americans responded vigorously to the creation of blackness as a category of inferiority and shame. Until later in the twentieth century, however, few white Americans listened.

The Christian mythic grounding for ideas of whiteness and blackness was powerful but unstable, subject to constant argument and revision. In the twentieth century, this grounding was radically overturned in part through a reimagination of the same Christian thought that was part of creating it in the first place. Black Christians who formed the rank–and–file of the civil rights movement demolished the political structures of segregation, and with them some of the folklore of blackness as inferiority that had enslaved so many Americans for so many centuries.

Yet, the category of blackness lives on, supported now more by cultural prejudices and the simple weight of history than by any widespread belief in the religious mythologies that created and undergirded it. The category of blackness transmitted through religion lives on perhaps most strongly in American popular music, with its dependence on black musical forms. Blues artists, in particular, have made use of traditional forms of religious mythology and blackness—in images from standing at the crossroads, selling one's soul to the devil in exchange for musical prowess, to boasting about being a "mojo man," or warning that "I put a spell on you, because you're mine." These lyrics play upon positive images of essential blackness, some sort of intuitive spiritual connection not entirely available to white people, images drawn deep from the roots of slave religion, conjure, and supernaturalism. In this way, and many others, mythoracial ideas still exert a perversely strong hold on the American imagination of blackness and whiteness.

NOTES

1. Winthrop Jordan, *White over Black: American Attitudes toward the Negro, 1550–1812* (Chapel Hill: University of North Carolina Press, 1968), 24.

2. Albert Raboteau, *Slave Religion: The Invisible Institution in the Antebellum South* (New York: Oxford University Press, 1978), 100.

3. Ibid., 65.

4. Jordan, *White Over Black*, 20.

5. Ibid., 201.

6. Larry Tise, *Proslavery: A History of the Defense of Slavery in America* (Chapel Hill: University of North Carolina Press, 1984), 17–19.

7. Jordan, *White over Black*, 199–200.

8. Raboteau, *Slave Religion*, 102–3.

9. Ibid., 100.

10. Jordan, *White over Black*, 19.

11. John Fletchers, *Studies on Slavery in Easy Lessons* (Mississippi, 1852).

12. Raboteau, *Slave Religion*, 103.

13. Ibid., 175.

14. See Paul Harvey, *Redeeming the South: Religious Cultures and Racial Identities among Southern Baptists, 1865–1925* (Chapel Hill: University of North Carolina Press, 1997), chapter 2.

15. Raboteau, *Slave Religion*, 283.

16. Yvonne Chireau, "Supernaturalism," in *Themes in American Religion and Culture*, ed. Paul Harvey and Philip Goff (in progress).

17. George Frederickson, *The Black Image in the White Mind: The Debate on Afro–American Character and Destiny, 1817–1914* (New York: Harper and Row, 1971), 87–88.

18. "Caucasian," *Anthropology for the People: A Refutation of the Theory of the Adamic Origin of All Races* (Richmond, 1891).

19. Ibid., 30.

20. Ibid., 29.

21. Ibid., 193, 213, 215, 228.

22. For an analysis of spectacle lynchings, see Grace Elizabeth Hale, *Making*

Whiteness: The Culture of Segregation in the South, 1890–1940 (New York: Pantheon, 1998).

23. George Wilson Brent, "The Ancient Glory of the Hamitic Race," *A.M.E. Church Review* 12 (October 1895): 272–75; George Wilson Brent, "Origin of the White Race," *A.M.E. Church Review* 10 (January 1893): 287–88.

SUGGESTIONS FOR FURTHER READING

Fredrickson, George. *The Black Image in the White Mind: The Debate on Afro-American Character and Destiny, 1817–1914.* New York: Harper and Row, 1971.

Jordan, Winthrop. *White over Black: American Racial Attitudes toward the Negro, 1550–1812.* Chapel Hill: University of North Carolina Press, 1968.

Peterson, Thomas Virgil. *Ham and Japheth: The Mythic World of Whites in the Antebellum South.* Metuchen, N.J.: Scarecrow Press, 1971.

Spencer, Jon. *Blues and Evil.* Knoxville: University of Tennessee Press, 1993.

Tise, Larry. *Proslavery: A History of the Defense of Slavery in America, 1701–1840.* Chapel Hill: University of North Carolina Press, 1987.

Chapter 2

Myth and African American Self-Identity

Eddie S. Glaude, Jr.

Religion and the Making of a Self

Religious language has been a critical resource in the construction of African American identity. From the Christian slaves' identification with the Exodus story to the religious views of the Nation of Islam, African Americans have articulated—through various religious traditions—their own sense of peoplehood, secured for themselves a common history, and imagined a future for their children. These efforts have occurred within the context of a society fundamentally shaped by white supremacy.[1] And, it is precisely in the African American struggle against the dehumanizing effects of racism that their religious imagination served as one of the key sources in the construction of an African American self.

It is important to note that the idea of an African American self is rooted in historical processes. Identities are made: they are not something static or fixed. Often our views about black identity stem from some set of assumptions about common historical experiences and shared vocabularies that provide us with stable, unchanging frames of reference in spite of the shifts and changes that make up our actual lives.[2] This singularity of reference and meaning is seen as the essence of black folk, determining how we understand ourselves in relation to others, the scope and extent of our political aspirations, and—perhaps most importantly—the manner in which we conceive of our obligations to one another.[3] But identities are much more complicated than this sort of account suggests. They are formed and reformed as we experience forces that impinge on us, and exact choices that shape who we are and will become. Through this view, identity is less about "essences" and more about the *conse-*

quences of human interaction: the product of our beliefs, choices, and actions as we engage our world.

Now, it doesn't follow from this particular view that our identities are hopelessly open ended—that there is no "self," so to speak. Rather, the claim is simply that our identities are *relatively* stable: that selves are really the organization of habits (always subject to modification) that constitute our characters as they have been shaped, in part, by our previous experiences and brought to consciousness in narrative. In short, what we have done and are doing and the kinds of stories we weave about these experiences are constitutive of who we take ourselves to be. And it is here—in the storytelling, the interpretative activity—that religious myth has been so critical to the construction of African American identity.

Myth and Ideology

Myths are sometimes thought of, at least in common parlance, as fictions or illusions. They are not quite lies: myths are seemingly accorded a grander status than that. But they do smack of something that's not quite true or, at least, as something beyond being true or false. When we think of, for example, the myth of the hypersexual black slave or the myths surrounding black intelligence,[4] we rarely accord them any truth-value (unless we're committed to a certain kind of racial politics). Yet we often recognize that such myths are part of a broader set of discursive meanings that produce tangible, that is to say, *real* effects in the lives of many Americans.

Myths can also be understood as true stories. The essays in this book maintain that myths authorize and legitimate ways of being in the world. Myths acquire this status precisely because they are believed to express the truth, and insofar as they are deemed credible, myths authorize beliefs, practices, choices, and actions that animate a particular community of experience. So, whether we view myths as fictions or as true stories, there is the recognition that this particular way of seeing the world has real effects on how we understand ourselves, interact with our fellows, and interpret our world. Obviously, true or not, myths matter.

I like to think of myths in this way: they are, at bottom, an interpretative activity "addressed to questions of origin, of moral ambiguity, of the meaning of suffering and death, and of the anomalous phenomena that cannot be assimilated to existing conceptual systems."[5] Myths, then, are all about making sense of and accounting for the various experiences that constitute our living—particularly those experiences that tend to go beyond our more common ways of making sense of phenomena and events. They are general and specific, sometimes idiosyncratic, ways of understanding what happens to us, and as such, myths can offer those who believe in them the conceptual tools to order (or at least attempt to order) the tumultuous events of their world. They can offer the conceptual resources to hold off the potentially debilitating effects of human limitation: the limits of our understanding, of our ability to endure, and of our moral insight.[6] To be sure, we come to our experiences with these conceptual resources ready at hand, and we interpret experiences, generating narratives that provide us with some semblance of stability in a constantly changing world.

For some, however, myths work ideologically. That is to say, when we engage in this kind of interpretative activity we are, in fact, reproducing a particular ideology. How ideology is understood varies.[7] It could mean something like this: a body of ideas that helps to legitimate the interests of a ruling class, and these interests are maintained by way of something called "mystification." Here values and beliefs that serve particular dominant interests are rendered in such a way that they are understood to be natural, self-evident, and universal. As such, we are unable to see the vast contradictions that make up our conditions of living and fail to mount a challenge to ruling interests. On this understanding of ideology, myths, as Roland Barthes maintained, give "an historical intention a natural justification, and mak[e] contingency appear eternal. [T]his process is exactly that of bourgeois ideology."[8] In short, myths mystify.

But there is another way of understanding ideology. We can think of it in terms of the production of ideas, beliefs, and values that make up the entirety of a particular form of life, *and* it is within this whole complex of meanings and processes that various battles are waged as individuals and groups reflect on their conditions of living. In this view, we are not faced with the appearance-reality distinction that informs the earlier account of ideology: that somehow those of us not in the ruling class have failed to see what is really going on and, by relying on religious myths, are living lives of illusions. (Remember, Karl Marx called for the "abolition of religion as the illusory happiness of men.")[9] Instead, what we see are various individuals and groups drawing on a range of resources within their reach—including myths—to make the case for their struggle.

Ideology is not simply conservative and coercive. Rather, following Kenneth Burke, I understand ideology as "an aggregate of beliefs sufficiently at odds with one another to justify opposite kinds of conduct."[10] So, when I say that myths are, at bottom, an interpretative activity I also mean to imply that this interpretative activity involves an active effort to determine what our experiences are doing to us, and what *that* effort is doing to our experiences.[11] We see this quite clearly, I believe, in the case of African American uses of religious myth to wage the battle against white supremacy in the United States.

African American Religious Myths and the American Ideology

America has often been figured as the shining city on the hill, and its citizens have been imagined as the New Israelites. It's really our Puritan inheritance. New England Puritans imagined their voyage from the Old World to the New as an exodus to a New Canaan and as an errand into the wilderness. This religious construction of their journey elevated to biblical drama the mundane events of the Puritans' efforts to escape religious persecution, and provided them with a rich source of metaphors not only to explicate an unfolding history but also to construct an identity.[12] John Winthrop's famous sermon, "Modell of Christian Charity," serves as a great example of the use of religious language in this way, what Werner Sollors calls *typological ethnogenesis*: the sense of peoplehood that emerges through the use of biblical typology. Winthrop, the leader of the expedition to the Massachusetts Bay Colony, described in his sermon the "covenantal" obligations to God of those who were making the journey across the Atlantic, linking it to the Sinaitic covenant of Israel. Here obligation to God was the basis for a group identity, because through their figural participation in the biblical narrative the Puritans, in effect, came to see themselves as a new Israel—a nation persecuted by the enemies of God. Their history then was rhetorically elevated and transformed into biblical drama, their transatlantic voyage interpreted as a new exodus, "their mission as an errand in the wilderness, and their role as that of a chosen people."[13]

As Albert Raboteau notes, Winthrop even paraphrased at the conclusion of his sermon Moses' last instructions to Israel:

Beloved there is now sett before us life, and good, deathe and evil in that
wee are Commaunded this day to the Lord our God and to love one another, to walke in his ways and to keepe his Commanundements and his
Ordinance, and his lawes, and the Articles of our Covenant with him that
wee may live and be multiplied, and that the Lord our God may blesse us in
the land whither we goe to possesse it: But if our heartes shall turne away
soe that wee will not obey, but shall be seduced and worship. . . other Gods,
our pleasures, and profits, and serve them; it is propounded unto this day,
wee shall surely perishe out of the good Land whither wee passe over this
vast Sea to possesse it.[14]

Here the ideas of migration, pilgrimage, and progress so central to the religious construction of American national identity come together to exhort the faithful to recognize that their success and, eventually, America's
success were contingent upon their obligations to God. America's destiny
then was linked to divine Providence, its history sacralized and its people
understood to be chosen by God.

To be sure, our Puritan inheritance bequeathed to us a religious language for the symbolic construction of an American national identity.
America, with the success of its Revolution and the power of its economy,
represents the *complete* break with the Old Israel and the fulfillment of
prophecy with the creation of the New Israel. It is the Redeemer Nation, a
beacon of freedom and the principle carrier of liberty. The religious construction of this national identity brings together in powerful and often
startling ways issues of history and memory, particularly with regard to
our interpretations of the nation's beginnings and how we remember
them to have shaped our moral comportment and our sense of national
cohesion. But, on a certain level, the point in all of this is quite straightforward: a religious myth has been absolutely central to the construction
of America's national identity. We tend to understand ourselves in religious terms despite the so-called secular nature of our social and political
organization. We are indeed the New Israelites. America is the New
Canaan. That is, unless you're black.

African Americans in the antebellum period often drew on religious
myths to come to terms with their status as slaves, to struggle for dignity
and freedom in American society, and to imagine a future for their children in the context of a radical experiment committed to democratic
ideals *and* slavery. For these peculiar Americans, the image of America as
the New Canaan was reversed. America was Egypt. As Vincent Harding

notes, "One of the abiding and tragic ironies of our history [is that] the nation's claim to be the New Israel was contradicted by the Old Israel still enslaved in her midst."[15] Here we have an example of how battles are waged within ideologies, drawing on the same languages for quite different ends. What is particularly interesting are the manifold ways African American efforts to make sense of their experiences of American racism redefined what it means to be American.[16] Like the nation in general, African Americans, through biblical analogy, saw themselves as the children of God and linked the freedom of the Israelites with their own eventual liberation. This appropriation of the Exodus story aided in African American articulations of their own sense of peoplehood, and also stood as a form of critique of American society for betraying its ideals. For example, Richard Allen, the first bishop of the African Methodist Episcopal Church, drew on the images of Exodus as he informed the nation that God would act to end slavery.

> I do not wish to make you angry, but excite your attention to consider how hateful slavery is in the sight of God who hath destroyed kings and princes for their oppression of the poor slaves. Pharaoh and princes, with the posterity of King Saul were destroyed by the protector and avenger of slaves. . . . When you are pleaded with, do not reply as Pharaoh did, "Wherefore do ye, Moses and Aaron let the people from their work, behold the people of the land are many, and you make them rest from their burden." We wish you consider God himself as the first pleader of the cause of slaves. . . . If you love your children, if you love your country, if you love the God of love, clear your hands of slavery.[17]

Allen presupposed that this biblical story was in wide circulation. In fact, it was precisely the familiarity of these tropes that made his passionate plea so powerful: he was in some ways striking the chord of the central religious myth of America. Moreover, Allen's use of this story signaled a conception of African American collective identity. Pharaoh refers to the *people* of Israel; their debased condition makes possible the idea of communal identification and solidarity (not only because of Pharaoh's actions but in the efforts to resist those actions, the Israelites—read African Americans—come to construct a particular conception of themselves as a people). The biblical analogy in the context of the United States then produces meanings in and around the conditions of African Americans that become paradigmatic for the construction of black identity and politics.

In fact, the Exodus story has been central to most political efforts in African American history. During slavery, the story provided Christian slaves with the languages to imagine a future in which they would be truly free. The events of the Civil War and the mass migrations of the late 1870s were described as re-enactments of the Exodus story. Thomas B. Wester, a black Union soldier, wrote in December 1864 "that he and his comrades were overthrowing 'Pharaoh' as 'in the days of old.'"[18] Sojourner Truth described the magnitude of efforts to relocate African Americans to Kansas in terms of the biblical narrative: "I have prayed so long that my people would go to Kansas, and that God would make straight the way before them. Yes, indeed, I think it is a good move for them. I believe as much in that move as I do in the moving of the children of Egypt [sic] going out of Canaan [sic]—just as much."[19]

Participants in the Great Migration of the interwar period utilized the metaphors of the story to interpret the unfolding events of urbanization and the background institutional terror that, in part, precipitated that mass movement. And, of course, Martin Luther King, Jr., in his last sermon drew on the power and persistence of this narrative in African American history to assure us that freedom was to come.

> We've got some difficult days ahead. But it really doesn't matter with me now. Because I've been to the mountaintop. Like anybody I would like to live a long life. Longevity has its place. But I'm not concerned about that now. I just want to do God's will. And He's allowed me to go up to the mountain. And I've seen the Promised Land. And I may not get there with you. But I want you to know tonight that we as a people will get to the Promised Land.[20]

King's invocation of this religious myth connected with a long history that involved not only African American struggles for freedom, but the nation's covenantal beginnings. The battle waged over the symbolic construction of America then necessarily involved the interpretation and reinterpretation of its central myth.

I've said that myths are, at bottom, an interpretative activity. They "serve as an interpretation of a community's experience."[21] White supremacy has fundamentally shaped the experiences of black America. In their uses of the Exodus story along with a number of other religious narratives, African Americans have attempted to make sense of those experiences and, in the process, have provided themselves with the tools to re-member past events and to imagine a future.

History, Identity, and African American Myths

African American religious myths deployed in the struggles against white supremacy have produced particularly charged conceptions of history, identity, and memory (which range across the political spectrum). We have already seen how a specific reading of the Exodus story challenged the fundamental symbolic construction of America. Wilson Moses main-tains, in fact, that the rhetorical power of this African American myth re-sides in its familiarity to the American public.[22] We all know the story. In different ways, of course, it is *our* story. But many uses of religious myths among African Americans reject identification with America. This rejec-tion begins with a basic reconfiguration of historical beginnings that makes possible the construction of an identity that stands over and against "the idea of America."

Psalms 68:13, "Princes shall come out of Egypt and Ethiopia shall soon stretch forth her hands unto God," has been a central part of African Americans' religious and political imagination, particularly in their ef-forts to make sense of unjustified suffering in the context of America's racial violence. This oft-quoted verse aided in the formulation of an African monumental history and in the articulation of a common racial mission or destiny in the world.[23] Here Africa was imagined as the birth-place of humanity and the home of grand civilizations only to have fallen from the grace of God. Alongside this view of an African past stood the claim that Africa's descendants would in fact redeem the world and re-claim their lost glory. This Ethiopian configuration, as Theophus Smith calls it, not only helped motivate black Christian missionaries to return to Africa and spread the Gospel, it also promoted black emigration back to Africa (as it did in the movement led by Marcus Mosiah Garvey in the 1920s).[24] With this particular use of religious myths, African Americans often presumed the United States to be beyond redemption. The nation, in some ways, required for its flourishing the continued subordination of African Americans, and this fact necessitated that they imagine a future elsewhere—an elsewhere that could extend to actual geographical loca-tions, such as Africa or Haiti, or to the end of history itself.

James Theodore Holly, in 1884, offered such a view in which the end of history marked the ascendance of the darker races. For him, Africans or "the Hamites" (for more, see chapter 1, by Paul Harvey in this volume) would instantiate God's words in the world and represent the fulfillment of a golden age prophesied in Revelations 20:1–7. Holly wrote:

> The African race has been the servant of servants to their brethren of the other races during all the long and dreary ages of the Hebrew and Christian dispensations. And it is this service that they have so patiently rendered through blood and tears that shall finally obtain for them the noblest places of service in the Coming Kingdom. That what has been a curse to them under Gentile tyranny will become a blessing to them under the mild and beneficent reign of Christ. . . . The curse of Canaan, dooming him to be a servant of servants unto his brethren, which lowered him to a place of dishonor under the earthly governments, will turn to a blessing unto him and exalt him to the posts of honor under the heavenly government of God.[25]

In the face of the terror of white supremacy in the United States, Holly and others sought to overcome the brutal realities of their condition of living; through myth, they "theologized" history and reached "forward" to a moment when their life's aspiration for freedom would be fulfilled. The Ethiopian configuration, along with uses of the Exodus story, not only provides an interpretation of the past, it also constructs a future— one linked to Providence and the special role African Americans have in bringing about the kingdom of God on earth.

With this formulation, I've put together the notions of *messianism* and *millennialism*. Wilson Moses defines *messianism* "as the perception of a person or group, by itself or by others, as having a manifest destiny or a God-given role to assert the providential goals of history and to bring about the kingdom of God on earth."[26] Timothy Fulop defines *millennialism* as "the belief rooted in Christian tradition and thought that history will be fulfilled in a golden age. The term itself comes from Revelation 20:1–7, which predicts a thousand year reign of Christ with the resurrected martyrs while Satan is bound and confined to the abyss."[27] Both highlight the relationship between history and agency that is so central to the work of these myths. More specifically, a theology of history is imagined as the site within which African Americans *act* in the name of God. This convergence of history and agency in the deployment of these religious myths then provide, to some degree, vocabularies of agency needed to engage the racist structures of America and the languages required to see beyond what was often an opaque condition.

Up to this point I have emphasized the appropriation of biblical narratives central to black Christianity. But African Americans have used religious myths from a variety of traditions to forge an identity and tell a history. Appropriations of the Exodus story, for example, have led some to claim that African Americans descended from the lost tribes of Israel. Slavery had stripped African Americans of their true identity, which is that of black Jews, and their task is to reclaim this more authentic way of being black in the world.[28] For example, Wentworth A. Matthew founded in the 1920s the Commandment Keepers Congregation of the Living God. Matthew held the belief that African Americans were "Ethiopian Hebrews" and Judaism was Ethiopia's true religion.

African Americans have also embraced Islam as a way of interpreting their experiences in the United States. In 1913, Noble Drew Ali formed the first Moorish Science Temple in Newark, New Jersey. Ali preached that African Americans were really "Asiatics" whose original homeland was Morocco. Members read from something called "The Holy Koran," a compendium of various teachings that translated the historical experiences, events, and personalities of African American life into a divine narrative. The book bore little resemblance to the actual *Qur'an* of Islam. Ali held the view that a true knowledge of African Americans' historical beginnings would better equip them to struggle against racism in the United States. The Socratic dictum "Know thyself" then became a mantra in Ali's efforts to reconstruct a lost past and forge an identity amid the brutal realities of black urban living. Members were given new names and identification cards. They were Moorish Americans, and this identity signaled a new orientation to the United States and to history.

Another variant of African American Islam emerged in the 1930s. The Nation of Islam, founded by Wallace D. Fard, declared that African Americans were Muslims, members of the lost-found tribe of Shabazz (for more, see chapter 6 by Aminah Beverly McCloud). Like Ali, Fard preached that a true knowledge of African American history was a necessary condition of black liberation. Fard's mysterious disappearance in 1933 resulted in Elijah Muhammad's ascendance to leadership of the movement until his death in 1975.

The Nation of Islam provided its members with a cosmology that interpreted the experiences of white supremacy in America. An ultimate, collective, and this-worldly belief in salvation defined the organization's general outlook. As Martha Lee describes, the doctrine of the Nation of Islam maintained that "the white world and its oppressive political institutions would fall; from their ashes would rise the Black millennium."[29]

The Nation's interpretation of the march of history included a set of startling inversions intended to reorient its members' racial psychology. Human origins, for example, were couched in an elaborate mythical structure aimed at disrupting the effects of years of racial subordination. Whites were grafted devils, the results of experiments of an evil scientist. Blacks, specifically black men, were gods, the direct reflection of Allah himself. The myth also explained the present state of Black America and the power of White America as the result of Allah allowing the white race to rule the earth for 6,000 years. The end of this period of rule would mark, in some ways, the end of history and the ascendance of the Black Nation to rule a new world.

The Nation of Islam, like black Christians throughout the United States, utilized religious language to interpret the political realities of black America. The organization certainly did not identify with the United States. The Nation preferred strict segregation between blacks and whites, argued for separate land as reparations for slavery, and encouraged black self-sufficiency in business and education. In fact, the Nation prophesied the fall of America and used every rhetorical means to articulate what they understood to be inevitable. The most powerful voices to emerge from this organization have been those of Malcolm X and Louis Farrakhan. And, to be sure, their efforts have helped foster a distinctive sense of black identity and gave a particular timbre to African American politics.

James Baldwin, with an amazing sense of clarity, showed the relationship between the religious myths of the Nation of Islam and those of black Christianity. In *The Fire Next Time*, Baldwin wrote:

> There is nothing new in [the Nation's] merciless formulation except the explicitness of its symbols and the candor of its hatred. Its emotional tone is as familiar to me as my own skin; it is but another way of saying that *sinners shall be bound in Hell a thousand years*. That sinners have always, for American Negroes, been white is a truth we needn't labor, and every American Negro, therefore, risks having the gates of paranoia close on him.[30]

Baldwin acknowledged the family resemblance between this unorthodox black religious expression and mainstream African American religion.

For him, the Nation's specific religious interpretation of the condition of African Americans had a long history, and that history made their efforts and, for that matter, that of black Jews in the United States intelligible.

A broader point to be made about this particular use of religious myth is this: that for many African Americans the religious pieties of white Christianity are no longer suitable, that their religious conversion questions their allegiances to the state, and that their pieties are of a different order all together. I mean African American conversion to Islam, in particular, has a different public effect than taking on the life practices of Buddhism or Hinduism; it represents, for some at least, a *political* gesture of a certain kind. So, on one level, African American conversion to Islam can be understood as not only an acceptance of a particular religious practice, but also as a rejection of American Christianity and the racist order of things in the United States.[31] Despite the particular ideological inflection of these efforts, religious myths remain central to the making of a new African American self and the location of that self in history.

African Americans often inscribe their political struggles within religious narratives and formulate their aspirations for freedom and, in some cases, citizenship as divinely sanctioned ends. These efforts involve a sense of the sacred that aids in the construction of a racial identity, which consolidates the idea of "the black community" and makes possible the expression of a prior unity among otherwise different individuals. In some ways it is a battle waged over history, memory, and the future. The political implications of this use of religious myth vary from Martin Luther King, Jr., to Malcolm X, from Cornel West to Louis Farrakhan. But, in every instance, the stories provide an interpretative framework in which experiences can be made sense of and hope can be sustained.

NOTES

1. See Cornel West, *Prophesy Deliverance! An Afro-American Revolutionary Christianity* (Philadelphia: Westminster Press, 1982), chapter 3.

2. Stuart Hall, "Cultural Identity and Diaspora," in *Colonial Discourse and Post-Colonial Theory: A Reader* (New York: Columbia University Press, 1994), 393.

3. See my essay, "Pragmatism and Black Identity: An Alternative Approach," *Nepantla* 2, no. 2 (2001).

4. There is a possible slippage here. The myths of black, slave hypersexuality

and black intelligence suggest that the word can easily be used interchangeably with stereotype.

5. Wayne Proudfoot, *Religious Experience* (Berkeley: University of California Press, 1985), 42.

6. I have in mind here Clifford Geertz's discussion of that part of his definition of religion that relates to "formulating conceptions of the general order of existence." Religious myths are critical tools in the work of holding chaos at bay. Geertz writes: "There are at least three points where chaos—a tumult of events which lack not just interpretations but interpretability—threatens to break in upon man: at the limits of his analytic capacities, at the limits of his powers of endurance, and the limits of his moral insight. Bafflement, suffering, and a sense of intractable ethical paradox are all, if they become intense enough or are sustained long enough, radical challenges to the proposition that life is comprehensible and that we can, by taking thought, orient ourselves effectively within it— challenges with which any religion, however, 'primitive,' which hopes to persist must attempt somehow to cope." Clifford Geertz, *The Interpretation of Culture* (New York: Basic Books, 1973), 100.

7. Ideology can be understood in at least five ways: (1) as false ideas that legitimate dominant political power, (2) ideas that are characteristic of a particular class or group, (3) the process of production of a particular social group or class, (4) the means by which human choices and actions are made to be natural, and (5) the way we make sense of our world. See Terry Eagleton, *Ideology: An Introduction* (London: Verso, 1991), chapter 1. Also see Tom Bottomore, ed., *A Dictionary of Marxist Thought* (Cambridge, Mass.: Harvard University Press, 1983), the entry for "ideology."

8. Roland Barthes, *Mythologies*, trans. Annette Lavers (New York: Hill and Wang, 1972), 142.

9. Robert C. Tucker, ed., *The Marx-Engels Reader*, 2nd ed. (New York: W. W. Norton, 1978), 53–54.

10. Kenneth Burke, *Counter-Statement* (Berkeley: University of California Press, 1968), 163.

11. See Giles Gunn's *Thinking across the Grain: Ideology, Intellect, and the New Pragmatism* (Chicago: University of Chicago Press, 1992), specifically chapter 2.

12. Albert Raboteau, *A Fire in the Bones: Religious Reflections on African American History* (Boston: Beacon Press, 1995), specifically chapter 1.

13. Werner Sollors, *Beyond Ethnicity: Consent and Descent in American Culture* (New York: Oxford University Press, 1986), 41. Also see my book, *Exodus! Religion, Race, and Nation in Early 19th Century Black America* (Chicago: University of Chicago Press, 2000), 44.

14. Quoted in Raboteau's brilliant essay, "African-American, Exodus, and the American Israel," in *Fire in the Bones*, 39. The sermon is reprinted in Conrad

Cherry, ed., *God's New Israel: Religious Interpretations of American Destiny* (Englewood Cliffs, N.J.: Prentice Hall, 1971), 43.

15. Vincent Harding, "The Uses of the Afro-American Past," in *The Religious Situation, 1969*, ed. Donald R. Cutter (Boston: Beacon Press, 1969), 829–840.

16. See Ralph Ellison's essay, "What America Would Be Like without Blacks," in *The Collected Essays of Ralph Ellison* (New York: Modern Library, 1995), and James Baldwin's essay, "The Discovery of What It Means to Be an American," in *Price of the Ticket: Collected Nonfiction 1948–1985* (New York: St. Martin's Press, 1985).

17. Richard Allen, *The Life, Experience and Gospel Labors of the Rt. Rev. Richard Allen* (Nashville: Abingdon, 1983), 52–53.

18. Quoted in David Blight, *Race and Reunion: The Civil War in American Memory* (Cambridge, Mass.: Harvard University Press, 2001), 23.

19. Quoted in Theophus Smith, *Conjuring Culture: Biblical Formations of Black America* (New York: Oxford University Press, 1994), 68.

20. See James M. Washington, ed., *A Testament of Hope: The Essential Writings and Speeches of Martin Luther King, Jr.* (San Francisco: Harper and Row, 1986), 286.

21. Proudfoot, *Religious Experience*, 41.

22. Wilson Moses, *Black Messiahs and Uncle Toms*, rev. ed. (University Park: Pennsylvania State University Press, 1993), 1.

23. Albert Raboteau has written the best essay on this subject. He isolates three important themes in African American uses of this Psalm: "the African Race," "the redemption of Africa," and "the mission of the darker races." See his essay, "Ethiopia Shall Soon Stretch Forth Her Hands: Black Destiny in Nineteenth-Century Black America," in *Fire in the Bones*, 37–56.

24. Theophus Smith, *Conjuring Culture*, 70.

25. Quoted in Albert Raboteau, "Ethiopia Shall Soon Stretch Forth Her Hands: Black Destiny in Nineteenth-Century Black America," in *Fire in the Bones*, 55.

26. See Moses, *Black Messiahs and Uncle Toms*, 4.

27. Timothy Fulop, "The Future Golden Day of the Race: Millennialism and Black Americans in the Nadir, 1877–1901," in *African American Religion: Interpretative Essays in History and Culture* (New York: Routledge, 1997), 230.

28. Figures like William Saunders Crowdy, organizer of the Church of God and Saints in Christ, and Prophet Cherry in Philadelphia also organized congregations around the idea of African Americans as Hebrews. The idea continues to circulate today. The Hebrew Israelite Nation, under the leadership of Prince Asiel Ben-Israel, continues to attract members.

29. Martha Lee, *The Nation of Islam: An American Millenarian Movement* (Syracuse, N.Y.: Syracuse University Press, 1996), 2.

30. James Baldwin, *The Fire Next Time* (New York: Vintage, 1991), 67.

31. This is certainly not to suggest that all African American Muslims hold this particular view of the United States. I am referring to a *perception* of black conversion to Islam as being as much a political conversion as it is a religious one.

SUGGESTIONS FOR FURTHER READING

Glaude, Eddie. *Exodus! Religion, Race, and Nation in Early Nineteenth-Century Black America*. Chicago: University of Chicago Press, 2000.

Moses, Wilson. *Black Messiahs and Uncle Toms: Social and Literary Manipulations of a Religious Myth*. University Park: Pennsylvania State University Press, 1993.

Raboteau, Albert. *Canaan Land: A Religious History of African Americans*. New York: Oxford University Press, 2001.

———. *Fire in the Bones*. Boston: Beacon Press, 1995.

Smith, Theophus. *Conjuring Culture: Biblical Formations of Black America*. New York: Oxford University Press, 1995.

Chapter 3

Almost White

The Ambivalent Promise of
Christian Missions among the Cherokees

Joel Martin

On July 10, 1817, white missionaries serving at Brainerd, a new mission school in southeastern Tennessee, received a visit from a young Cherokee woman who desired to enroll. The missionaries, New England Protestants sponsored by the American Board of Commissioners for Foreign Missions, responded with skepticism.[1] The woman's appearance triggered a strong and negative reaction that revealed much about the missionaries. They felt the woman, whose name was Catharine Brown, "had a high opinion of herself and was fond of displaying the clothing and ornaments in which she was arrayed."[2] They later wrote, she "was proud and haughty, loaded with earrings and jewelry."[3] As this encounter and their judgments revealed, to New England missionaries appearances counted. Because they equated "conversion" with "civilization," aesthetics mattered and looks meant something that scholars have yet to fully appreciate. Saving the other's soul also meant changing how she dressed. Missionaries *modeled* more than piety. In what follows, we will track the double-sided conversion of Catharine Brown, paying as much attention to her clothing as to her prayer habits. We will also compare her transformation with that of a male Cherokee. This will reveal how gender mattered to missionaries and affected their reactions to Cherokee appearances. In conclusion, we will step back to evaluate the ambivalent politics that characterized the missionary project and produced tensions with harsher, race-based policies of exclusion and removal.

Nearly every New Englander who met Catharine Brown had something to say about her appearance. Moody Hall wrote in his diary: "She I suppose is about eighteen: fair complexion, well formed, her appearance genteel and prepossessing—nature has done much for her."[4] He also reported that some missionaries harbored initial "unfavorable impressions,"[5] evidently troubled by her beauty and wealth. They feared that she was too accustomed to luxury to ever be at home in "our humble accommodations," too pampered to tolerate the missionaries' "discipline."[6] Although their initial resistance was evident to her, Brown probably did not realize how or why her appearance disturbed them. By the standards of southeastern Indians, who coveted a look very different from that of the New Englanders, she had dressed appropriately.

At the time of her arrival at Brainerd, Catharine Brown dressed like other southeastern Indians of her day. She blended indigenous and European fabrics, styles, and garments in a hybridized or composite look that embodied the cultural meshing of the polyglot Southeast, a region where Europeans, Africans, and Native Americans from many nations interacted regularly. This look emerged in the eighteenth century as Cherokees and other southeastern Indians traded vigorously with French, English, Spanish, and African newcomers and gained access to colorful cloth, metal goods, and glass beads. William Bartram, a colonial naturalist writing before the Revolution, described the typical dress of southeastern Indian women of his era: a long petticoat, "reaching almost to the middle of the leg . . . a little short waistcoat, usually made of calico, printed linen, or fine cloth, decorated with lace, beads, and c."[7] Both men and women were "fond of decorating themselves with external ornaments."[8] Many sported tattoos, slit and stretched ears, silver nose and ear ornaments.[9] Bartram asserted that women "never cut their hair, but plait it in wreaths, which are turned up, and fastened on the crown, with a silver broach, forming a wreathed top-knot, decorated with an incredible quantity of silk ribbands, of various colours, which stream down on every side, almost to the ground."[10]

Decades later, in 1833, John Howard Payne observed an affluent Creek woman wearing "a white muslin gown; a black scarf, wrought all over with flowers in brilliant colors; an embroidered white collarette . . . gold chains, coral beads, and jewelled ear-rings . . . her hair beautifully dressed in the Parisian style; a splendid tortoise-shell comb, gemmed; and from one large tuft of hair upon one temple to that upon the other there passed a beautiful gold ornament."[11] Catharine Brown, a member of the

Cherokee elite, shared a similar aesthetic. Elaborate self-decoration was nothing unusual. Among other "ornaments," Brown wore earrings and knobs, rings, and a large necklace.[12] To whites in the early nineteenth century, however, it all looked like "Indian superabundance" of finery, something excessive.[13] Her look alarmed the missionaries.

Fashion remains a matter of great social and economic importance in North America and beyond, but it does not mean today exactly the same things it meant in an earlier period. For New Englanders and Europeans of the eighteenth and nineteenth centuries, fashion served as a crucial boundary marker, a way of distinguishing who was "civilized" from who was not. Educated people were expert at interpreting the "social symbolics of dress."[14] As Roxann Wheeler explains, clothing "was key to the constitution of religious, class, national, and personal identity in the eighteenth century. In the Christian tradition, clothes were an aspect of social and moral conduct. Conventionally, clothing functioned as an index of character: it was supposed to reflect a person's quality of mind." Fashion also helped reinforce proper expressions of maleness and femaleness and maintained boundaries between social classes. In colonial New England, for example, legal courts required dozens of nonelite men and women to explain why they wore "silk contrary to the law" or "long hair and other extravagancies."[15] These courts, created by Protestant Christians, sought to conform society to moral and ethical teachings gleaned from the Bible. The apostle Paul, one of the most important advocates of early Christianity and author of several portions of the Bible, had counseled early Christians to stay within their social station and to submit to earthly authorities. New Englanders, eager to model their social order on a biblical one, thought that people should not dress beyond their means or represent themselves falsely through their apparel, speech, or behavior.

Saint Paul had also established the dominant tone of the Christian tradition's teachings regarding the appearance of women. He wrote in 1 Timothy 2:8: "I desire then that in every place the men should pray lifting holy hands without anger or quarreling; also that *women should adorn themselves modestly and sensibly in seemly apparel, not with braided hair or gold or pearls or costly attire, but by good deeds, as befits women who profess religion*" (New Standard Revised edition, emphasis added). Subsequent church leaders built upon this admonition. Tertullian wrote an entire volume, *On the Apparel of Women.*

Central Christian myths communicated a negative view of the human body and especially of women. From the biblical story of the Garden of

Eden, Christians learned that it was the woman, Eve, who tempted Adam to break God's law. As a consequence, God banished Adam and Eve (and thus, all humanity) from the Garden. Adam and Eve, newly aware of their own nakedness and ashamed of their bodies, sought clothing. The message was harsh. Through a woman, sin had entered the world. Through a woman's duplicity and a man's complicity, sin had become humanity's fate.

But the Christian story did not end there. Thankfully, the gracious intervention and sacrifice of the new Adam, Jesus Christ, broke the cycle for some. Christ made it possible for some to be saved, through no merit of their own. Evil did not end, however. Temptations still abounded. Sin was the rule; salvation the exception. Christians needed to practice vigilance, to seek biblical guidance, and to submit to godly authorities.

To keep sin at bay and promote the spiritual well-being of their communities, New Englanders regulated not just how people worshiped, but how they behaved and presented themselves in public. Guided by deep Christian myths and teachings that conveyed grave concerns about women's sexuality, New Englanders knew that if a woman wanted to be a good Christian, she needed to dress appropriately.

In short, for New England missionaries among the Cherokees, dress held religious significance and could strengthen or weaken morality. As their diaries reveal, missionaries among the Cherokees felt dress could stimulate or suppress "carnality," a powerful pull to sin that could cause emotional chaos and spiritual ruin.

Proper clothing covered the body without attracting attention in order to protect the soul. This aesthetic and ethic shaped and disciplined the missionaries at Brainerd, and they applied both without hesitation to the Cherokees they schooled. But these classic Christian concerns about clothing, modesty, and sexuality were further exacerbated and magnified by prevalent stereotypes about Indians. Put in another way, contact with Indians stimulated and intensified certain anxieties. Like most New Englanders, missionaries associated Indians with moral and physical danger. To be precise, these dangers were gender coded. Indian women were tied to erotic license; Indian men to frontier violence.

As historian Kathleen Brown has noted, European "travellers often communicated the aesthetic and erotic appeal of Indian women's bodies and demeanour, frequently casting Indian women as seductresses, playthings, or beautiful and virtuous allies of Europeans."[16] For example, William Bartram, author of perhaps the most influential and famous account of eighteenth-century southeastern Indians, depicted native women as promiscuous. Describing a party he witnessed in northern Florida, he wrote: "White and red men and women without distinction, passed the day merrily with these jovial, amorous topers, and the nights in convivial songs, dances, and sacrifices to Venus, as long as they could stand or move; for in these frolicks both sexes take such liberties with each other, and act, without constraint or shame."[17] In what sounds like late eighteenth century soft porn, Bartram elsewhere describes the sexual excitement produced in "hearty young [British] men" who "enjoyed a most enchanting view" of strawberry fields where "companies of young, innocent Cherokee virgins, some busy gathering the rich fragrant fruit, others having already filled their baskets . . . disclosing their beauties to the fluttering breeze, and bathing their limbs in the cool fleeting streams; whilst other parties, more gay and libertine, were yet collecting strawberries, or wantonly chasing their companions, tantalising them, staining their lips and cheeks with the rich fruit."[18] The lascivious writings of men like Bartram eroticized Cherokee women, rendering them as highly sexual natural beings, fruitful, fertile like the mythologized American continent itself.

Even when missionaries could look beyond cultural stereotypes and encounter individuals, they could not accept the normal behavior of Cherokee women, such as teenaged women swimming together with men in the nude and frankly discussing sex and their bodies. Cherokee women of this era, even married Cherokee women, enjoyed considerable sexual freedom, more than their Choctaw and Muskogee sisters, and far more than that available to Euro-American women.[19] Such freedom and openness scandalized missionaries. No wonder they doubted that a young, beautiful, wealthy, bejeweled Cherokee woman could conform to their expectations. In the end, however, they did decide to admit Catharine Brown to the school.

A deep religious faith and a strong sense of mission motivated the missionaries at Brainerd. Devout Christians, they dedicated enormous psychic energy to the cultivation of their interior lives, praying, writing uplifting letters and self-castigating diaries, and giving erudite sermons. At a time when massive numbers of white and black Americans were joining the Methodists' American Board of Commissioners for Foreign Missions (ABCFM), missionaries harkened back to an older style of Puritanism, the faith of their fathers. Withdrawing from their familiar culture and leaving friends and family behind, they traveled great distances to live in foreign lands in order to serve Christ and to rescue a people whom they perceived as "perishing in sin." So great was their dedication that some of the unmarried male missionaries took an oath of celibacy.[20] This was a severe measure, unusual for Protestants other than Shakers, but it concorded with the missionaries' overall goal of ordering their lives solely around matters of the spirit. It was as if these people were trying to sanctify every aspect of their lives. It should not surprise us that they worried about their own sensuality and that of the Cherokees. These worries colored how they viewed the dress and deportment of Cherokee women and men and caused them to change the clothing of the students at the boarding school.

Because appearance provided an exterior measure of one's spiritual rectitude, missionaries correlated changes in Brown's beliefs and behavior with a transformation in her appearance, and vice versa. Soon after arriving at Brainerd, Catharine Brown increased her involvement in devotional exercises. She committed the Lord's Prayer to memory and enjoyed repeating it by herself after evening prayers.[21] Within three months, she was reading the Bible and inquiring about the Savior. She shared her inner struggles with Mrs. Hall and other missionaries. Trust grew and a strong bond emerged. In essence, Brown became attached to the missionaries, psychologically and emotionally dependent upon them for insight, correction, and inspiration. They became surrogate parents.

As Brown became more involved in Christianity, she changed her appearance, toning down her dress, modifying it to suit the more restrained aesthetic sense of the New Englanders. As she grew in faith, Brown shed her jewelry. She contributed most of it to the cause of missions, but gave a portion of the necklace to a beloved missionary sister, signifying a strong bond with this woman. Stripping away her finery, she transformed herself from a female having an excessive "fondness of dress"[22] into a woman the missionaries deemed "extremely modest,"[23] "neat in her person," and "industrious in her habits."[24] Thus, her inner journey to Christ was mirrored in her external appearance. A native woman wearing too many ornaments became a Christian woman who, according to a missionary publication "would *be* an ornament, to any boarding school in New-England."[25] Changes in clothing provided an index of this and other pilgrims' progress. Saint Paul would have been pleased.[26]

A few years later, Lucius Verus Bierce, a traveler, saw her at her father's inn in Creek Path, Alabama. His description confirmed the result the missionaries sought: "She was probably one fourth Indian, beautiful form, thick set for one of her tribe, dressed in the American style, and but for the small, dark eye, prominent cheek bones and glossy hair would have passed well for an American lady."[27] But Bierce's description also revealed the growing importance of racial categories among non-Natives, that is, the increasing tendency among whites to judge human beings by physical traits that were presumed to reveal their membership in discrete "races" possessing distinctive characters and capabilities. Another way to put this is to say that to some observers Catharine Brown was almost, but not quite, "white." Missionaries, optimistic about the capacity of American Indians and especially Cherokees to civilize, emphasized the "almost" part; their critics, more committed to racialized thinking and apartheid politics, focused on the "not quite" part.

Missionaries eagerly publicized their successes in journals, circular letters, memoirs, and fiction. They featured prominently the story of Catharine Brown, "the first fruits of our labor in this heathen land."[28] In 1819, someone in Connecticut who was familiar with the details of Catharine Brown's story published a short play about her transformation, "Catharine Brown, The Converted Cherokee, A Missionary Drama, Founded on Fact, Written by a Lady." Predictably, this text connected evangelizing with civilizing and conversion to Christ with changes in dress and deportment. The first scene, set in New England among whites only, argues that Indians are not just "monsters of cruelty. . . with tomahawk and scalping knife," but are "capable of improvement." Brainerd, treated in the second scene, provides "occular [*sic*] demonstration of the practicability of civilizing the Savages."[29] According to the stage directions, Catharine Brown arrives "dressed in all her finery: Jewels, wampum, and c." After meeting her, a male missionary concludes that her greatest "love" is for "Indian finery" but he expresses hope that the Almighty might yet save her from "burning."[30]

Meanwhile, two Indian women come to the mission to remove their male children from the supervision of the missionaries. The boys' fathers, the women complain, had taken their sons away from their mothers before they had "fixed" them "fine. You come here, without clothes. They give you them clothes, the missionaries did; but there is no wampum [beads] on them."[31] The boys cry and persuade their mothers to let them stay at Brainerd, where they will continue to dress without "wampum." Almost immediately a fresh shipment of Anglo-style clothing arrives from "the ladies in Philadelphia." The boys receive "jackets and trowsers, and the girls frocks, stocking and shoes; and some calico bonnets."[32]

"Scene Three" reveals that Catharine Brown, now among the "hopeful converts . . . dresses in a becoming manner, and is modest and humble in her deportment . . . neat and plain."[33] When interrogated about her former love of finery, frolicking, and dance, she affirms that she gladly sacrificed them for religion. Much as the boys gave up the chance to wear wampum, she has sacrificed her ornaments. "All my costly jewels and trinkets; my gay ribbons and plumes; I have most willingly given to the charity-box, and keep only these single drops, which I wear in honour to a friend I have lost."[34] A missionary who meets the transformed Brown pronounces her "dignified" and Cherokee chiefs praise her as "pleasant—charming as a bright summer's morning." The chiefs conclude that it is time to forsake "Indian ways" to learn the "religion of the good white men."[35]

The play concludes, however, on a cautionary note, lest readers think the project of evangelizing and civilizing has triumphed. As actually happened at an early point in her education at Brainerd, Catharine Brown's parents assert their control and take their tearful daughter away from the missionaries.[36] In reality, her parents eventually relented and allowed her to return to school. Because this reunion took place after the play was written, it does not appear in the text. Indeed, the last line of the play challenges New Englanders to recommit themselves to the cause of Indian missions and invokes the image of an exiled Catharine Brown. "Oh ye, who with delight, sit under the droppings of the sanctuary, and enjoy the communion of saints, remember Catharine in your prayers."[37] And, the playwright might well have added, "send clothes to Brainerd," so close was the tie between conversion and clothing.

The concern about proper clothing was not just theoretical or theological. Supplying appropriate clothing to their Cherokee students consumed an enormous amount of the energies and funds of missionaries and staff at Brainerd and beyond. Initially, the female staff of the mission—missionary wives, teachers, and daughters—attempted to make the clothes needed to outfit Brainerd's scholars. This repeated the precedent established a decade earlier in Cherokee country by Presbyterian missionary Gideon Blackburn and his wife, but it soon proved too taxing, as it had for the Blackburns.[38] As a mission journal entry recorded, "the continued heat of a southern summer debilitates the nerves of northern people very much—sister Hall is frequently so feeble as to require nursing, and continually unable to labor, except a little at very light work: and some of our children came almost naked."[39]

The journal writer requested help from the Christian women of New England. "Surely our dear sisters at the north would gladly take part with their sisters here in the labor of making clothes for these naked sons of the forest, if they knew their need. We trust this will soon be made known to them, and arrangements made for sending clothes ready made for these children. This would be a great relief, and enable us to take more children without any additional female help." New England women responded quickly, creating female societies and other benevolent organizations to meet the need. An impressive network, staffed largely by local women but administered by male ABCFM officials located in Boston, began supplying Brainerd with clothing, sending hundreds, even thousands of garments. The Brainerd Mission journal entry from November 4, 1819, is typical: "One box was from members of the Female Academy of Litchfield, Con. containing 13 shirts, 4 pr pantaloons, 6 frocks, and 3 hunting shirts. One from females in Northampton, Mass. by Mary Williams Agent, containing 182 articles of clothing, including caps, handkfs, aprons and c—1 towel, 1 pillow case, 39 yds cloth of various kinds, 1 penknife, thread and pins, 1 Bible and a quantity of Tracts."[40]

Subsequently, many dozens of boxes and chests brought hundreds, even thousands of garments, some new, some used, along with tracts, beddings, cloth, homewares, and sundry other items. Boxes came from the Elliot Society, Philadelphia; the Brainerd Society, Philadelphia; the Female Alms Society Benson, Vermont; the Cherokee Society of South Hadley; and from dozens of towns in New England. A box from Yale College arrived February 1821 and brought 113 garments, 40 yds of cloth, and a "pattern for a dress for sister Catharine Brown."[41] Clothing from Philadelphia supporters played a role in the transformation of one of Brown's closest male friends, a fellow convert named John Arch. Examining the stories missionaries told about Arch reveals their anxieties about the "nature" of Indian men.

Arch, reaching Brainerd about a year after Brown, triggered strong reactions from the missionaries. Their first impressions were mixed:

A Cherokee man who does not know his age, thinks he is about 25, apparently not quite so old, offered himself as a schollar. He spoke english, and his countenance indicated a mind that might admit of improvement; but having the dress and dirty appearance of the most uncultivated part of the tribe, and withal a mind and body for so many years under the influence of these habits, we were sorry to hear him say any thing about entering the school.[42]

They later recalled that "his dress and appearance . . . showed . . . he had spent so many years in savage life."[43]

Significantly, Arch arrived at the mission with his gun. The weapon did not alarm the missionaries or seem unusual in 1819 in the hills of eastern Tennessee, but missionaries seized upon the gun as a symbol, an icon of unredeemed male Indianness. "His willingness to part with his gun (a piece of property so dear to the Indian)" the missionaries "considered a favorable omen."[44] The missionaries "agreed to take his gun and pay him for it in clothes as he should want them."[45] This exchange pleased the missionaries, because it epitomized the specific type of changes they sought to encourage among native men under the auspices of a federally sponsored program sometimes referred to as the "civilizing" mission. Indian men, according to the view promoted by federal officials including, Presidents George Washington and Thomas Jefferson, needed to give up their guns and settle down, to stop hunting and start farming. As the 1819 play about Brown put it, Indian boys needed "to leave off hunting, and wandering, for the sake of being industrious and to learn [their] book."[46] Arch's posthumous memoir, published a decade later, traced this very movement. Telling the story of how Christianity tamed a wild man, the memoir revealed just how deeply missionaries and other New Englanders conflated outward appearance with moral character.

Published by the ABCFM in 1829, the memoir depicted Arch's youth as one almost entirely devoted to hunting. Arch's mother, the memoir noted early on, died when he was a small child.

> His father taught him scarcely any thing except to hunt deer and other wild animals of the forest. This was his father's occupation.
>
> The old man, when traveling through the woods in search of game, used to carry his son on his back, and on discovering a deer, would stop and make the little boy over his shoulder till he could see the animal, and then would creep up and shoot it, with John still on his back. As the son grew older, and became expert in discovering deer at a distance, the father would sometimes rest his gun on a bush or log, and make him shoot them. Thus John killed several deer before he could raise a gun to his face, or walk alone through the woods.

As soon as he could run about, and take some care of himself, his father used to leave him all day at the hunting camp; and though he generally returned in the evening, he would sometimes be absent through the night.[47]

By emphasizing Arch's wildness, his immersion in nature, and his precocious prowess as a hunter, the memoir evoked the culturally dominant colonial myth of the Indian male as a wild, roaming savage raised to violence.[48] But the memoir did not stop there. If it had, it would merely have supported anti-Indian, anti-mission sentiments coalescing at that very moment around the ex-Indian fighter and dispossessor Andrew Jackson, who became president in 1829 and enforced the politics of Indian Removal. The memoir continued to relate how Arch converted to Christianity, served the mission as an interpreter and translator, and died with his new faith intact. The message conveyed to New Englanders was simple: Indians could be saved. ABCFM missionaries could domesticate the wildest man in America and turn gun toters into Bible quoters.

But this transformation, missionaries warned, could occur only if other Christians rallied to support the missionary cause. Viewing themselves as humble beggars on behalf of the desperate heathen, they sought to convey to New Englanders the importance of their gifts, especially gifts of clothing. Material gifts communicated Christian values and opened the way to conversion, they affirmed.[49] The gifts from New Englanders were

not merely clothing the naked and relieving the distressed; but . . . [were] preaching Christ; and in that manner calculated to engage the attention, and interest the feelings, of the rudest savage. He beholds his child, the object of his warmest affections, decently and comfortably clad. And who has done this? A Christian [struck through] person whose situation precludes the possibility of his expecting, or receiving, any return from his beneficiary. Every dollar given to supply the mission fund, may be considered not merely as going to support missions, but itself becoming a missionary.[50]

As this metaphor indicates, the missionaries posited a seamless link or unbroken exchange between material and spiritual realms.

Because they connected spirit and body, piety and appearance, religion and gender roles, the missionaries could not be satisfied with change in only one dimension of Cherokee life. Correct belief was not enough, nor was civilized appearance alone sufficient. Influenced by Christian traditions of modesty but also by discourses of Indians as natural beings, missionaries worked hard to radically restructure Cherokee everyday life. Brainerd, after all, was a Christian boarding school designed in a comprehensive way to transform Cherokee boys and girls into New England Protestants.[51]

As historian William G. McLoughlin explains, in addition to being a formal school employing the Lancastrian model of education, where older students taught younger ones, "Brainerd was designed to be a model farm. . . . [The boys] learned the principles of the three-field system of planting, how to care for horses and cattle, how to plough, harvest, and grind corn at the mission gristmill and how to saw wood at the mission sawmill. Some were apprenticed to blacksmiths or other mechanics. . . . The students became in fact an essential part of the labor force."[52] Brainerd was a place where young men learned practical outdoor skills. Hence, the boys' dorm's location near the garden.

A model farm, Brainerd was also a model home where female students were taught to handle "domestic concerns," to sew, clean, cook, iron, nurse, and babysit. Hence, the location of the girls' schoolhouse near the mission house. While John Arch and other boys were in the fields or at the mills, Catharine Brown and other girls were inside working at household tasks under the guidance of female teachers and missionary wives. They were learning how to be housewives, training for life in a social order organized in accord with emerging white gender roles. The only other vocational option modeled for girls was that of missionary, missionary teacher, or missionary wife.[53]

If boys and girls attended different classrooms and learned different practical skills, they were taught common virtues: "the habits of obedience, hard work, promptness, tidiness, thoroughness, and self-discipline."[54] And they received the same religious training, beginning their days at 5:30 A.M. with prayer and hymns, passing the morning with Bible lessons, praying before meals and at bedtime. Throughout the day, individual students would receive words of spiritual encouragement, guidance, correction, and inquiry from vigilant missionaries. Missionaries monitored their students closely for signs of contrition, repentance, and salvation. And they disciplined them for infractions of Christian order, dismissing them for sins such as theft or fornication. Designed as a model farm and home, Brainerd was intended also to be a model community, united in Christ.

Viewed generations later from a more critical vantage point, Brainerd seems less benign, the missionaries' idealism limned with unconscious bigotry. Some postcolonial critics might label the missionaries' project one of "cultural genocide," that is, the intentional destruction of a people's distinctive way of being in the world. Thus many Cherokees withdrew their children from Brainerd and returned the clothing provided by missionaries. But if the ABCFM missionaries' program seems to anticipate the totalistic programs that were later institutionalized at post–Civil War boarding schools like Carlisle Indian Industrial School in Carlisle, Pennsylvania—where incoming students were stripped of all signs of "Indianness" and forced to speak English—we need to avoid anachronistically equating Brainerd with later models. We need to consider Brainerd in its own historical context and note how it contrasted with more pernicious policies and approaches advanced by powerful contemporary whites, including the seventh president of the United States, Andrew Jackson.

For all of its parochialness, the missionaries' project affirmed the Cherokees' humanity, their capacity for reason, learning, literacy, and public life. Missionaries were ethnocentric and some were racists, but not all were hardcore racists. Their very focus on religion and their near obsession with clothing reveals this. Confession and clothing concerned them far more than did skin color or pedigree.

Because of this peculiar kind of conservatism, missionaries could sometimes act in oppositional ways, running afoul of public opinion and public policy. Missionary leaders, in spite of widespread white prejudice, defended intermarriage. Jeremiah Evarts, a leading policymaker for the American Board of Commissioners for Foreign Missions, chided whites obsessed with race. He regarded the phenotypic difference between Europeans and Cherokees as "a small variance in complexion."[55] Promoting integration, he clashed with supporters of Indian removal, an American version of apartheid. As race-based thinking spread, missionaries' old-fashioned Christian universalism brought them into direct conflict with townsfolk in New England, states in the South, and with federal authorities.[56]

During the 1810s and 1820s, missionaries and Cherokees had co-constructed a rich project of redemption, revitalization, and *redress*, but it would not save the Cherokees from novel forms of massive violent assault and state-sponsored apartheid. In spite of the missionaries' and the Cherokee converts' best efforts, the idea of "civilizing" Indians, let alone supporting their sovereignty or autonomy in their ancestral lands, lost public support. Racialistic thinking and racist policies gained force. In the age of Jackson, Cherokees could change their clothes all they wanted and it would not matter. The promise of conversion had always been tainted by the missionaries' ethnocentrism, now it was contradicted by their opponents' racism. No matter how sincerely Catharine Brown prayed or how properly she behaved, her eye would always remain "dark," her cheekbones "prominent," and her hair "glossy." She, like her sisters, could not finally pass "for an American lady" anymore than John Arch, like his brothers, could gain full acceptance beyond Cherokee country. In a nation with Andrew Jackson as its president, male and female Cherokees could change their clothes and quote the Bible all they wanted and more, but this conversion would not prevent the forced removal of most of their nation or the theft of most of their lands.

NOTES

The author would like to acknowledge the constructive responses to earlier versions of this work provided by the late John Andrew, and by Jon Sensbach, Patricia Galloway, Justine Smith, Theda Perdue, Misty Bastian, David Thomson, Reshela DuPuis, Karen Seat, and Christine Heyrman. An earlier version of this essay, given as a talk at the conference "Rituals and Spirits: Religious Contact and Change in the Early Atlantic World," held at the University of Florida in October 2000, is being published separately along with other talks from that gathering.

1. Founded by Massachusetts Congregationalists in 1810, the American Board of Commissioners for Foreign Missions supported missions across the globe, including the foreign parts of North America. In 1816, the Board sent Samuel J. Mills, William Goodell, and Cyrus Kingsbury into Indian country to identify nations suited for mission work. These men determined that southern Indians were the most likely candidates for civilization, and of these, the Cherokees the easiest to transform into a people "English in language, civilized in habits, and Christian in religion" (William Ellsworth Strong, *The Story of the American Board* [New York: Arno Press, 1969], 36).

2. Rufus Anderson, ed., *Memoir of Catharine Brown, A Christian Indian of the Cherokee Nation* (2d ed., Boston: Crocker and Brewster, 1825), 17.

3. Isaac, Donald, and Campbell to the Prudential Committee, May 29, 1818, American Board of Commissioners for Foreign Missions Papers, quoted in Wade Alston Horton, "Protestant Missionary Women as Agents of Cultural Transition

among Cherokee Women, 1801–1839" Ph.D. diss. Southern Theological Seminary, 1992, 184.

4. M. Hall to Jeremiah Evarts, February 14, 1824, 18.3.1, v. 3, American Board of Commissioners for Foreign Missions Papers (ABCFM Papers). Houghton Library, Harvard University, Cambridge, Massachusetts.

5. M. Hall to Jeremiah Evarts, February 14, 1824, 18.3.1, v. 3, ABCFM Papers.

6. Ibid.

7. Native men mixed clothing genres with equal creativity. An affluent Cherokee man, for example, might wear a combination of domestically produced and market-provided fabrics: deerskin, wool, silk, and cotton. A head-and-shoulders portrait of a prominent Creek leader, dated 1790, shows him in a "cloth turban, ornamental feathers, earbobs, trade-bead necklace, silver gorget, ruffled shirt, and great coat with metal buttons," in Kathryn E. Holland Braund, *Deerskins and Duffels: The Creek Indian Trade with Anglo America, 1685–1815* (Lincoln: University of Nebraska Press, 1993), 108.

8. William Bartram, *Travels through North and South Carolina, Georgia, East and West Florida, the Cherokee Country, the Extensive Territories of the Muscogulges, or Creek Confederacy, and the Country of the Choctaws* (New York: Penguin, 1988 [1791]), 393.

9. William G. McLoughlin, *Cherokees and Missionaries, 1789–1839* (New Haven: Yale University Press, 1984), 71.

10. Bartram, *Travels*, 395.

11. John Howard Payne, "The Green-Corn Dance," *Continental Monthly* 1 (1862): 17–29, quotation on 28.

12. Initially, Brainerd attracted the children of the Cherokee elite, the numerically small, relatively affluent, culturally hybridized category of slave-owning Cherokees that included Catharine Brown. Hunger for education drew Brown to the school. Brown had learned to read simple texts with the help of Cherokee friends and possibly African American slaves. Additional students had encountered formal education before reaching Brainerd. After briefly attending a white school in his childhood, John Arch harbored "the hope of learning" and "cultivating his mind at school" (*Memoir of John Arch* [Boston: Massachusetts Sabbath School Union, 1829], 10–11). Upon arrival at Brainerd, neither he nor Brown expressed interest in Christianity itself. If anything, they communicated indifference; Brown later said she thought Christianity was something for white people only. This nonchalance did not alarm the missionaries, but their style of dress and self-presentation presented a tangible and preexisting condition that the missionaries sought to erase.

13. Payne, "The Green-Corn Dance," 28.

14. Roxann Wheeler, *The Complexion of Race: Categories of Difference in Eighteenth-Century British Culture* (Philadelphia: University of Pennsylvania Press, 2000), 17.

15. Quoted in Robert Blair St. George, *Conversing by Signs: Poetics of Implication in Colonial New England Culture* (Chapel Hill: University of North Carolina Press, 1998), 148. St. George's ideas also influenced other points in this paragraph.

16. Kathleen Brown, "Native Americans and Early Modern Concepts of Race," in Martin Daunton and Rick Halpern, eds., *Empire and Others: British Encounters with Indigenous Peoples, 1600-1850* (Philadelphia: University of Pennsylvania Press, 1999), 79–100, quotation on 91–92.

17. Bartram, *Travels*, 214. Bartram continues, however, to explain that excessive consumption of alcohol caused the lewd behavior and that Seminoles would ordinarily have avoided or punished such debauchery.

18. Ibid., 289.

19. Theda Perdue, *Cherokee Women: Gender and Culture Change, 1700–1835* (Lincoln: University of Nebraska Press, 1998).

20. Journal of Daniel Sabin Butrick, March 27, 1827, 18.3.3, v. 4, ABCFM Papers.

21. M. Hall to Jeremiah Evarts, February 14, 1824, ABCFM Papers.

22. Anderson, *Memoir of Catharine Brown*, 28.

23. Laura W. Potter to Jeremiah Evarts, November 1824, 18.3.1, v.4, ABCFM Papers.

24. M. Hall to Jeremiah Evarts, February 14, 1824, 18.3.1, v.3, ABCFM Papers.

25. "Catharine Brown, the Converted Cherokee, a Missionary Drama, Founded on Fact, Written by a Lady" (New Haven, 1819), 13.

26. M. Hall to Jeremiah Evarts, February 14, 1824, ABCFM Papers.

27. Lucius Verus Bierce, Travels in the Southland, 1822–23 (Columbus: Ohio State University Press, 1966), 93–94, quoted in Larry J. Smith, ed., *Guntersville Remembered* (Albertville, Ala.: Creative Printers, 1989), 18.

28. Journal of the Cherokee Missions, Brainerd, January 25, 1818, ABCFM Papers.

29. "Catharine Brown, the Converted Cherokee," 4–5.

30. Ibid., 6.

31. Ibid., 6.

32. Ibid., 7.

33. Ibid., 8, 9.

34. Ibid., 10.

35. Ibid., 17.

36. On January 25, 1818, the missionaries baptized Catharine Brown, making her their first full convert. The missionaries had rushed the rite, because Brown's parents insisted upon withdrawing her from Brainerd. They intended to take her west to the Arkansas region where they hoped to avoid white harassment and exploitation. She left with them, an unhappy but dutiful daughter. Later, her parents relented and allowed her to return to the school.

37. "Catharine Brown, the Converted Cherokee," 27.

38. Gideon Blackburn, "Letter III," *Panoplist* (December 1807), 323. See also McLoughlin, *Cherokees and Missionaries*, 57.

39. *The Brainerd Mission Journal*, June 18, 1818, in Joyce B. Phillips and Paul Gary Phillips, *The Brainerd Journal: A Mission to the Cherokees, 1817–1823* (Lincoln: University of Nebraska Press, 1998), 65.

40. Ibid., November 4, 1819, 136.

41. Ibid., February 15, 1821, 207.

42. Ibid., January 26, 1819, 104.

43. *Memoir of John Arch*, 9.

44. *The Brainerd Mission Journal*, January 26, 1819, in Phillips and Phillips, 104.

45. Ibid.

46. "Catharine Brown, the Converted Cherokee," 11.

47. *Memoir of John Arch*, 5–7.

48. Richard Slotkin, *Regeneration Through Violence* (Middletown, Conn.: Wesleyan University Press, 1973).

49. *The Brainerd Mission Journal*, January 8, 1819, in Phillips and Phillips, 102.

50. Note how the rhetoric glorifies a single male benefactor and overlooks the largely female labor of making and collecting clothes for the missions.

51. E. D. Graham, "American Indian Slavery as an Issue in Mission Work," typescript (1956), 44, ABCFM Papers. For more details about the design of the school and daily instructional and devotional patterns, see Joel Martin, *The Land Looks after Us: A History of Native American Religion* (New York: Oxford University Press, 2001), 68–70. This and some subsequent paragraphs repeat some ideas and phrases from my earlier work.

52. McLoughlin, *Cherokees and Missionaries*, 139.

53. Ibid. See also Martin, *The Land Looks after Us*, 68–70.

54. McLoughlin, *Cherokees and Missionaries*, 138.

55. Jeremiah Evarts to Rev. Calvin Chapin, July 5, 1825, in E. C. Tracy, *Memoir of the Life of Jeremiah Evarts*, Esq. (Boston: Crocker and Brewster, 1845), 222–23.

56. See John Andrew, "Educating the Heathen: The Foreign Mission School Controversy and American Ideals," *American Studies* 12/3 (1978): 331–342.

SUGGESTIONS FOR FURTHER READING

Andrew, John. *From Revivals to Removal: Jeremiah Evarts, the Cherokee Nation, and the Search for the Soul of America*. Athens: University of Georgia Press, 1992.

McLoughlin, William G. *Cherokees and Missionaries, 1789–1839.* New Haven: Yale University Press, 1984.

Perdue, Theda. *Cherokee Women: Gender and Culture Change, 1700–1835.* Lincoln: University of Nebraska Press, 1998.

Phillips, Joyce B. and Paul Gary Phillips. *The Brainerd Journal: A Mission to the Cherokees, 1817–1823.* Lincoln: University of Nebraska Press, 1998.

Tinker, George E. *Missionary Conquest: The Gospel and Native American Cultural Genocide.* Minneapolis: Fortress Press, 1993.

Treat, James, ed. *Native and Christian: Indigenous Voices on Religious Identity in the United States and Canada.* New York: Routledge, 1996.

Chapter 4

Indigenous Identity and Story
The Telling of Our Part in the Sacred Homeland

Nimachia Hernandez

This chapter is about Native peoples' stories and the way these stories shape identity and spiritual practices. I argue that Native American identity is inseparable from the land and the cosmos, and it is from Native experience of the land and the cosmos that our stories emerge. Before addressing those stories, it is important to provide a context for interpreting their significance. This context involves the manner in which Western culture and academics have demeaned Native ways of knowing, and particularly the Native use of story. Discussing this history is an essential step toward gaining an understanding of the role of story, or "myth," in the maintenance of Native identity. Race has played a role in understanding Native peoples and stories, but this is because outside understandings of Native peoples are subject to racial thinking, not because traditional Native stories deem race an essential part of beliefs about the inherent nature of the world and people.

Contextualizing Native Stories: "Scientific" Racism, Genocide, and the Suppression of Native Spirituality

For centuries, Western academics have held that the "knowledge" that is defined as such by the rules and traditions of Western perspectives is what constitutes real or true (i.e., superior to other cultures') knowledge. While indigenous story-based knowledge is a long-standing, viable tradition around the world, literature on Native Americans has not considered

oral traditions to be relevant to the process, purpose, or findings of research. It has excluded Native knowledge and its foundational structures
and expressions from serious consideration as representative of a dis-
tinctly Native religious philosophy. Western philosophers, using Western
scientific principles, have debated the possibility that "primitive" cultures
around the world may have "religious philosophies" and have generally
decided that their culture's conception of a philosophy of religion precludes culturally distinct perspectives on the issue. The Western concern
with the universality of Truth and the assumption that what is right, true,
or functional within one culture would be right for all collides with the
indigenous perspective that every culture may have what is right for it.

By declaring one type of religious system "legitimate" (i.e., those that
posit one universal truth, as the Judeo-Christian tradition does), all other
types of knowledge become superstitions, paranoia, perspectives, beliefs,
neuroses,[1] magic, supernatural, witchcraft, pseudoscience, parasciences,
demonology, metaphysics, spiritism, superstitions, the occult,[2] and the
like. Western perspectives thus never really grant traditional Native stories the status of "truth" that is rooted in Western concepts of religion.

Long before academic disciplines such as linguistics, folklore, anthropology, and religious studies developed, Euro-Americans were trying to
understand indigenous peoples and were imposing Judeo-Christian-in-
formed perceptions upon Native knowledge or "beliefs" and their accompanying practices.[3] As many of the belief systems of the European immigrants to the Americas were founded on culturally exclusive and sometimes racist principles, they interpreted Native peoples' beliefs as
reflecting an inferior, often "evil" religion (an interpretation that included accusations of devil worship, cannibalism, and infanticide, coupled with claims that Natives' "heathen ways" were due to their childlike
minds).[4] An alternative to these claims was that Natives had no religion at
all, that they held nothing as sacred.[5] The latter belief was a common perception among European immigrants to Canada, while the former interpretation of indigenous peoples as Satan worshipers prevailed in the
United States. Although Enlightenment ideas came to the New World by
1700, Calvinist Protestantism with its stark dualisms and its strong belief
in the devil remained central to the perceptions of Natives throughout
the colonial period.[6]

The fear of different races and their presumed satanic practices that
arrived in the New World with the Puritans influenced the treatment of
indigenous peoples, and it continues to pervade the perception of Natives

today.[7] Such fears not only justified whites' increased intolerance, but also inspired an all-out war against the beliefs and practices deemed most sacrilegious, rendering Natives as God's enemies. Various churches, with civil and military backing, acted against native peoples.[8] The result has been centuries of atrocities against Natives, including massacres, government prohibition of Native ceremonies, imprisonment of anyone suspected of participating in or conducting such ceremonies, legalized abduction of young children followed by forced attendance at boarding schools (for years at a stretch), and forced indoctrination into several Christian denominations,[9] causing "cultural genocide in the classroom."[10] Native children's mandatory attendance at Anglo schools has historically been and continues to be part of a conscious, deliberate, and systematic effort to suppress and extinguish Natives' practices and beliefs.[11] Legalized hostilities against indigenous communities still exist, destroying the traditional network of authority and social and spiritual cohesion.[12]

All indigenous nations have endured policies aimed at starvation, land theft, and widespread destruction of Native sustenance systems—physical, spiritual, and otherwise. For instance, it was widely believed that Native "medicine" posed the most serious challenge to efforts to convert and "civilize" Indigenous peoples:[13]

> The holy men of the Indian nations were ridiculed, imprisoned, and often times, killed. The spirituality of the indigenous people was forced to go underground in order to survive. It was brought out on special occasions, such as on White holidays, and cleverly disguised as part of the local celebration. But for the most part, it was practiced in secret, thereby lending ammunition to the preachings of the local ministers intent on destroying it, that its believers were practicing black magic and were devil worshippers.[14]

The debasement of Native spirituality extended to nearly all aspects of indigenous life:

> In an unrelenting attack, the priests sought to ridicule outright the Indians' "foolish beliefs" and "superstitions" in act and deed. They brazenly interrupted Indian ritual with their prayers, poked fun at Indian concerns with dreams, challenged and denigrated hunting ceremonies, and scoffed at the threats of the . . . "devil." Some of their most divisive ploys included insulting or humiliating shamans in public, debasing idols, rolling away

sacred stones, destroying objects used in a dog feast, and in one case, casting the carcass of the dog itself into a nearby river.[15]

By the 1800s, territorial expansion was a key aim of the U.S. government and Native peoples stood in the way of this expansion. One proposed solution to the problem of Native resistance was forcible removal from sacred land bases[16] to reservations.[17] The impact of this removal cannot be overstated. Native peoples understood the ecological relationships of their homeland as the basis of ceremonial life:

> Traditional religious practices of Native Americans are inseparably bound to land and natural formations. These may be places were spirits dwell, where sources of power are, spots where spirits often reveal themselves. A relationship to specific physical areas is fundamental in traditional Native American religions. From one generation to the next, continuity of spiritual and traditional beliefs is maintained through the natural world. Tribal religions do not incorporate a set of established truths (theological doctrines) as do Western religions; rather they are based on the performance of rituals and ceremonies, many at specific sites, which have the ability to generate new "revelations." These sites are often related to tribal creation stories and other historical events of religious significance. For many tribal religions, there is no alternative place of worship. When freedom of religion is discussed in the context of traditional Indian religion, it is the right of practitioners to maintain relationships with the natural world that is at issue. . . . As has historically been the case in regard to the Indian's relationship with the land, the institutions of the federal government frequently have failed to respect the needs of Indians where incompatible with the needs and philosophy of Western society.[18]

The forced removal from sacred lands was thus a significant way in which traditional Native spiritual practices have been interfered with and homelands destroyed:

> A central issue of Native American religious practice is the overriding value attributed to nature and ecological integrity. . . . For traditional Native Americans there is a sacred unity of nature, humanity, and "supernatural powers" that requires the moral acknowledgment of wild nature. The consequence of these beliefs is that spirits of nature are fully integrated into all aspects of social, cultural, and environmental activity, and are

therefore definitive in traditional religious practice. . . . Affirming this ecological orientation of Native American religions is the fact that land is central in their traditions. Specific geographic provinces are understood as
places of origin, home of ancestors and relatives, as well as the loci of other
significant matters in religious life. Accordingly, Native American religions
are not easily understood within the common framework of the role of religion in Western society.[19]

The significance of environmental knowledge and its interrelatedness
with the social and spiritual life of indigenous peoples is reflected in their
traditional stories. They underscore the need to understand the ties to
land and environment that are the foundations of the rules for traditional indigenous existence.

Casting the Natives' way of life as demonic and ridiculing traditional
ways was, and continues to be, instrumental in rationalizing abuse of Native people by emissaries of both church and state. By reinforcing images
of barbarism and savagery in the American imagination, they made it acceptable to dehumanize Natives, leaving them susceptible to manipulation or annihilation.[20] As these views of Natives have taken hold, an understanding of the centrality of their stories about themselves, and the inseparability of the people from the land in the Native mind, has been lost.

Commonly called "myths," the stories that form the basis of Native
cultures everywhere have been studied in different ways, with different
goals. Studies have aimed to determine linguistic and thematic concepts,
gender relationships and associations, historical evidence for land occupation or trade routes, religious affiliations with other Native nations,
kinship systems, and other aspects of culture.

Undoubtedly, some sought genuine understanding of Native worldviews and wanted to explore Native conceptions of ultimate reality or
philosophy, of which cosmology (the understanding of the universe) has
a part.[21] But the racist premise basic to much science persisted in the different studies of "primitive man."[22] In the nineteenth century it became
obvious to a majority of the "civilized" people of the world that there was
only one human species, but this did not prevent the ordering of the
"races" into a hierarchy justified by "science," with Native peoples occu-
pying one of the lower rungs.[23] This vision of the social order validated
the looting of indigenous burial sites for the purpose of measuring (i.e.,
proving) the biological (i.e., racial) inferiority of Natives compared to
"whites."[24]

A discussion of this history may initially seem unnecessary because in the academic world today, there has been a growing awareness of a need to seek more open perspectives on Native issues, and Native topics have been increasingly welcomed in the academy. But this trend, less than a generation old, gives the impression that deep wounds have healed and that misunderstandings have been put aside. Both non-Natives and Natives are still struggling with the prejudices and mistrust that developed over centuries of Euro-America's aggressive determination to terminate the traditional way of life for Native peoples. It continues today as many Christian ministers refer to practitioners of Native spirituality as "heathens" and call their stories "heresy."

Moreover, the stories of Native peoples have traditionally been considered unworthy of serious study as sources of religious philosophy. Yet they are the vehicles for carrying on the teachings that form the backbone of the various indigenous peoples' cultures.[25] Indigenous peoples' stories have purposes that reach far beyond the need simply to deal with the fear of striving to exist in a world of harsh climates, unpredictability, danger, and proximity to death on a daily basis. The stories help to explain the world, and express a sense of unity and oneness with the energy forces of all life. They represent knowledge traditions that are respected within their framework, and the telling of the stories is the important link for access to this knowledge.

It is possible, of course, to access knowledge through means other than the Western framework, and to hold such knowledge in as much esteem. Traditional indigenous knowledge informs us about a unique way of knowing and of pursuing and considering knowledge that is rooted in the land and cosmos, encompassing the entire universe. While many of the positions regarding the nature of truth and ways to understand truth have been thoroughly discussed within academic circles, much still has not been addressed adequately regarding how these positions reflect—or fail to reflect—the existence or reality of Native peoples. In part because few Natives are included in the discourse, Native viewpoints are often overlooked, with important ramifications.

Many indigenous people object to the classification systems inherent in some academic discourse (including the use of terms such as "myth"). The mere translation of a cultural narrative into the English language has the potential to substantially distort its meaning. Words in indigenous languages (as in all languages) gain their meanings from distinctive contexts and are subject to nuances accessible only to those who not only speak the languages, but also share those contexts. The main objection to the distortion of "Native reality," then, does not primarily have to do with which discipline happens to be analyzing it, but with the nature of academic language and how it alters Native reality.

In this context, scholars like S. J. Gould[26] exhort us to realize how deeply the oral tradition has been excised from Western culture, and to observe the effect: we value one type of mind over others. In short, to understand how orality functions in a culture, we must attend to the ways it is perceived by those doing the investigating. Indigenous stories relate realities in a domain in which knowledge is multiple, context dependent, collectively asserted, and spiritually derived.[27] Indigenous stories are about the metaphysics of pan-consciousness and a sociopolitics of interdependence and cooperation, with storytellers serving as collectively voiced community autobiographers.[28] This is as true of the stories told by the most modern storytellers as it likely was long ago.

How Do We Know Who We Are? The Stories Tell Us

With the historical and academic context explained above in mind, let us begin to discuss the stories themselves and how they are understood by Native peoples. Indigenous peoples take for granted a clear relationship between cosmology and what Westerners have termed "religion" (a term for which there is no equivalent in any Native language). From this perspective, religion and cosmology are seen as parts of the same whole. Numerous Native peoples have been of interest to academics in part because their traditional cultural ways and beliefs clearly connect their understanding of the cosmos with their broader, more general perspectives on knowledge. This connection is taught through the religious practice and ceremony of a variety of indigenous peoples around the world, with many examples from the Americas.[29] Naked-eye astronomy used by the "prophet-scientists" of times past was one of the first scientific approaches that formed the foundation of various societies' cultural, religious, and philosophical constructions.[30] Native narratives orient lifeways in accordance with planetary cycles. Despite the variety of contexts, indigenous self-conceptions also generally accept that all Native peoples have traditions rooted in their unique geographical surroundings that are functional enough—scientifically, historically, socially, and spiritually— for those who live by them. Attempting to understand these traditions and narratives from outside Native culture has led to much confusion since aspects of these narratives such as the role of stories in history, the validity of "very ancient or mythical events,"[31] first or secondhand accounts,[32] and the use of "sacred" time subvert not only the Euro-American narrative but many "commonsense" notions about the nature of time itself.[33]

Sacred Earth, Sacred Sites, and Harmony and Identity with Nature

What we know about who we are as indigenous people is a reflection of what we know about our relationship with the land and its accompanying cosmos. Native peoples' traditions are bound to the environmental, ecosystemic, and cosmic contexts in which they have been originally conceived and practiced. It makes sense to attempt an understanding of Native concepts of peoplehood beginning with their natural geographical and astronomical surroundings. Elements of both are considered sacred and have a strong influence on ceremonial life. Ceremonies and traditions are at the root of indigenous systems of knowing all things, including identity. One characteristic of the predominantly oral culture of many Native "ways" is that the basic precepts and practices of those "ways" are transferred to younger generations by oral tradition and by practicing those traditions in their appropriate settings.[34] The land, and the stories of our relationship to it, tells us who and what we are.

The oral tradition has taught Native peoples for thousands of years. The spiritual directives handed down from generation to generation have come in the form of stories. Each Native culture has developed a use and structure of language that helps make the connections necessary to understand the phenomena of life. People believe in stories not from careful analysis to try to ferret out the "truth," or because they can pin down the precise date for every occurrence. What is important is that a way of life that was offered as a model of rightness, or as an alternative to other more maladaptive strategies for survival, has continued, and that its worth is reaffirmed through the practice of the stories.

Within my own Blackfoot tradition, there are a number of stories that model goals and practices that reflect the Blackfoot philosophy and identity with the land and cosmos. Some of the "persons" who play key roles in defining the Blackfoot's present relationship with the Blackfoot homeland, and who appear throughout the stories, include the Sun, Moon, Morning Star, and those who live on the sacred Earth, including Katoyis, Scarface, Napi (Trickster), and Feather and Elk Woman. A thorough understanding of the roles these "persons" play in the creation of the Blackfoot homeland is necessary to understand how identity is still being lived by the Blackfoot in the same space/place where the first beings were created, and where the Blackfoot were created. The local mountains, rivers, coulees, cliffs, and prairies are part of the concept of "land," as are the stars and planets, the wind, and the directions. As Gregory Cajete explains,

> Within the contexts of Native American mythologies, certain geographical features personify ties between natural processes. Generally, such features are looked upon as sacred places. These natural features may be specific formations, springs, lakes, rivers, mountains, or other natural places. All these features, physically, visually, and metaphysically represent concentric rings in Nature. Many are symbols of life sustainers such as corn, deer, buffalo, fish, rain, clouds, and forests. An understanding of the relationships inherent in these ties is essential to survival. Therefore, much attention is given to ways of knowing and learning about important natural phenomena. Myths represent a way of mapping a particular landscape. Relating the stories associated with a particular geographic place is a way to begin developing a cognitive map of that place and of its concentric rings of interrelationship.[35]

The following excerpt exemplifies the ancestral relationship that the present-day Blackfoot people share with the universe. Since there is only enough space to share one version of one of these stories here, it is difficult to demonstrate the ways in which they are interconnected and intertwined, how they circle back on themselves, and how they continue to influence present interpretations of identity. For present purposes, the following story sample known as "Star Boy (Scarface)" shows how the Blackfoot can use the "reliving" of these stories through their retelling and reenacting of them. The evolution or progression of *who the Blackfoot are* is also explained through this story:[36]

> We know not when the Sun-dance had its origin. It was long ago, when the Blackfoot used dogs for beasts of burden instead of horses; when they stretched the legs and bodies of their dogs on sticks to make them large,

and when they used stones instead of wooden pegs to hold down their lodges. In those days, during the moon of flowers (early summer), our people were camped near the mountains. It was a cloudless night and a warm wind blew over the prairie. Two young girls were sleeping in the long grass outside the lodge. Before daybreak, the eldest sister, So-at-sa-ki (Feather Woman) awoke. The Morning Star was just rising from the prairie. He was very beautiful, shining through the clear air of early morning. She lay gazing at this wonderful star, until he seemed very close to her, and she imagined that he was her lover. Finally, she awoke her sister, exclaiming, "Look at the Morning Star! He is beautiful and must be very wise. Many of the young men have wanted to marry me, but I love only the Morning Star." When the leaves were turning yellow (autumn), So-at-sa-ki became very unhappy, finding herself with child. She was a pure maiden, although not knowing the father of her child. When people discovered her secret, they taunted and ridiculed her, until she wanted to die. One day while the geese were flying southward, So-at-sa-ki went alone to the river for water. As she was returning home, she beheld a young man standing before her in the trail. She modestly turned aside to pass, but he put forth his hand, as if to detain her, and she said angrily, "Stand aside! None of the young men have ever before dared to stop me." He replied, "I am the Morning Star. One night during the moon of flowers, I beheld you sleeping in the open and loved you. I have now come to ask you to return with me to the sky, to the lodge of my father, the Sun, where we will live together, and you will have no more trouble."

Then So-at-sa-ki remembered the night in spring, when she slept outside the lodge, and now realized that Morning Star was her husband. She saw in his hair a yellow plume, and in his hand a juniper branch with a spider web hanging from one end. . . . So-at-sa-ki replied hesitatingly, "I must first say farewell to my father and mother" but Morning Star allowed her to speak to no one. . . . He directed her to shut her eyes. She held the upper strand of the spider web in her hand and placed her feet upon the lower one. When he told her to open her eyes, she was in the sky. They were standing together before a large lodge. Morning Star said, "This is the home of my father and mother, the Sun and the Moon," and bade her enter. It was day-time and the Sun was away on his long journey, but the Moon was at home. Morning Star addressed his mother saying, "One night I beheld this girl sleeping on the prairie. I loved her and she is now my wife." The Moon welcomed So-at-sa-ki to their home. In the evening when the Sun Chief came home, he also gladly received her. . . . So-at-sa-ki lived happily in the sky with Morning Star, and learned many wonderful things. When her child was born, they called him Star Boy. The Moon then gave So-at-sa-ki a root digger, saying, "This should only be used by a pure woman. You can dig all kinds of roots with it, but I warn you not to dig up the large turnip growing near the home of Spider Man. You now have a child and it would bring unhappiness to all."

Everywhere So-at-sa-ki went, she carried her baby and the root digger. She often saw the large turnip, but was afraid to touch it. One day, while passing the wonderful turnip, she thought of the mysterious warning of the Moon, and became curious to see what might be underneath. Laying her baby on the ground, she dug until her root digger stuck fast. Two large cranes came flying from the east. So-at-sa-ki besought them to help her. Thrice she called in vain, but upon the fourth call, they circled and lighted beside her. The chief crane sat upon one side of the turnip and his wife on the other. He took hold of the turnip with his long sharp bill, and moved it backwards and forwards, singing the medicine song: "This root is sacred. Whenever I dig, my roots are sacred."

He repeated this song to the north, south, east, and west. After the fourth song he pulled up the turnip. So-at-sa-ki looked through the hole and beheld the earth. Although she had not known it, the turnip had filled the same hole through which Morning Star had brought her into the sky. Looking down, she saw the camp of the Blackfeet, where she had lived. She sat for a long while gazing at the old familiar scenes. The young men were playing games. The women were tanning hides and making lodges, gathering berries on the hills, and crossing the meadows to the river for water. When she turned to go home, she was crying, for she felt lonely, and longed to be back again upon the green prairies with her own people. When So-at-sa-ki arrived at the lodge, Morning Star looked at this wife and he exclaimed, "You have dug up the sacred turnip!" When she did not reply, the Moon said, "I warned you not to dig up the turnip, because I love Star Boy and do not wish to part with him." Nothing more was said, because it was daytime and the great Sun Chief was still away on his long journey. In the evening, when he entered the lodge, he exclaimed, "What is the matter with my daughter? She looks sad and must be in trouble." So-at-sa-ki replied, "Yes, I am homesick because I have today looked down upon my people." Then the Sun Chief was angry and said to Morning Star, "If she has disobeyed, you must send her home." The Moon interceded for So-at-sa-ki, but the Sun answered, "She can no longer be happy with us. It is better for her to return to her own people." Morning Star led So-at-sa-ki to the home of the Spider Man, whose web had drawn her up into the sky. He placed on her head the sacred Medicine Bonnet, which is worn only by pure women. He laid Star Boy on her breast, and wrapping them both in the elk-skin robe, bade her farewell, saying, "We will let you down into the center of the Indian camp and the people will behold you as you come from the sky." The Spider Man then carefully let them down through the hole to the earth.

It was evening in midsummer, during the moon when the berries are ripe, when So-at-sa-ki was let down from the sky. Many of the people were outside their lodges, when suddenly they beheld a bright light in the northern sky. They saw it pass across the heavens and watched, until it sank to the ground. When the Indians reached the place where the star had fallen, they saw a strange-looking bundle. When the elk-skin cover was opened, they found a woman and her child. So-at-sa-ki was recognized by her parents. She returned to their lodge and lived with them, but never was happy. She used to go with Star Boy to the summit of a high ridge, where she sat and mourned for her husband. One night she remained alone upon the ridge. Before daybreak, when Morning Star rose from the plains, she begged him to take her back. Then he spoke to her, "You disobeyed and therefore cannot return to the sky. Your sin is the cause of your sorrow and has brought trouble to you and your people."

Before So-at-sa-ki died, she told all these things to her father and mother, just as I now tell them to you. Star Boy's grandparents also died. Although born in the home of the Sun, he was very poor. He had no clothes, not even moccasins to wear. He was so timid and shy that he never played with other children. When the Blackfeet moved camp, he always followed barefoot, far behind the rest of the tribe. He feared to travel with the other people, because the other boys stoned and abused him. On his face was a mysterious scar, which became more marked as he grew older. He was ridiculed by everyone and in derision was called Poia (Scarface).

When Poia became a young man, he loved a maiden of his own tribe. She was very beautiful and the daughter of a leading chief. . . . Poia sent this maiden a present, with the message that he wanted to marry her, but she was proud and disdained his love. She scornfully told him that she would not accept him as her lover, until he would remove the scar from his face. Scarface was deeply grieved by the reply. He consulted with an old medicine woman, his only friend. She revealed to him that the scar had been placed on his face by the Sun God, and that only the Sun himself could remove it. Poia resolved to go to the home of the Sun God. The medicine woman made moccasins for him and gave him a supply of pemmican.

Poia journeyed alone across the plains and through the mountains, enduring many hardships and great dangers. Finally he came to the Big Water (Pacific Ocean). For three days and three nights he lay upon the shore, fasting and praying to the Sun God. On the evening of the fourth day, he beheld a bright trail leading across the water. He traveled this path until he drew near the home of the Sun, where he hid himself and waited. In the morning, the great Sun Chief came from his lodge, ready for his daily journey. He did not recognize Poia. Angered at beholding a creature from the earth, he said to the Moon, his wife, "I will kill him, for he comes from a good-for-nothing-race," but she interceded and saved his life. Morning Star, their only son, a young man with a handsome face and beautifully dressed, came forth from the lodge. He brought with him fried sweet grass, which he burned as incense. He first placed Poia in the sacred smoke, and then led him into the presence of his father and mother, the Sun and the Moon. Poia related the story of his long journey, because of this rejection by the girl he loved. Morning Star then saw how sad and worn he looked. He felt sorry for him and promised to help him.

Poia lived in the lodge of the Sun and Moon with Morning Star. Once, when they were hunting together, Poia killed seven enormous birds which had threatened the life of Morning Star. He presented four of the dead birds to the Sun and three to the Moon. The Sun rejoiced when he knew that the dangerous birds were killed, and the Moon felt so grateful that she besought her husband to repay him. On the intercession of Morning Star, the Sun God consented to remove the scar. He also appointed Poia as his messenger to the Blackfeet, promising, if they would give a festival (Sundance) in his honor, once every year, he would restore their sick to health. He taught Poia the secrets of the Sun-dance, and instructed him in the prayers and songs to be used. He gave him two raven feathers to wear as a sign that he came from the Sun, and a robe of soft-tanned elk-skin, with the warning that it must be worn only by a virtuous woman. She can then give the Sun-dance and the sick will recover. Morning Star gave him a magic flute and a wonderful song, with which he would be able to charm the heart of the girl he loved.

Poia returned to the earth and the Blackfeet camp by the Wolf Trail (Milky Way), the short path to the earth. When he had fully instructed his people concerning the Sun-dance, the Sun God took him back to the sky with the girl he loved. When Poia returned to the home of the Sun, the Sun

God made him bright and beautiful, just like his father, Morning Star. In those days Morning Star and his son could be seen together in the east. Because Poia appears first in the sky, the Blackfeet often mistake him for his father, and he is therefore sometimes called Pok-o-piks-o-aks, Mistake Morning Star.

It is impossible to explain how each aspect of this story is essential to the Blackfoot sense of identity. Some elements of the story, such as the interrelationships (literally as "family" or "kin") that exist between humans and all other aspects of the universe, are primary. By emphasizing universal familial relations with all other forms of life, human identity necessarily takes its cue from this context. To be a Blackfoot person, then, is to have had ancestors who participated in the acts described in stories, located in the sacred homeland, and reenacted in various ways by the descendants of the beings in the stories.

The Earth-to-cosmos connection confirmed through stories like the one above is based on important teachings, including respect for the interdependence and mutuality of human interrelationships. This interdependence is reflected in the natural environment, whether earthbound or astronomically located. Stories teach respect for the interdependence of humans, all Earth life, and the larger circle of the universe because they are inseparable. They are connected and their relationships are reciprocal. The respect for land and its sacredness is so crucial to the indigenous worldview that when Native peoples' land is destroyed, so too is the culture.[37] Close interrelationships between the environment/land, stories, and Native peoples' health—physical and otherwise—are practically universal, as in the case of the Winnebago[38] and the Hopi.[39]

The thorough knowledge of the environment contained in indigenous teachings and traditions has the potential for improving global environmental[40] and social health.[41] Specifically, indigenous peoples view the land (world) as a living being, a social being[42] with whom they create and define a social relationship and modes of acceptable behavior. The world is seen as having the power to exert itself and its expectations upon humans, who should learn to listen to and receive insights in order to survive. This knowledge is passed from one generation to the next through stories and the rituals they contain and instruct.

Early settlers' Western concepts of land and nature as material, mechanical, and devoid of spirit stood in stark contrast with Native traditions picturing nature as an extended family or society of living, ensouled beings.[43] Rather than fostering an attempt to control nature, their outlook offers the prospect of a political society in harmony with nature,[44] with moral and spiritual dimensions to this relationship. Indigenous peoples' traditional teachings emphasize an awareness of a great power—the energy or moving force of the universe. Their stories are important because they tell us about our relationship to the various manifestations of this force.

Indigenous peoples' stories take place at sites found all over traditional homelands. It is significant that stories of creation take place on areas around the traditional homelands from time immemorial, or tell of a migration to that sacred homeland. This significance is not lost on those who know the stories. They indicate the homesites of uncounted ancestors and the long-standing relationship with the universe established and nurtured by the ancestors. For indigenous peoples throughout the world, in their traditional relationship with the land, all land is alive and filled with the ancestors of the entire people, and these are the powers that the people seek out. To disrespect the land is to disrespect one's identity as a member of that people, society, community, or nation (however this is defined by outsiders). The ongoing relationship with the traditional homeland, and the people's responsibility to take care of the Earth, is reaffirmed by the many examples of negative consequences to humans when they disrespect it. Such concern for the proper treatment of the land and the powers that live within it has its source in the long history of the people's relationship to the land.

Elders highlight the underlying background inherent in the teachings of stories about the nature of the reciprocal relationship between humans and the rest of the natural world. The stories express a responsibility to maintain good relations between the different parts of nature, including animals and plants, because all of it is considered to be alive, and to share in the power given to all of creation by the Creator. There is an assumed respect and responsibility in the role of caretaker of that balance. Prayer, through song, action, word, or even just intent, is believed to influence this delicate balance. The energies of the world find ways to make their presence known when they are disrespected, or when humans have obligations or responsibilities they are not fulfilling.

Sociocultural resource management practices are based on a body of aboriginal knowledge that includes this cosmological framework and its associated sacred geography. Spiritual stewardship represents a cosmic sanctioning of ethics that ensures the continued future supply of strategic life-supporting resources and thereby ensures the future of the people who depend on them for cultural and physical survival.[45] The practice of spiritual stewardship involves the ritual taking and use of natural resources according to cultural protocols established in tribal stories and validated within a cosmology that views human beings as part of an interacting life force continuum that includes animals and spirit beings. Animals and fish are viewed as intelligent societies having the power to influence events; as such, they must be treated with respect according to instructions encoded in the stories and teachings of the people's oral traditions. Involvement with creation, also called 'nature,' includes a primary relationship with the Sun, Creator, or giver-of-life, and encourages a practice of balance and a recognition that humans must live in harmony with the Earth and with each other.

Stories should be understood as giving meaning and expression to an understanding of "the way things are," or a "religious philosophy," based on a spiritual relationship between humans and their natural environment. Native peoples have always had stories that tell about why and how things are the way they are. In this way, the "what" and the "how" of the ways of the world are explained to the next generation of culture bearers. What can attention to the ways in which this knowledge is structured, relayed, and practiced ultimately tell us about Native identities? The stories serve as repositories of the foundational ideals, goals, processes, and purposes behind "knowing" and emphasize that knowing your Creator is about knowing yourself, knowing who you are. The best understanding of the meanings of these stories is accessible to those who choose to practice the way of life that is outlined and guided by the stories' teachings. The traditional languages, geographical and astronomical homelands, social structures, musical traditions, and even artistic or architectural designs are just some examples of the ways spiritual knowledge is manifested and transferred in indigenous traditions.

The Native peoples of the world understand cultural traditions and spiritual practices as having their source in the stories that tell about the origins of the people's existence. The creation stories in particular tell about the relationships between the larger universe and the Earth and all that lives on it. The explanations include all sources of life on Earth (e.g., animals, plants, rocks, trees, etc.) and all forces that give life (e.g., thunder/rain, wind, snow/blizzard, etc.) or play a prominent role in its continuance. The stories explain the creation of the unique ecological, geographical, cosmological, etc., surroundings of a people, and the stories essentially map out the terrain: What has to be learned about the living space? The traditions embedded in the stories teach how to conduct oneself in the world as well as what the parameters and dimensions are of that and other related worlds.

Native stories about stars tell of the relationship between the cosmos and the Earth. They often explain the basic origins of how people came to be. They link the Earth with the rest of the cosmos, and therefore humans to the rest of life. They also provide a context within which a member of that indigenous community may see the foundations of the core values they are to follow. Sometimes these are expressed through negative examples. Often, however, stars may be beings who had an important role in bringing teachings to humans and may offer insights into how to maintain harmonious relationships with all of life, extending from the outer cosmos, through the human interaction level, to the nearest bug, fish, or blade of grass. Their lessons are reenacted with each telling of the story, so the story re-creates our life.

The ancient Native storytelling traditions also encourage healing through the telling of traditional stories[46] and connect indigenous peoples to their ancient identities, thus ensuring their survival in the natural world. Together, humans and the rest of life share unity as the "primary aesthetic." Through story they reconstruct traditional relationships, subtly reinforcing the principle of homecoming, unity, and wholeness for the audience as well as the characters.[47] Even the recounting of deeds, as has often been noted by observers of Native life, is a traditional way to reinforce beliefs and values.[48]

Native peoples' stories tell about the first humans and animals, when and how the geographical formations of the sacred homeland took shape, the happenings along this same terrain, and how people were, and are, involved. The stories include the songs that have a crucial role in ceremonies and inform about the correct protocols to follow in ceremonies in order for the teachings to take place properly. These narratives hold the keys to the practice and continuance of the most powerful community knowledge.

Tipi rings, rock paintings, boulder or mound configurations, and even architecture also reflect—and sometimes represent the only available geographical remains of—the ancient astro-Earth connections in which many indigenous peoples have traditionally participated.[49] What initially appear to be simple linear observations of a few visible planets or constellations is the basis of more complex ideas based on observation of the planetary systems.[50] The complexity of the natural world's patterns, rhythms, and expectations or rules of life on Earth is brought into relation with humans and all other life in the telling of creation stories.[51] Such stories are similar among many Native peoples: an image of cosmic union runs through the thought patterns and is expressed in myth, ceremony, and even social organization.[52] All Native peoples relate culturally, geographically, and cosmologically unique stories about the creation and the circumstances of their origins.

The stories are the heart—the values, lessons, songs, experiences—of the reconstructions, the re-creations, and the literal reliving of the conditions under which those people in the stories learned. To renew and repeat those conditions is to validate the story as real and to continue to learn through these practices. To continue to use the same, original articles (e.g., tobacco) that came to be used in the original event the stories tell about, keeps them "real." There is nothing artificial or imitated in traditional indigenous spirituality.

Often, the first experience one might have had with these types of stories was as a child. The Native language and the home context began the development of a larger, more encompassing "background" in the indigenous traditions. Even though these stories were originally told to children, their impact and lessons become increasingly relevant with experience, since each new telling brought new lessons as life circumstances changed. The lessons about identity emphasize that since people come as part of the Earth and the spirit world, so should the methods used to teach them about this connection. We are part and parcel of the lessons taught in the creation stories. The repetitions of the conditions/practices (sweats, vision seeking) re-create anew the original spiritual context for learning, so it can be as powerful for those learning from these methods now as it has been for those who have learned in this context since time immemorial. These repetitions bring about learning through firsthand experience, and their value is sought by the individual for the benefit of/service to the entire community.

Interpretations of these stories have changed, in part as a result of new developments in language and problems with translation into English. Although the stories vary (sometimes significantly), elders agree that the basic meanings and main points remain the same across different versions. Traditionally, the power of the teachings is not and was not diminished by the existence of different versions of the stories, nor need it be today. There is immense knowledge to be explored through the story character's relationships as they travel from place to place, and through various dimensions, encountering those who are considered "alive."

Stories connect the "background" referred to earlier to everyday, modern experiences of Native life. Together these form a continuum of sorts, through time and space, and have as their residing place the power and permanence of the indigenous language itself. The teachings offered through the stories are varied, and their contexts range from everyday comments to the most sacred of ceremonies. The continuum of knowledge accessed through Native language, stories, and ceremonies are viewed as lifetime learning. Elders say, "I'm still learning. It's every day and if you're unsure about something it doesn't hurt to ask." Western conceptions of time are bridged by story and ceremony as Elders explain, "History simultaneously occurs with the present.... This is history happening today." This concept is made concrete through firsthand experiences that guide us to the realization that understanding the stories requires that we practice the ways taught by the story people. The protocols and the strict rules involved through the re-creation of story events (e.g., in ceremonies) and the telling of the story provide knowledge about who we are as people. We pass on the stories of our ancestors from generation to generation. And it is this connection to our ancestors that cements our relationship to our land. Our ancestors are buried in that land. We all came from the land. We live from the land. We are the land and the land is us.

NOTES

1. See Sigmund Freud, *Totem and Taboo: Some points of agreement between the mental lives of savages and neurotics* (New York: W. W. Norton, 1952).

2. See L. E. Shepard, *Encyclopedia of Occultism and Para-psychology: A compendium of information on the occult sciences, magic, demonology, superstitions, spiritism, mysticism, metaphysics, psychical sciences, and parapsychology, with biographical and bibliographical notes and comprehensive indexes* (Detroit: Gale Press, 1978).

3. The reverse is also true. Natives' observations of the "White man" left with them unfavorable impressions of him when measured against their cultural values and practices. See J. P. Ronda, "Exploring the Explorers: Great Plains Peoples and the Lewis and Clark Expedition," *Great Plains Quarterly* 13/2 (1993): 81–90; see also W. Stevenson, "Beggars, Chickabbooags, and Prisons: Paxoche (Ioway) views of English society, 1844–1845," *American Indian Culture and Research Journal* 14/4 (1993): 126–139.

4. For examples of this sort of attitude, see A. A. Cave, "New England Puritan Misperceptions of Native Shamanism," *International Social Science Review* 67/1 (1992): 15–27; Raymond J. DeMallie, "The Lakota Ghost Dance: An ethnohistorical account," *Pacific Historical Review.* 51/4 (1982): 385–405; S. Kan, "Shamanism and Christianity: Modern-day Tlingit elders look at the past," *Ethnohistory* 38/4 (1991): 363–387; D. S. Lovejoy, (1994). "Satanizing the American Indian," *New England Quarterly* 67/4 (1994): 603–621; R. H. Pearce, "The 'Ruines of Mankind': The Indian and the Puritan mind," *Journal of the History of Ideas* 13 (1952): 200–217; C. Ramsey, "Cannibalism and Infant Killing: A system of "demonizing" motifs in Indian captivity narratives," *Clio* 24/1 (1994): 55–68; W. S. Simmons, "Cultural Bias in the New England Puritans' Perception of Indians," *William and Mary Quarterly* 38/1 (1981): 56–72; F. Shuffelton, "Indian devils and Pilgrim Fathers: Squanto, Hobomok, and the English conception of Indian religion," *New England Quarterly* 49/1 (1976): 108–116; and J. D. Thiesen, "Rodolphe Petter and General Conference Missions," *Mennonite Life* 40/3 (1985): 4–10.

5. See P. Desy, "A Secret Sentiment (devils and gods in 17th century New France)," *History logy* [Great Britain] 3 (1987): 83–121; and A. R. Gualtieri, "Indigenization of Christianity and Syncretism among the Indians and Inuit of the Western Arctic," *Canadian Ethnic Studies* [Canada] 12/1 (1980): 47–57.

6. Lovejoy, "Satanizing the American Indian."

7. Cave, "New England Puritan Misperceptions of Native Shamanism."

8. The illegalization of traditional scaffold burials, for example, forced indigenous peoples to join a church in order to bury their dead.

9. Different denominations competed for members, and it is not uncommon for a reservation today to continue to have several denominations.

10. See J. Hamley, "Cultural Genocide in the Classroom: A history of the federal boarding school movement in American Indian education, 1875–1920," in *Education Administration, Planning, and Social Policy* (Cambridge, MA: Harvard University Graduate School of Education, 1994); 272.

11. D. Bryan, "Cultural Relativism—Power in Service of Interests—the particular case of Native-American education," *Buffalo Law Review* 32/3 (1983): 643–695; M. Coulter, "The Sun Dance of the Blackfoot Indians" (Cambridge, MA: Peabody Museum, 1992); R. J. DeMallie, "The Lakota Ghost Dance: An ethnohistorical account," *Pacific Historical Review.* 51/4 (1982): 385–405; J. P. Robb, "Discourse in the Sun Dance War, 1880–1914: An analysis of the narratives of suppression, resistance, reaction, and revitalization in the successful struggle by the plains Indians to defeat the Canadian government's orchestrated campaign to destroy their central religious ceremony," *Anthropology/History* (Carleton University, Canada) (1995): 347; G. C. Webster, "The U'Mista Cultural Centre," *Massachusetts Review* 31/1–2 (1990): 132–143.

12. T. E. Mails, *Plains Indians: Dog soldiers, bear men and buffalo women* (Carrolton, TX: Promontory Press, 1973).

13. N. Point, "Religion and Superstition: Vignettes of a wilderness mission," *American West* 4/4 (1967): 34–43, 70–73.

14. T. A. Giago, "Spirituality Comes from the Heart, Not from a Book [Native Americans]," *American Indian Religions: An Interdisciplinary Journal* 1 (Winter 1994): 98.

15. James Axtell, *The Invasion Within: The contest of cultures in colonial North America* (New York: Oxford University Press, 1985), 95.

16. M. D. Spence, "Dispossessing the Wilderness: The preservationist ideal, Indian removal, and national parks," in *United States History* (Los Angeles: University of California Press, 1996), 348.

17. Archeological excavations date occupation and active use of buffalo drives in the traditional Blackfoot homelands at A.D. 800–1500; see T. F. Kehoe, "The Boarding School Bison Drive Site," *Plains Anthropologist* 12 (1967): 1–165.

18. Jack F. Trope, "Protecting Native American Sacred Sites and Religious Freedom," *Wicazo Sa Review* 7/1 (Fall 1991): 53.

19. C. Vecsey, *Imagine Ourselves Richly: Mythic narratives of North American Indians* (San Francisco: HarperCollins, 1991), 457–459.

20. C. Ramsey, "Cannibalism and Infant Killing: A system of 'demonizing' motifs in Indian captivity narratives," *Clio* 24/1 (1994): 55–68.

21. M. Davidson, *The Stars and the Mind: A study of the impact of astronomical development on human thought* (London: Watts, 1947); P. Radin, *Primitive Man as Philosopher* (London: Appleton, 1928), and *Primitive Religion: Its nature and origin* (London: Hamilton, 1937); D. Runes, *On the Nature of Man: An essay in Primitive philosophy* (New York: Philosophical Library, 1956).

22. R. E. Bieder, *Science Encounters the Indian, 1820–1880: The early years of American ethnology* (Norman: University of Oklahoma Press, 1986); J. S. Haller, Jr., "Race and the Concept of Progress in 19th Century American Ethnology," *American Anthropology* 73 (1971): 710–724; A. Kuper, *The Invention of Primitive Society: Transformations of an illusion* (London: Routledge, 1988); N. Thomas, *Out of Time: History and evolution in anthropological discourse* (Ann Arbor: University of Michigan Press, 1988).

23. Haller, "Race and the Concept of Progress in 19th Century American ethnology," 710–724; and Haller, "Concepts of Race Inferiority in 19th Century Anthropology," *Journal of Historical Method* 25 (1970): 40–51.

24. R. E. Bieder, "The Collecting of Bones for Anthropological Narratives," *American Indian Culture and Research Journal* 16/2 (1992): 21–35.

25. Vecsey, *Imagine Ourselves Richly.*

26. S. J. Gould, "Speaking a World into Existence: A writer's debt to oral culture [Native American lesbians]," *Women's Review of Books* 9 (July 10–11, 1992): 12.

27. L. J. Krumholz, "Ritual, Reader, and Narrative in the Works of Leslie Marmon Silko and Toni Morrison," in *Modern & American Literature, Woman's Studies* (Madison: University of Wisconsin Press, 1991), 406.

28. C. C. Norden, "Native and Non-Native: A rhetoric of the contemporary fourth world novel," in *General & Modern Literature*, (Madison: University of Wisconsin Press, 1991), 345.

29. A. F. Aveni, *Native American Astronomy* (Austin: University of Texas Press, 1977); Aveni, *World Archeoastronomy: Selected papers from the 2nd Oxford International Conference on Archeoastronomy held at Merida, Yucatan, Mexico, January 13–17, 1986* (Cambridge, U.K.: Cambridge University Press, 1989); Aveni, *Conversing with the Planets: How science and myth invented the cosmos* (New York: Times Books, 1992); B. S. Bauer, *Astronomy and Empire in the Ancient Andes: The cultural origins of Inca skywatching* (Austin: University of Texas Press, 1995); J. Broda, "Astronomical Knowledge, Calendrics, and Sacred Geography in Ancient Mesoamerica," in *Astronomies and cultures*, Clive L. Ruggles and Nicholas J. Saunders, eds. (Niwot: University Press of Colorado, 1993): 253–295; D. Carrasco, "Star Gatherers and Wobbling Suns: Astral symbolism in the Aztec tradition," *History of Religions* 26 (1987): 277–294; V. D. Chamberlain, *When Stars Came down to Earth: Cosmology of the Skidi Pawnee Indians of North America* (Los Altos, CA: Ballena Press, and College Park, MD: Center for Archeoastronomy, University of Maryland, 1982); C. Classen, *Inca Cosmology and the Human Body* (Salt Lake City: University of Utah Press, 1993); J. M. Malville, "Lunar Standstills at Chimney Rock," *Archeoastronomy: Supplement to Journal for the History of Astronomy* 16 (1991): 43–50; S. C. McCluskey, "Calendars and Symbolism: Functions of observation in Hopi astronomy," *Archeoastronomy: Supplement to Journal for the History of Astronomy* 15 (1990): 1–16; R. A. Williamson, "Native Americans Were Continent's First Astronomers," *Smithsonian* 9/7 (1978): 78–85; M. J. Young, "The Interrelationship of Rock Art and Astronomical Practice in the American Southwest," *Archeoastronomy: Supplement to Journal of History of Astronomy* 10 (1986): 43–58; M. Zeilik, "The Ethnoastronomy of the Historic Pueblos I: Calendrical sun watching," *Archeoastronomy: Supplement to Journal for the History of Astronomy* 8 (1985): 1–24, and Zeilik, "The Ethnoastronomy of the Historic Pueblos, II: moon watching," *Archeoastronomy: Supplement to Journal for the History of Astronomy* 10 (1986): 1–22.

30. W. H. Calvin, *How the Shaman Stole the Moon: In search of ancient prophet scientists from Stonehenge to the Grand Canyon* (New York: Bantam Books, 1991); J. Cornell, *The First Stargazers: An introduction to the origins of astronomy* (New York: Scribner, 1981); E. Hadingham, *Early Man and the Cosmos* (New York: Walker, 1984); N. S. Hetherington, ed., *Cosmology: Historical, literary, philosophical, religious and scientific perspectives* (New York: Garland Press, 1993); E. C. Krupp, *Beyond the Blue Horizon: Myths and legends of the sun, moon, stars, and planets* (New York: Oxford University Press, 1991); and Krupp, *Echoes of the Ancient Skies: The astronomy of lost civilizations* (New York: Harper and Row, 1983).

31. P. Sakmann, "The Problems of Historical Methods and of Philosophy of History in Voltaire," *Hist. Theor. Beiheft* 11 (1971): 24–59.

32. J. Tompkins, "'Indians': Textualism, morality, and the problem of history," *Critical Inquiry* 13/1 (1986): 101–119.

33. R. A. Lake, "Between Myth and History: Enacting time in Native American protest rhetoric," *Quarterly Journal of Speech* 77/2 (1991): 123–151.

34. "Way" is more appropriate than "culture," "practice," "belief," etc., because it encompasses all of these and more, and is a more accurate way to describe Native understandings of these events.

35. G. Cajete, *Look to the Mountain: An ecology of indigenous education* (Durango, CO: Kivaki, Press, 1994), 121.

36. Walter McClintock, *The Old North Trail: Life, legends and religion of the Blackfeet Indians* (Lincoln: University of Nebraska Press, 1968), 491–499.

37. S. Romeo, "Concepts of Nature and Power: Environmental ethics of the northern Ute," *Environmental Review* 9/2 (1985): 150–170; R. C. Ward, "The Spirits will leave—Preventing the desecration and destruction of Native-American sacred sites on federal land," *Ecology Law Quarterly* 19/4 (1992): 795–846.

38. B. A. Bigony, "Folk Literature as an Ethnohistorical Device: The interrelationships between Winnebago folk tales and Wisconsin habitat," *Ethnohistory* 29/3 (1982): 155–180.

39. J. D. Loftin, "Emergence and Ecology: A religio-ecological interpretation of the Hopi way," *Philosophy of Religion* (1983): 484.

40. A. B. J. Harwell, "Writing the Wilderness: A study of Henry Thoreau, John Muir, and Mary," *American Literature: Philosophy, Environmental Science* (Knoxville: University of Tennessee Press, 1992), 297; M. G. Holly, "The Persons of Nature versus the Power Pyramid: Locke, land, and American Indians," *International Studies in Philosophy* 26/1 (1994): 13–31; M. E. Oelschlaeger, *Postmodern Environmental Ethics* (Albany: SUNY Press, 1995).

41. V. Plumwood, "Nature, Self, and Gender: Feminism, environmental philosophy, and the critique of rationalism," *Hypatia* 6 (Spring 1991): 3–27.

42. G. W. Stickel, "This Land as a Social Being: Ethical implications from societal expectations," *Agriculture and Human Values* 7/1 (Winter 1990): 33–38.

43. J. B. Callicott, "Traditional American Indian and western European attitudes toward Nature: An overview," *Environmental Ethics* 4 (Winter 1982): 293–318.

44. M. V. McGinnis, "Myth, Nature, and the Bureaucratic Experience," *Environmental Ethics* 16/4 (Winter 1994): 425–436.

45. M. E. Tyler, "Spiritual Stewardship in Aboriginal Management Systems," *Environments* 22/1 (1993): 1–8.

46. J. Shi, "Healing through Traditional Stories and Storytelling in Contemporary Native American fiction," in *American Literature, American Studies* (Bethlehem, PA: Lehigh University Press, 1995), 394.

47. K. C. Walter, *Native American Aesthetics in Twentieth-Century Inter-American Literature* (University Park: Pennsylvania State University Press, 1994), 148.

48. W. McClintock, "Dances of the Blackfoot Indians," *Masterkey* (1937): 15, 19.

49. S. C. Haack, "A Critical Evaluation of Medicine Wheel Astronomy," *Plains Anthropologist* 32 (1987): 77–82; C. D. Hunter, "A Bibliography of Writings Concerning the Big Horn Medicine Wheel, Big Horn National Forest," *Annals of Wyoming* 57/1 (1985): 13–20; T. F. Kehoe and A. B. Kehoe, "Stones, Solstices, and Sun Dance Structures," *Plains Anthropologist* 22 (1977): 85–95; J. D. Keyser, "Variations in Stone Ring Use at Two Sites in Central Montana," *Plains Anthropologist* 24 (1979): 133–144.

50. C. Hardman, Jr., and M. H. Hardman, "Linear Solar Observatory Theory: The development of concepts of time and calendar," *North American Archeologist* 13/2 (1992): 149–172.

51. P. G. Zolbrod, *Dine' Bahane': The Navajo creation story* (Albuquerque: University of New Mexico Press 1984).

52. R. Ridington, "Images of the Cosmic Union: Omaha ceremonies of renewal," *History of Religions* 28/2 (1988): 135–150.

SUGGESTIONS FOR FURTHER READING

Cajete, G. *Look to the Mountain: An Ecology of Indigenous Education*. Durango, CO: Kivaki Press, 1994.

Gunn Allen, P. *The Sacred Hoop: Recovering the Feminine in American Indian Traditions*. Boston: Beacon Press, 1992.

Harrod, H. *The Animals Came Dancing: Native American Sacred Ecology and Animal Kinship*. Tucson: University of Arizona Press, 2000.

Knudtson, P. and David Suzuki. *Wisdom of the Elders*. Toronto: Stoddart Press, 1993.

Lindquist, M. A. and Martin Zanger, eds. *Buried Roots and Indestructible Seeds: The Survival of American Indian Life in Story, History, and Spirit*. Madison: University of Wisconsin Press, 1993.

Sarris, G. *Keeping Slug Woman Alive: A Holistic Approach to American Indian Texts*. Berkeley: University of California Press, 1993.

Thornton, R. ed. *Studying Native America: Problems and Prospects*. Madison: University of Wisconsin Press, 1998.

Vecsey, C. *Imagine Ourselves Richly: Mythic Narratives of North American Indians*. San Francisco: Harper, 1991.

Chapter 5

Jew and Judaist, Ethnic and Religious
How They Mix in America

Jacob Neusner

The Ethnic and the Jewish

The Jews in Western democracies, especially in the United States and Canada, form an ethnic group, and in the state of Israel they constitute a nation. They share a common history and memory, seeing themselves as a community of fate, not of faith. For instance, certain food in certain places is regarded as "Jewish," meaning, a Jewish ethnic specialty. At one time bagels were a Jewish food, so Jews were called "bagel eaters," just as in ancient times they called themselves "garlic eaters." But if we know how to bake bagels, we do not necessarily know anything about how Judaism, the religion, views God or virtue or salvation.

Religion and Ethnicity

Judaism is a religion, with normative beliefs and practices. Jews who practice Judaism always belong to the ethnic group, the Jews. But matters are not so simple. Thus, by converting to Judaism, the religion, a gentile becomes not only a Judaist—one who practices Judaism—but a Jew. Such a one is then part of the Jewish community as much as of the community of Judaism.

So, in the Jewish framework religion and ethnicity are difficult to separate. In the United States and Canada, Western Europe, and Hispanic America, the Jews form an ethnic group, part of which also practices the religion, Judaism. In the state of Israel, the Jews form the vast majority of the population of a nation, only part of which also practices the religion, Judaism. There Judaism is not the culture of an ethnic group, nor is it the nationalism of a nation-state, even though it is nourished by, and helps to define, both.

What is required to sort out the ethnic and the religious in the Jewish context is first to distinguish the religious and the ethnic. For the sake of analysis they are to be treated as though they represented components of a community's life and culture that can be differentiated. Then we have, second, to show how, in reality, Jews actually combine the religious faith with ethnic culture and sentiment, the sacred with the secular. The reality shows a community of Jews who are mostly Judaists, practitioners of Judaism—but on their own, ethnic terms. In much of contemporary American Judaism, the religion serves as a medium of ethnic identification.

The Religious and the Ethnic in Contemporary Judaism

The ethnic group and the religion shape each other's life, but the fate of Judaism as a religion is not the same as the fate of the Jews as a group. If the Jews as a group grow few in numbers, the life of the religion, Judaism, may yet flourish among those that practice it. And if the Jews as a group grow numerous and influential but do not practice Judaism (or any other religion) or practice a religion other than Judaism, then Judaism will lose its voice, even while the Jews as a group flourish. The upshot is simple. A book (that is, a set of religious ideas, divorced from a social entity) is not a Judaism, but the opinions on any given subject of every individual Jew also do not add up to a Judaism.

To have a Judaism we require a group of Jews who together set forth a way of life, a worldview, and a theory of who and what they are. Many of the great debates among Judaisms over history have focused on the definition of the word "Israel," meaning not the nation-state, the state of Israel of our own day, but the people, Israel, of which Scripture speaks. That is not a question of the here and now but an issue of what it means to form the people descended from the saints and prophets of that "kingdom of priests and holy people" that God calls into being at Sinai, that defines itself within the Torah. So, once more, we see how the ethnic shades over into the religion as much as the religious nourishes ethnic identification.

The Paradox of Ethnicity in Judaism

Here then is a religion that addresses all humanity with a message of what God wants of all creation but is identified with a particular ethnic group, the Jews. The universality of its focus—the religion's concern for the entire history and destiny of the human race and its message of salvation—is framed in terms that involve a specific group of people. In the time that everyone who belonged to that people believed in God and practiced Judaism, these "people" corresponded in Judaism to "the Church, the mystical body of Christ" in Christianity—that is to say, "people" stood for "holy community," a religious group. Then, as everyone understood, to form "Israel" was not the same thing as to form a nation or an ethnic, secular community. It meant to form a holy community.

But in modern times some Jews gave up the practice of Judaism without adopting any other religion. Furthermore, these people remained part of the group, which, consequently, lost its clear-cut character as a religious community and came to be seen as an ethnic group. The group defined itself by common traits of ethnicity—for instance, its customs and ceremonies—rather than by a common religion involving divine commandments and sacred rites. But within the group, many continue to practice Judaism. Not only so, but as we shall see, people who convert to the religion, Judaism, as a matter of common practice are admitted also to the ethnic group as well. And Jews who give up Judaism for another religion are regarded as having left the ethnic group. Clearly, matters are complicated.

The Universal Religion of an Ethnic Group

Then, when it comes to the Jews, we see a fine case of the mixture of secularity and religiosity, ethnicity and faith. Jews form an ethnic group, but Judaism is a universal religion. The puzzle comes about because only some of the Jews practice Judaism, but all of them regard all those who practice Judaism as not only "Judaists" (people who observe the Judaic religion) but also as "Jews" (members of the ethnic community).

Public Religion versus Plural Ethnicity

No one confuses the Catholic faith with the ethnic culture of Italians, Poles, Austrians, Spaniards, or Brazilians—Catholics all. To be a Lutheran is not necessarily also to be a Finn, Dane, Swede, Norwegian, or German. Everyone understands that there is a Catholic or a Lutheran faith that is distinct from the various ethnic cultures that take shape in dialogue with that faith, that transcends the particularities of circumstance. Brazilian and American Pentecostals know the difference between nationality and religion. So, too, Judaism is not an ethnic religion, and the opinions of an ethnic group cannot serve to define that religion. Practice of the singular faith takes diverse forms in different circumstances, so that the national culture of the state of Israel, infused though it is with Judaism, is not the same thing as Judaism, nor is the ethnic culture of American Jews.

Some Jews may declare themselves atheists. But Judaism teaches that one, unique God created the world and gave the Torah. Other Jews may not believe in the resurrection of the dead. But Judaic worship, whether Orthodox or Reform, affirms that God raises the dead and "keeps faith with those that sleep in the dust." A public opinion poll might produce broad Jewish consensus in favor of abortion. Judaism, the religion, in its classical formulation condemns abortion from the ninetieth day after conception. (Some contemporary Judaic formulations do not concur.)

Many Jews regard "Judaism" as the foundation for liberal opinion, even quoting verses of Scripture to prove their point. But among the faithful—that is, among those who practice a Judaism of one kind or an-other—considerable debate takes place on whether Judaism is conserva-tive or liberal, or even whether these contemporary political categories apply at all. Because of these simple facts, the confusion of the ethnic and the religious must be addressed head-on. Otherwise, the representation of Judaism in these pages, based as it is on the classical sources of Judaism and contemporary practice of Judaism in synagogues by the faithful, will conflict with the impressions we gain from everyday life.

Why does personal opinion take the place of public religious doctrine? The reason is that Judaism, the religion, in North America, Europe, Latin America, the South Pacific, and South Africa, finds itself wrapped around by Jewishness, the ethnic identity of persons who derive from Jewish par-ents and deem "being Jewish" to bear meaning in their familial and social life and cultural world. In considering the facts of Judaism around the world, therefore, we always have to remember that the Jews form a community, only part of which practices Judaism. Some may even join synagogues to attend public worship mainly to be with other Jews, not to engage in public worship. They may wish to utilize the synagogue to raise their children "as Jews," while in their homes they practice no form of Judaism. A key institution of Judaism, the Sabbath, is praised by a secular thinker in these words: "More than Israel has kept the Sabbath, the Sabbath has kept Israel." That is, the Sabbath is treated as instrumental, Israel the secular group as principal. But in Judaism, the Sabbath is a holy day, sanctified by Israel, the holy people, and not a means to some ethnic goal of self-preservation.

Israel: Location or Holy Community

To explain the mixture of the ethnic and religious, a simple case serves for illustration. The word "Israel" today generally refers to the overseas political nation, the state of Israel. When people say, "I am going to Israel," they mean a trip to Tel Aviv or Jerusalem, and when they speak of Israeli policy or issues, they assume they are referring to a nation-state. But the word "Israel" in Scripture and in the canonical writings of the religion, Judaism, speaks of the holy community that God has called forth through Abraham and Sarah, to which God has given the Torah ("teaching") at Mount Sinai, of which the Psalmist speaks when he says, "The One who keeps Israel does not slumber or sleep"(Ps. 121). The Psalmists and the Prophets, the sages of Judaism in all ages, the prayers that Judaism teaches, all use the word "Israel" to mean "the holy community." "Israel" in Judaism forms the counterpart to "the Church, the mystical body of Christ" in Christianity. Among most Judaisms, to be "Israel" means to model life in the image, after the likeness, of God, who is made manifest in the Torah. Today "Israel" in synagogue worship speaks of that holy community, but "Israel" in Jewish community affairs means "the state of Israel."

That example of the confusion of this-worldly nation with holy community by no means ends matters. In the Jewish world outside of the state of Israel, Jews form a community, and some Jews (also) practice Judaism. To enter the Jewish community, which is secular and ethnic, a gentile adopts the religion, Judaism; his or her children are then accepted as native Jews, without distinction, and are able to marry other Jews without conversion. So the ethnic community opens its doors not by reason of outsiders' adopting the markers of ethnicity—the food or the association or the music—but by reason of adopting what is not ethnic but religion. And to leave the Jewish community that is ethnic, one takes the door of faith. Here comes a further, but not important, complication. While not all Jews practice Judaism, in the iron-consensus among contemporary Jews, Jews who practice Christianity cease to be part of the ethnic Jewish community, while those who practice Buddhism remain within. Buddhism, not a monotheism (not even theistic), is viewed as a philosophy, not a competing religion. Christianity, monotheist as is Judaism—reaching back to the same Scriptures, viewing the history of humanity within the same structures, sharing much in the traditions of ethics—is a competing religion; for Jews and the diverse Judaisms, moreover, the long and bloody record of Christian antipathy to the Jews and Judaism, the massacres and pogroms and "Christ-killer" epithets, the annual Passion narratives with their dreadful portrayal of "the Jews"—these serve to place Christianity outside the range of commitments that the Jewish ethnic community can tolerate. And, as to those who practice Judaism, to adopt any other religion is to apostatize, pure and simple.

The Books Describe Judaism, the People Practice Jewishness (Ethnicity)

The holy books of Judaism speak to people who are always and only Jews. Not only so, but they are Jews by God's choice, subject to an eternal covenant between God and Israel, which they cannot abrogate but may only violate. But the social platform of American and Canadian Jews rests on the principle that Jews are (also) Americans or Canadians, integrated by choice, not segregated by choice. And in addition, within the American or Canadian populations, they form an ethnic group comprised of three things: Americans by nationality, Jews by ethnicity, Judaists by religion. They suffer no obligations except those they voluntarily accept; and a votive obligation is an oxymoron. "Israel" is Israel because a person feels like it, wants it, affirms it, always voluntarily; never coerced by God, on the one side, or by a hostile society, on the other (or even by a friendly and welcoming society, for that matter). And at that point, the books become simply implausible: they speak of an "Israel" no one knows or wants to comprise. To those who may choose to be Jews or not, who may decide to live only among Jews or to live with gentiles as well, books that speak only of holy Israel, a people that dwells apart, deliver a puzzling message, one to be negotiated, to be affirmed but also interpreted.

The holy books did not always present the faithful with implausible premises. For it is a matter of simple fact that for a very long time, from late antiquity to the eighteenth century, a single Judaism predominated, and it was a Judaism that took for granted that Jews were always, and solely, "Israel," defining the social entity, "Israel," as against the nations. In such a Judaism, no provision accommodated what we may call integrationism: the desire to be Jewish but something else in addition. Such Judaism and its holy books did not distinguish the ethnic from the religious. During this long period, the principal question facing Jews was how to explain the success of the successor religions, Christianity and Islam, which claimed to replace the Judaism of Sinai with a new testament, on the one side, or a final and perfect prophecy, on the other. Both religions affirmed but then claimed to succeed Judaism, and the Judaism of the dual Torah (written, meaning the Pentateuch, and oral, ultimately written down in the Talmuds and related documents of late antiquity) enjoyed success among Jews in making sense of the then-subordinated status of the enduring people and faith of Sinai.

The Ethnic Group Which Is the Religious Community

The way we know what people do is to ask. Social science, particularly the demographic wing of sociology, through its mastery of correct polling techniques and of statistics, provides a generally reliable account of how people say they behave. True, opinion polling produces its embarrassments, as "President" Dewey could testify in 1948. But, tested over decades, demography—the statistical description of social behavior—has shown itself to be accurate.

To describe the ethnic group in its religious dimension, I present figures that outline a broad consensus. The issue of the contrast between books' descriptions and peoples' behavior emerges when we examine the behavior of that vast middle, encompassing the different Judaisms of North America, the best known being Reform, Orthodoxy, Reconstructionist, and Conservative (but there are many others). These are the Jews who cherish the books but also form a pattern of measurable behavior clearly different in some ways from what the books describe as the Judaic way of behaving; and who profess beliefs not entirely, or even not much, shaped within the lessons of those books. They form the problem: How do we play across the gap between books and behavior when we study religion? To state what I think is at issue for that huge middle, encompassing better than 90 percent of the Jews of the United States and Canada, we examine neither entire integrationists nor complete segregationists, but people who want both to practice Judaism and also to be Jewish, but not so Jewish that they do not, also, participate in the mainstream of American or Canadian life (however the currents in those streams may flow). How they sort out the demands of books that presuppose they are *only* Jewish and also *only* Judaic defines the problem, and their solutions to the problem form the theory of the matter.

Jews by Religion

Current social studies of Judaism in America yield a consensus that all surveys have produced.[1] Among the many religious occasions and obligations set forth by the Torah, American Jews in the aggregate practice some but not others. Take demography for starters. The United States counts as a "Jewishly identified population" some 6.84 million. Of these, 4.2 million identify themselves as born Jews and claiming Judaism as their religion. They embody all the Judaisms that flourish in North America. Another 1.1 million say they were born Jews but have no religion. Jews by choice ("converts") number 185,000. The remainder have ethnic Jewish connections but practice a religion other than Judaism.[2] It follows that the "core Jewish population" is 5.5 million, of which approximately 80 percent—4.4 million—are Jews by religion.

Are the Jews a Religious Community or an Ethnic Group?

The further figure that affects our study—besides the 4.4 million who are Jews by religion, which defines its parameters—concerns intermarriage patterns. At this time, 68 percent of all currently married Jews by birth (1.7 million) are married to someone who was also born Jewish. But, as Barry Kosmin's 1991 survey makes clear, well over half of the marriages in recent years involve Jews who marry Gentiles, and only 5 percent of these marriages involve Gentiles who convert to Judaism. Mixed couples are being created at twice the rate of couples where both partners are Jews. Jack Wertheimer comments on the matter of intermarriage, in these terms: "Intermarriage has exploded on the American Jewish scene since the mid-1960s, rapidly rising in incident to the point where as many as two out of five Jews who wed marry a partner who was not born Jewish." In Reform Judaism, he reports, 31 percent of the lay leaders of Reform temples reported having a child who was married to a non-Jewish spouse.[3] So the first thing that captures our attention is that the single most important building block of Judaism, the family—the expression in the here and now of the sacred genealogy of Israel, that is, "the children of Israel"—wobbles.

Religious Beliefs: Judaism in America

Restricting our attention to the Judaists and the secular Jews (Kosmin's born Jews whose religion is Judaism and his born Jews with no religion), what do we learn about religious beliefs?

1. The Torah is the actual word of God: 13 percent concur (but 10 percent of those born Jews but having no religion do too—not a very impressive differential).
2. The Torah is the inspired word of God, but not everything should be taken literally word for word: 38 percent of Judaists concur, as do 19 percent of secularists.
3. The Torah is an ancient book of history and moral precepts recorded by man: 45 percent of Judaists and 63 percent of secular Jews concur. And 4 percent of the Judaists and 8 percent of the secularists had no opinion.[4]

It follows—by the criterion of belief in the basic proposition of the Judaism of the dual Torah—that 13 percent of the Judaists concur that the Torah is the word of God; another 38 percent agree that the Torah is the inspired word of God but not literally so; and another 45 percent value the Torah. If we were to posit that these numbers represent Orthodox, Conservative, and Reform Judaisms, we should not be far off the mark.

In fact, the denominational figures that Kosmin's report gives are shown in table 5.1 (current Jewish denominational preferences of adult Jews by religion = our Judaists).

TABLE 5.1.
Jewish Denominations in America (in percentages).

	Proportion of Those Polled	Proportion of Households
Orthodox	6.6%	16%
Conservative	37.8%	43%
Reform	42.4%	35%
Reconstructionist	1.4%	2%
"Just Jewish"	5.4%	

Of the Judaists, 80 percent are Reform or Conservative, approximately 7 percent Orthodox;[5] and the high level of identification with Orthodoxy is strictly a phenomenon in the greater New York City area. Elsewhere, the percentage of Orthodox Jews in the community of Judaists is still lower.[6] The denominational choice of the rest is scattered. It is not clear whether the distinction between Jews and Judaists is reflected in these figures, but the upshot is not in doubt.[7]

What about the religious practice of the Judaists—the center of concern for this inquiry? With regard to public worship practices the figures cover only three matters:[8]

1. Fast on the Day of Atonement   61%
2. Attend synagogue on high holidays   59%
3. Attend synagogue weekly   11%

Every study for several decades has replicated these results: lots of people go to Passover seders, a great many also observe the so-called High Holy Days (in the Torah: "the days of awe," that is, Rosh Hashanah, the New Year, and Yom Kippur, the Day of Atonement). So we may ask, why do people who in community do not pray weekly (or daily) come to synagogue worship for the New Year and the Day of Atonement, that is to say, why do approximately half of the Judaists who worship in community at all do so only three days a year?

As to rites at home and household practices, Kosmin shifts to entirely Jewish households, rather than mixed Jewish and gentile households, that is, from the Judaist to the Jewish (and a sensible shift at that):[9]

1. Attend Passover seder   86%
2. Never have Christmas tree   82%
3. Light Hanukkah candles   77%
4. Light Sabbath candles   44%

5. Belong to a synagogue   41%
6. Eat kosher meat all the time   17%

What makes Passover different from all other holidays? Clearly, that question must come up first of all. What makes Sabbath candles (all the more so, the weekly Sabbath as a holy day of rest) only half so important as Hanukkah candles (one week out of the year)?

Since the Torah devotes considerable attention to the foods that may sustain the life of holy Israel, and since the ethnic Jews too identify foods as particularly Jewish, we may ask about the matter of observance of dietary rules in Conservative Judaism, which affirms them and regards them as a key indicator of piety. Charles S. Liebman and Saul Shapiro report that among the Conservative Jews they surveyed, 5 percent of the men and 6.4 percent of the women report that they observe the dietary laws both at home and away (by the standards of Conservative Judaism, which are somewhat more lenient than those of Orthodoxy); 29.2 percent of the men and 28.8 percent of the women have kosher homes but do not adhere to dietary taboos away from home.[10] Approximately one-third of the Conservative homes, then, appear to be conducted in accord with the laws of kosher food. Liebman and Shapiro comment that the home of the parents of those in this group also was kosher, and observance of the dietary laws correlates with Jewish education:

> Of the children receiving a day school education, 66% come from kosher homes; of all those who attended Camp Ramah [a Jewish education summer camp run by the Conservative movement], 53% came from kosher homes; this despite the fact that only 34% of the parents report their homes are kosher. The differences are even more dramatic if one bears in mind that a disproportionate number of older Conservative synagogue members have kosher homes, which means that their children were educated at a time when day school education was much less widespread in the Jewish community.[11]

Along these same lines, Steven M. Cohen introduces the metaphor of "an artichoke syndrome," where, he says,

> the outer layers of the most traditional forms of Jewish expression are peeled away until only the most essential and minimal core of involvement remains, and then that also succumbs to the forces of assimilation . . .

according to assimilationist expectations, ritual observance and other indi-
cators of Jewish involvement decline successively from parents to
children.[12]

But current studies do not "support a theory predicting uniform decline
in ritual practice from one generation to the next. Rather, it suggest inter-
generational flux with a limited movement toward a low level of observance entailing Passover Seder attendance, Hanukkah candle lighting,
and fasting on Yom Kippur."[13] In yet other studies, Cohen speaks of
"moderately affiliated Jews," who nearly unanimously "celebrate High
Holidays, Hanukkah and Passover, belong to synagogues when their children approach age 12 and 13, send their children to afternoon school or
Sunday school, and at least occasionally support the Federation [United
Jewish Appeal] campaigns."[14] Cohen speaks of "broad affection for Jewish
family, food, and festivals." Here, Cohen's report provides especially valuable data. He explains "why Jews feel so affectionate toward their holidays:"

> One theme common to the six items [celebrated by from 70 to over 90 per-
> cent surveyed] is family. Holidays are meaningful because they connect
> Jews with their family-related memories, experiences, and aspirations. Re-
> spondents say that they want to be with their families on Jewish holidays,
> that they recall fond childhood memories at those times, and that they es-
> pecially want to connect their own children with Jewish traditions at holi-
> day time. Moreover, holidays evoke a certain transcendent significance;
> they have ethnic and religious import; they connect one with the history of
> the Jewish people, and they bear a meaningful religious message. Last, food
> ... constitutes a major element in Jews' affection for the holidays.[15]

The holidays that are most widely celebrated in this report remain the
same as in the others: Passover, Hanukkah, and the High Holy Days. By
contrast, "relatively few respondents highly value three activities: observing the Sabbath, adult Jewish education, and keeping kosher."[16] The question comes to the fore once again: Why those rites and not others, why
those rites in preference to others?

Ethnicity, Philanthropy, and the State of Israel in American Jewry

What about Israeli matters? Among the Judaists, 31 percent have visited the state of Israel, 35 percent have close family or friends living there; among the ethnic Jews (not Judaists), the figures are 11 percent and 20 percent.[17] This brings up another question: What makes the state of Israel so important to the Judaists?

And, along the same lines come charity, including Israel-centered charity (United Jewish Appeal, for instance) (once more speaking of entirely Jewish households):[18]

1. Contributed to a Jewish charity in 1989   62%
2. Contributed to UJA/Federation campaign in 1989   45%
3. Celebrate Israeli independence day   18%

And, for comparison:

1. Contributed to a secular charity in 1989   67%
2. Contributed to a political campaign in 1988-1990   36%

The Ethnic and the Religious Joined

If, then, we wish to describe the large center of American Jews, those who are both ethnically Jewish and religiously Judaic—estimated by Steven M. Cohen to number about half of the American Jews—we may do so in the terms Cohen has provided. He gives these generalizations that pertain to our problem:

> The moderately affiliated are proud of their identity as Jews, of Jews generally, and of Judaism. They combine universalist and particularist impulses; they are ambivalent about giving public expression to their genuinely felt attachment to things Jewish. They are especially fond of the widely celebrated Jewish holidays as well as the family experiences and special foods that are associated with them. . . . They vest importance in those Jewish activities they perform; and they regard those activities they fail to undertake as of little import. Accordingly, they are happy with themselves as Jews;

they believe they are "good Jews." . . . They are voluntarists, they affirm a right to select those Jewish customs they regard as personally meaningful, and unlike many intensive Jews, most of the moderately affiliated reject the obligatory nature of halakhah [laws, norms]. They endorse broad, abstract principles of Jewish life (such as knowing the fundamentals of Judaism) but fail to support narrower, more concrete normative demands (such as regular text study or sending their children to Jewish day schools). . . . To the moderately affiliated, "good Jews" are those who affiliate with other Jews and Jewish institutions.[19]

We have before us the description of an ethnic community that, in the main, practices a single religion. They form a mass of Jews-Judaists, who in some ways conform, and in other ways do not conform, to book-Judaism. Their religion presents us with a problem of interpretation: How do these people know the difference between what matters and what doesn't, not only Passover as against Pentecost (Shabuot) fifty days later; but circumcision as against intermarriage; the Holocaust and anti-Semitism as against the state of Israel; the existence of God as against God's active caring? The key lies in Cohen's description: "they affirm a right to select." And that is the trait of the ethnic Jew by sentiment, not the religious Judaist acting in response to God's commandments. There is no shared myth that animates both religious and secular Jews.

NOTES

1. I consulted a variety of books and articles, but mainly rely upon Steven M. Cohen, *Content or Continuity? Alternative Bases for Commitment* (New York: The American Jewish Committee, 1991); Jack Wertheimer, "Recent Trends in American Judaism," in *American Jewish Yearbook, 1989* (New York and Philadelphia: American Jewish Committee and Jewish Publication Society, 1989) (from this point: Wertheimer); and Barry A. Kosmin, Sidney Goldstein, Joseph Waksberg, Nava Lerer, Ariella Keysar, and Jeffrey Scheckner, *Highlights of the CJF [Council of Jewish Federations] 1990 National Jewish Population Survey* (New York: Council of Jewish Federations, 1991) (from this point: Kosmin) Kosmin survey may also be found online at http://web.gc.cuny.edu/dept/cjstu/highint .htm; Michael Satlow provided, in addition, these items: M. Sklare and J. Greenbaum, *Jewish Identity on the Suburban Frontier: A Study of Group Survival in the Open Society* (New York: Basic Books, 1967), 49–96; Charles Liebman and S. Shapiro, "A Survey of the Conservative Movement and Some of Its Religious At-

titudes" (unpublished; dated New York, 1979), 17–24; Samuel Heilman and Steven M. Cohen, *Cosmopolitans and Parochials: Modern Orthodox Jews in America* (New York: Basic Books, 1987), 39–111, 207–216, 222–227, 235–244; Samuel Heilman and Steven M. Cohen, "Ritual Variation among Modern Orthodox Jews in the United States," *Studies in Contemporary Jewry* (Jerusalem) 2 (1986): 164–187; and S. Cohen, *American Assimilation or Jewish Revival?* (Bloomington: Indiana University Press, 1988), 71–81, 130. Professor Calvin Goldscheider provided the following: Calvin Goldscheider, "Jewish Individuals and Jewish Communities: Using Survey Data to Measure the Quality of American Jewish Life" (unpublished, prepared for the Third Sydney Hollander Memorial Conference on Policy Implications of the 1990 National Jewish Population Survey, July 1991); Calvin Goldscheider, "The Structural Context of American Jewish Continuity: Social Class, Ethnicity, and Religion" (unpublished paper, presented at the American Sociological Association, Cincinnati, 1991). Note also Gary A. Tobin, "From Alarms to Open Arms," *Hadassah Magazine* (December 1991): 22ff; Arthur J. Magida, "The Pull of Passover," *Baltimore Jewish Times* (April 17, 1992): 58ff; Samuel C. Heilman, *Jewish Unity and Diversity: A Survey of American Rabbis and Rabbinical Students* (New York: American Jewish Committee, 1991).

2. Kosmin, 4.

3. Ibid.; Wertheimer, 92–94.

4. Kosmin, table 19.

5. Ibid., tables 22 and 29.

6. Wertheimer, 80.

7. Ibid., 80–81.

8. Kosmin, table 27.

9. Ibid., table 28.

10. In "A Survey of the Conservative Movement and Some of Its Religious Attitudes" (unpublished manuscript dated September 1979; Library of the Jewish Theological Seminary of America).

11. Ibid.

12. Cohen, *American Assimilation or Jewish Revival?* 80.

13. Ibid., 81.

14. Cohen, *Content or Continuity?*, 4. Cohen distinguishes between "the Jewish-identity patterns of the more involved and passionate elites from those of the more numerous, marginally affiliated Jews, those with roughly average levels of Jewish involvement and emotional investment. . . . One may be called 'commitment to content' and the other 'commitment to continuity.' alternatively . . . 'commitment to ideology' versus 'commitment to identity.'"

15. Ibid., 14–15.

16. Ibid., 16.

17. Kosmin, table 27.

18. Ibid., table 28.
19. Cohen, *Content or Continuity?*, 41–42.

SUGGESTIONS FOR FURTHER READING

Glazer, Nathan and Daniel J. Boorstin, eds., *American Judaism*, rev. ed. Chicago: University of Chicago Press, 1989.

Neusner, Jacob. *Understanding American Judaism: Toward the Description of a Modern Religion Vols. 1–2*. New York: Ktav, 1975. Reprint: Binghamton 2001: Global Publications/SUNY Press. In Academic Classics of Judaism Series. I. *Understanding American Judaism: Toward the Description of a Modern Religion—The Synagogue and the Rabbi.*

Neusner, Jacob. *Understanding American Judaism: Toward the Description of a Modern Religion Vols. 1–2*. New York: Ktav, 1975. Reprint: Binghamton 2001: Global Publications/SUNY Press. In Academic Classics of Judaism Series II. *Understanding American Judaism: Toward the Description of a Modern Religion—The Sectors of American Judaism: Reform, Orthodoxy, Conservatism, and Reconstructionism.*

Sklare, Marshall. *Conservative Judaism: An American Religious Movement.* New York: Schocken Books, 1972.

Chapter 6

Blackness in the Nation of Islam

Aminah Beverly McCloud

Why do I stress the religion of Islam for my people, the so-called American Negroes?

First, and most important, Islam is actually our religion by nature. It is the religion of Allah (God), not a European organized white man's religion.

Second, it is the original, the only religion of Allah (God) and His prophets. It is the only religion that will save the lives of my people and give them divine protection against our enemies.

Third, it dignifies the black man and gives us the desire to be clean internally and externally and for the first time to have a sense of dignity.

Fourth, it removes fear and makes one fearless. It educates us to the knowledge of God and the devil, which is so necessary for my people.

Fifth, it makes us to know and love one another as never before.

Sixth, it destroys superstition and removes the veil of falsehood. It heals both physical and spiritual ills by teaching what to eat, when to eat, what to think, and how to act.

Seventh, it is the only religion that has the divine power to unite us and save us from the destruction of the War of Armageddon, which is now. It is also the only religion in which the believer is really divinely protected. It is the only religion that will survive the Great Holy war, or the final war between Allah (God) and the devil.

Islam will put the black man of America on top of the civilization.[1]

Islam, today the fourteen-centuries-old worldview of 1.5 billion people, came to the shores of America in the sixteenth century with African slaves. Researchers estimate that a significant number, 15 to 20 percent of the African slaves sold or kidnapped into the slave trade, were Muslim. The Islamic worldview, with its monotheistic core, is unique in its simplicity. The word "Islam," in its most comprehensive definition, means the peace that comes with the surrender of the human will to the will of God. Those who believe in Islam, referred to as Muslims, practice a series of disciplines that help them to surrender their will. Each of the disciplines is embraced individually without the aid of clergy.

Muslims pray five times daily, restrain themselves from food, drink, and secular pleasures from sunrise to sunset during the lunar month of Ramadan, purify their wealth annually by giving away a percentage of it, and attempt to perform a pilgrimage to Mecca in Saudi Arabia at least once in their lifetimes, if they are able. Again, in Islamic practice, the performance of these disciplines is not mediated through clergy or congregation. Each individual Muslim is solely responsible to God for disciplining his or her will.

The scripture of Islam is the Qur'an , a recitation. Muslims around the world strive to memorize all of it and all Muslims memorize some of it. In the Muslim world, children begin to memorize the Qur'an around age seven. The African Muslims brought to the shores of the Americas were able to continue to practice the disciplines of Islam for at least one or two generations before knowledge faded. They had Qur'an schools, as many were teachers of Islam, and all had been schooled in the memorization of the Qur'an. They were known to have written letters and accounts of their enslavement.[2] These first Muslim slaves rarely converted to Christianity even as subterfuge and retentions remained in the black slave community for sometime.[3] Still, Islam in the form of a Muslim community did not reappear until the twentieth century.

The late nineteenth century witnessed the emergence of the social sciences, biblical criticism, Charles Darwin's new biology of humanity, geologist Charles Lyell's rewriting of the Genesis account of the origin and early history of Earth, and a plethora of new religious movements in Christianity. In this post–Civil War era of social and religious chaos, the presence of ex-slaves and their questionable legal status was problematic both for them and for the international face of America.

At the beginning of the twentieth century, descendants of slaves and ex-slaves found themselves largely illiterate, the objects of Jim Crow segregation, noncitizens, with few positive or even hopeful prospects for a future. Segregation, even in religion, was also a general rule as a plurality of white, Christian ministers in the North and the South preached the need to keep blacks separate from whites regarding matters of worship. The "blackness" of Africans was seen as cursed, and as their numbers grew after the end of slavery, they were no longer seen as necessary to the economic growth of the United States. Herbert Spencer's "social Darwinism" placed blacks at the bottom of the human evolutionary ladder and provided whites with "scientific" proof of their superiority. The social sciences of anthropology and sociology along with geology cemented the evolutionary place of blacks as little more than animals in the realm of social life.

While some white Christians saw twentieth-century modernity and biblical criticism as hailing the return of Jesus Christ and the end of the modern world, some black Christians saw the chaos as evidence of the beginning of change in the social order. Prophets, seers, and gods, male and female, emerged in the black community as the need for solace and the hope that prophets were thought to bring became even more pressing. Migrations from the South to the North did not solve the problems of unemployment, housing, and education, creating a climate of severe need. Blacks in the North and Midwest found themselves in stiff competition with new immigrant Europeans. From 1900 to 1910 nine million Irish, German, and other Europeans immigrated to the United States. Former immigration laws that were specifically concerned with the health, wealth, and sanity of potential U.S. citizens shifted to focus on race and color.

Immigration laws were reformulated to target northern European Protestant ethnic groups to increase the "white" population. Southern Europeans and other "dark" Europeans who did not fit the new racial descriptions of "white" were denied or discouraged from immigration, and people from "oriental" countries were generally denied admittance on the basis of race and color. The smaller population of ex-slaves, about three million, struggled to find, keep, and prosper from what little employment was available. Ethnic ghettos of immigrants and ex-slaves quickly emerged as sites of solace along with their prophets in the form of spiritual men and women and gangsters.

Prophets of doom and peace dueled with new fundamentalist and millennial movements. Mainstream, white, Protestant Christianity found itself at odds internally and externally as the rise of the social sciences threatened to undermine their understanding of God and pushed notions of modernity and scientific advancement. Some Protestant white churches promoted the "social gospel" as a way to reconstruct the mission of the church, while some focused their energies on promoting the inerrancy of the Bible as a central claim of Christianity. Simultaneously, white Christians invested energy in the white church to keep blacks out. The "Curse of Ham," a story in which black people are cursed because a son (Ham) witnessed the nakedness of Noah, his father (Ham was later mythologized to be the ancestor of all black people), was a central religious determinant of the status of black people as inferior for many in the white Christian Church (for more on Ham mythology, see the chapters by Paul Harvey and Eddie Glaude, Jr.). Black Christian theologians and ministers have spent a great deal of time either dismissing this story or refuting it, though it continues to be a factor in black/white Christian relations. Just as a strong positive identity was central to the concept of "whiteness" in the United States, a positive concept of "blackness" was central to the spiritual and psychological survival of blacks.

Miscegenation (procreation between the "races"), broken families, and forced marriages during slavery caused a loss of humanity and thus a loss of identity in the black community. Nuclear family structures did not and could not make up for this loss. Ongoing lynchings, discrimination, and other forms of racism prevented clear, positive identity formation other than that of servant or slave. In response, from the black Christian church emerged prophets who confronted both the spiritual and racial issues. Discussions of these issues were prominent in all black churches, whether they were mainstream or marginal, with race competing with spirituality as a focus. Some black prophets asserted alternative pasts and futures for black people that were understood as real.

While some blacks in offshoots of white churches continued to harbor hopes that one day whites would see them at last as equals in the sight of God, others labored to build sound black churches, and still others, most notably Father Divine, Daddy Grace, and Father Hurley, ventured to incorporate a different sense of self in black religious understandings. Father Divine, who established dozens of missions or "heavens" in the United States, Europe, Africa, and Australia, instructed his "angels" that the races could and should coexist in community. Blacks and whites did live in his community, where he was identified as God and guided the lives of his members. Unlike Father Divine's race mixing, Daddy Grace saw a banquet that could feed both the physical and spiritual hunger of the black community as a focus. Under his guidance, black folks would not have to beg for admittance into white churches or remain hungry in society.

Father Hurley provided an alternative past along with the safety of community for his followers where the negative aspects of "blackness" were assaulted. A self-proclaimed god, Father Hurley organized his main church in Detroit in 1923. He argued that "it was whites who bore the curse of Cain," not blacks. Writing in the *Aquarian Age* in the late 1930s, he asserted, "God throughout the ages had appeared in the form of Black men." For this black Christian, hell was the "hatred, jealousy, segregation, lying, poverty, and disease" present in society and sin was "hatred, prejudice, jim-crowism and segregationism."[4] The beginnings of the twentieth century also saw the simultaneous emergence of other religious traditions in the black community such as Judaism and Islam. Prophet F. S. Cherry organized one of the first black Jewish communities in 1919. He asserted that white Jews were frauds and the true Israelites of the Bible were black. Other communities of blacks chose their religious articulation inside the Islamic worldview and did so either by renouncing to an extent their American citizenship, as in the Moorish Science Temple founded by Timothy Drew (known as Noble Drew Ali), or claiming Islam through a kind of primordial memory of Islam as the monotheistic tradition of slaves, as in the Nation of Islam.

A Brief Overview of the Nation of Islam Regarding the Concept of Blackness

The considerations described above help explain why the Nation of Islam found Islam the most compatible religion for black people. The Nation of Islam was founded by W. Fard Muhammad and was led by the Honorable Elijah Muhammad from 1934 to 1975. The quote from *Message to the Blackman* at the beginning of this essay forms a part of the core philosophy of the Nation of Islam. Its goal is "to lift the so-called Negro out of the deteriorating social circumstances" that the absence of jobs and segregation create.

It is knowledge of self that the so-called Negroes lack which keeps them from enjoying freedom, justice and equality.

It is Allah's (God's) will and purpose that we shall know ourselves. Therefore He came Himself (God) to teach us the knowledge of self. Who is better knowing of who we are than god, Himself? He has declared that we are the descendants of the Asian black nation and of the tribe of Shabazz.[5]

The "god in person" spoken of here is W. Fard Muhammad. Members of the early Nation of Islam understood that Allah came to reveal Islam to them in the person of Fard Muhammad. Most accounts of Mr. Muhammad assert that he was an Arab peddler, as many Arab immigrants were, who began teaching about Islam in Detroit during the 1930s. Fard Muhammad spoke of the injustices perpetrated on black people and asserted that they needed to "come into" knowledge of who they were in human history. Fard taught that they were originally Muslims brought in chains to the shores of North America and they were descendants of the "original man."

This concept of the "original man" was designed to give black ex-slaves a place in the history of the world. In his teachings, the Honorable Elijah Muhammad provided answers for why black people's hair was "kinky," why Africans were taken into slavery, why black people were permitted to survive slavery, and what black people needed to do to move from one condition of being to another. After knowing "yourself," members of the Nation were and still are taught to "love self." Identifying the lack of "love of self" as the root cause of "hate, disunity, disagreement, quarreling, betraying, fighting and killing," Muslims were urged to "refrain from doing evil to each other." Education of the self about the self is considered paramount. Education about others can then be taught. When the mind is developing, black children, just like other children, must be given knowledge of self. Black people are "members of the original people or black nation of the earth."

The Honorable Elijah Muhammad reminded those who listened that "the slaves instead started not only without land and the money to purchase it but with few avenues open to earn and save money. Ownership of producing land is a prime and necessary part of freedom."[6]

How could one know oneself and learn to love that self when it is prohibited to assign value to blackness? The black child had little to inherit and build on whether it was business or property or heritage. The Nation of Islam strove to lay the groundwork for blacks to "do for self" despite the obstacles placed by white people. Without knowledge of self, whatever knowledge a black person gains, the knowledge will benefit others and not self nor the community, asserts the Nation.

My people should get an education which will benefit their own people and not an education adding to the "storehouse" of their teacher. We need education, but an education which removes us from the shackles of slavery and servitude.

Education for my people should be where our children are off to themselves for the first 15 or 16 years in classes separated by sex. Then they should seek higher education without the danger of losing respect for self or seeking to lose their identity. No people strive to lose themselves among other people except the so-called American Negroes. This they do because of their lack of knowledge of self.[7]

Central to knowledge of self is the story of Yakub.[8] To summarize this story, black people were the original people who lived in Arabia. Over six thousand years ago scientists predicted the birth of a brilliant young man named Yakub who would "change civilization." Yakub as a child demonstrated a precociousness through his persistence in scientific experiments. These experiments eventually grew into a primitive form of cloning, or rather a genetic manipulation, as he sought to make a human unlike himself (black) and anything else (with certain negative personality traits) on Earth at that time. Some people were drawn to follow this extraordinary man. The "humans" he made were troublemakers, peacebreakers, and destroyers. Yakub's ultimate goal was to create beings that would eliminate the black race. This process took about six hundred years. After the creation of these unusual beings, Yakub sought to create a civilization. For this task he was forced to get the germ-seeds from others in the kingdom.

Yakub bargained away his and his creation's freedom in the city in exchange for the ingredients for making a civilization. The resultant beings "were really pale white, with really blue eyes." They were called Caucasian. Caucasian was defined as "one whose evil effect is not confined to one's self alone, but affects others." It was also defined by skin and eye color. Yakub violated the bargained agreement after he and his newly created followers (Caucasians) moved out of Arabia by sending them back to cause chaos and hostility. The plan was to get "them fighting and killing each other then ask them to let you help settle their disputes, and restore peace among them. If they agree, then you will be able to rule." The people of Arabia revolted and drove the Caucasians out into West Asia (Europe), stripping them of everything except language.

It took some two thousand years for the Caucasians to start a civilization. They descended to the level of savages. According to this story, it was Moses who brought the white race into civilization again to their place as rulers. He is said to have done this according to Allah's plan. This two thousand-year sojourn was necessary if the "devils were to rule as a god of the world. They must conquer, and bring into subjection, all life upon earth." This is the myth that explains what happened to black people to bring them to the state they were in. Their subjugation, exploitation, and poverty were the result of a plan, and the release from this state involved their recognizing who they were and the necessity to set things right again. This was the task of the Honorable Elijah Muhammad, who further set out to make the "concept of blackness" positive through healthy living, healthy eating, and correct behavior. This creation story sufficed to repair some of the psychological damage done from slavery, segregation, and the ensuing physical violence. It provided a strong sense of "righteous" community against the vagaries of injurious behavior by the major white community.

The myth of Yakub has all of the aspects of so many other mythologies: description of the origin of a people, descriptions of right and wrong societal relations, an explanation of the status quo, and some information about a possible future. Here, the Nation of Islam assisted blacks in understanding their place in history.

The Nation of Islam's creation story does not begin with unmasking the concepts of black and white. Like all other creation stories, it begins with a primordial worldview. In the beginning the world was populated by the black race. Among them were the normal professions and trades that one expects to find in civilization. Among the scientists, the birth of one child, Yakub, heralded a new year. While his genius was supported by most, his desire to create a sort of Frankenstein was not. Fulfilling a prediction, he was able to find students and followers of his new science (gene manipulation) among the population. His experiments were successful and he did indeed create a new race of people.

One can analyze this story in at least two ways. In one scenario, the Yakub myth asserts that white (pale) people did not have a direct hand in their unexplainable viciousness toward black people. The genes that control violence toward or uncontrollable hatred of black people were introduced into the population thousands of years ago. Whites, then, have to be reeducated in order to quell what is, in a sense, natural. In another scenario, the plight of black people is part of a script or plan set in motion thousands of years ago that has to be lived out. Here, the task of black people is to recognize what they have to do for one set of circumstances to end and another to begin. The Honorable Elijah Muhammad asserted that when black people understood that they were a part of the original race and not semihumans without a history, they would act differently. This picture seems most like the understanding of Mr. Muhammad as he trained his followers to cleanse their bodies of intoxicating substances by fasting frequently and eating only one meal a day at other times.

Positive behavioral attitudes were encouraged by practicing courtesy in every situation, thus modeling behavior expected of the descendants of the original people. Blackness ceased to be a state of impurity, defilement, and rejection, becoming instead noble and worthy. Islam is the cement of the spiritual connection to God. There is no curse on blackness in Islam. Instead, there is a connectedness for American blacks to black Africa and the rest of the world. As Muslims, the nation can build and in a sense has "permission" to build while living in a predominately white society. Joining the world of Islam opens the world to black Americans such that they are not bound by the racism of America and can interact with people all over the globe as equally human.

For many decades the Nation of Islam was on the margins of more "mainstream" Islam because of its focus on the welfare of black people, its creation story, and its deification of Fard Muhammad. Despite this marginalization, however, many Muslims in seats of power in the Muslim world harbored hope that the community would one day reformulate its thinking on the creation story and the divinity of Fard Muhammad. This hope has come true in the teachings of Minister Louis Farrakhan, the successor to the Honorable Elijah Muhammad. Beginning in the late 1980s, Minister Farrakhan began the road to mainstream Islam while still finding a place for the Nation's struggle with the plight of black Americans. The Nation enlisted the help of quite a few Islamic scholars to teach Qur'anic studies, prayer, and Muslim world etiquette. Many Muslim governments and philanthropists have made Islamic education available and accessible to the Nation of Islam by providing airfare, tuition, and housing for families for decades. Members of the Nation of Islam have begun to take advantage of these opportunities. In the 1990s the Nation of Islam moved persistently forward in its push to bring the community into the mainstream of Islam. Members now follow all of the disciplines of Islam. This has caused many in other Muslim communities to be more accepting, though the process has been slow. The Nation is quickly repairing ties with "old" community members also.

In 1975, the Honorable Elijah Muhammad died, leaving leadership of the community to his son, Warithudeen Muhammad. Within two years of accepting the position of leader, Imam (the Arabic word for prayer leader, sometimes used as leader of a community) Muhammad shifted the focus of the Nation away from its marginality into the mainstream of Islam. This change caused many followers to leave, including Louis Farrakhan. In the early 1980s, Minister Farrakhan salvaged what was left of the Nation and began a rebuilding program based largely on the old tenets. While the two men, Imam Muhammad and Imam Farrakhan, have had long periods of silence between them, recently they have begun a repair process. Both men and their followers have been sharing meetings and conventions. Publicly, in annual conventions since 2000, they have made their intentions of working together known.

Some in the larger African American Muslim community have looked on these events with skepticism while others have warmly welcomed this healing of philosophies and religious tenets. Since the tragedies of September 11, 2001, Imam Farrakhan has been a leading spokesperson for American Muslims in the larger black community. The Nation of Islam still sees its greatest struggle in the survival of the black American community. The "conception of blackness" remains a dilemma for all black Americans. Though the Nation of Islam has pushed a positive conceptualization of blackness since its inception, the struggle with this conception continues.

NOTES

1. Elijah Muhammad, *Message to the Blackman*. Reprint under the auspices of the Honorable Louis Farrakhan and the Nation of Islam (Chicago: Muhammad's Temple No. 2, 1965), 84–85.

2. See Allan Austin ed., *African Muslims in Antebellum America: Transatlantic Stories and Spiritual Struggles* (New York: Routledge, 1997) and Sylvaine Diouf, *Servants of Allah: African Muslims Enslaved in the Americas* (New York: New York University Press, 1998).

3. See Alex Haley *Roots* (Garden City, NY: Doubleday, 1976).

4. Hans A. Baer, *The Black Spiritual Movement : A Religious Response to Racism* (Knoxville: University of Tennessee Press, 1985), 83.

5. Elijah Muhammad, *Message to the Blackman*, 31.

6. Ibid., 37.

7. Ibid., 39.

8. Ibid., 50.

SUGGESTIONS FOR FURTHER READING

Clegg III, Claude Andrew. *An Original Man: The Life and Times of Elijah Muham-mad*. New York: St. Martin's Press, 1997.

Lincoln, C. Eric. *Black Muslims in America*, 3d ed. New York: Africa World Press, 1994.

McCloud, Aminah Beverly. *African American Islam*. New York: Routledge, 1995.

Turner, Richard Brent. *Islam in the African-American Experience*. Bloomington: Indiana University Press, 1997.

Chapter 7

Theologizing Race
The Construction of "Christian Identity"

Douglas E. Cowan

Introduction

"Christian Identity" is the term commonly associated with a number of the more violent white supremacist groups in North America. Among others these include the Aryan Nations, the Church of Jesus Christ Christian, The Order, and the Posse Comitatus. While each has its own individual working agenda, all share a common mythology about the origins of race and ethnicity, as well as a common discourse about the meaning that mythology gives to their lives. As a result, sociologically speaking, they constitute less an *organization* with a set hierarchy and a well-defined leadership than a *social movement* of loosely affiliated groups oriented around similar themes, beliefs, and objectives.

In broad terms, three aspects define Christian Identity. First and foremost is the belief that whites are the true Israelites of the Old Testament, the so-called lost tribes of Israel. Second, in a racialist war between light and dark (one that is both real and metaphorical), Jews are believed to be the literal children of Satan, and nonwhites the descendants of various pre-Adamic "mud peoples." Third, in Identity mythology these beliefs demand that the races live physically separate from one another. As such, many Identity Christians are convinced that North America ought to be divided into a number of distinct geographical regions, each region devoted to a particular race or group of races. Because all of these aspects are believed to be God's will, Identity Christians explicitly link their racialist crusade with God's divine purpose for the world.

This application of a religious mythology to rationalized intolerance makes the Christian Identity movement considerably more dangerous than other racist movements. In human experience, religion has been one of the most powerful motivators, inspiring heroic self-sacrifice on one hand, and triggering the most terrifying violence on the other. And, in the context of a mythological holy war of the races, not only are Identity Christians prepared to sacrifice themselves, many are fully prepared to kill to further their ideals.

The belief that Jews and nonwhites are different, lesser races, the products of wholly separate creations, did not appear overnight. While Richard Girnt Butler's well-known Church of Jesus Christ Christian together with his Aryan Nations compound in Hayden Lake, Idaho, did not come into existence until the early 1970s, its roots run much deeper, emerging first in Britain more than a century earlier. Because it is the best known of the Christian Identity groups and incorporates all of its important features, in this chapter I will primarily use Butler's group to illustrate Identity's mythological construction of racial identity and the way in which that construction motivates Identity behavior.[1]

The Long Trek: British-Israelism and the Origins of "Christian Identity"

Christian Identity finds its roots in an ideology known as "British-Israelism," a nineteenth-century revision of ancient Near Eastern history that attempted to answer the question of the ten "lost tribes of Israel." As the biblical witness recounts, following the death of King Solomon in 930 B.C.E., civil war split the nation of Israel into two kingdoms: a northern kingdom (Israel) that comprised ten tribes, and a southern kingdom (Judah) made up of the remaining two (1 Kings 12). Two hundred years after Solomon's death, the Northern Kingdom was invaded by Assyria and its population was carried away into captivity. A century-and-a-half after that, the Southern Kingdom fell to the Babylonians, and a similar fate ensued.

Scripture records that the tribes of the Southern Kingdom were able to maintain their religion and culture in the midst of their exile, and after seventy years they were allowed to return to Jerusalem reasonably intact in order to rebuild the city (Ezra and Nehemiah). The precise fate of the ten northern tribes exiled over four hundred years earlier, however, remained a mystery. Most probably, they simply assimilated into their new environment, intermarrying both with their Assyrian captors and with the people of neighboring tribes, and gradually losing any tribal distinction they may have carried with them into exile. Various "lost tribes" theories, however, maintain that they did not lose their tribal integrity, but safeguarded it with them out of exile. Over time, different groups from places ranging from Persia to South Africa, from Afghanistan to the Crimea, the Caucasus, and Siberia, and from Peru to Japan have claimed to be descendants of these ten "lost tribes."

As its name suggests, British-Israelism contends that the "lost tribes" returned neither to Israel nor to any of these other countries. Rather, taking various routes away from Assyria they made their way overland across what is now Turkey, Greece, the southern republics of the former Soviet Union, and western Europe, arriving finally in Britain, where they became the ancestors of the various British races. According to Michael Barkun, while the *idea* of British-Israelism existed almost fifty years before anything approaching a British-Israelist *movement* began,[2] something of a movement did begin with John Wilson (d. 1871) and his book, *Lectures on Our Israelitish Origin* (1840). Rather than simply suggest that the peoples of the British Isles were the descendants of the "lost tribes," Wilson tried to demonstrate that fact linguistically. He searched for common words or words that sounded similar and concluded that they had a similar origin. A favorite stratagem for "lost tribes" theorists, the argument contends that if words from seemingly disparate groups of people look or sound the same, even if the similarity must be stretched or invented, then those groups of people must be connected in some way. This was the formula Wilson used to "discover" the genealogical relationship between the British peoples and the "lost tribes" of Israel. In the case of British-Israelism, for example, the equation is made between *berit-ish* (Hebrew for "man of the covenant") and "British." (Until recently, similar arguments were also made by the Worldwide Church of God, a non-supremacist Christian sect founded by Herbert W. Armstrong.)

Despite the fact that Wilson's book went through five printings and that he lectured tirelessly to promote his ideas, it took another man, Edward Hine (1825–1891), to start the movement. While he claimed to have been converted to Wilson's British-Israelism as a boy, Hine strongly disagreed with Wilson on one important point. Arguing theologically as well as linguistically, Hine believed that the various biblical prophecies concerning Israel could not be fulfilled if the nation of Israel was scattered all over Europe. In his *Forty-Seven Identifications of the Anglo-Saxons with the Lost Ten Tribes of Israel,* which was published the year his mentor died, Hine declared that only the British people were the true descendants of Israel. With Germanic and Scandinavian tribes excluded from the new "chosen people," the movement became a true "*British*-Israelism" (sometimes called "Anglo-Israelism").

As the movement crossed the Atlantic, however, it both returned to its pan-European character and assumed a sinister quality that had not been present in Britain. Although a variety of Americans gradually attached themselves to British-Israelism, it was William J. Cameron (1878–1955), the editor of Henry Ford's *Dearborn Independent* newspaper, who forged the link between British-Israelism and explicit, often virulent anti-Semitism. In the early 1920s Cameron published a series of anti-Semitic articles in the *Independent,* reprinting them in 1922 in a four-volume set called *The International Jew.* Subtitled "The World's Foremost Problem," volumes 3 and 4 of this set dealt with "Jewish Influences in American Life" and "Aspects of Jewish Power in the United States," respectively. In addition to this, as Barkun points out, these articles (for which a libel suit was filed against Cameron in 1925) "constituted the first and widest American popularization of *The Protocols of the Elders of Zion,* the czarist forgery that became the most famous anti-Semitic book of the twentieth century."[3] In this way, besides being the victims of random acts of anti-Semitism based simply on ignorance and negative popular perception, the Jewish people were now represented as the primary cause of any number of social problems. Less than a decade later, this same ideology would become explicit in Germany as signs bearing the slogan *Die Jüden sind unser Unglück* ("The Jews are our misfortune!") began to appear regularly at Nazi Party rallies.

Although Cameron may have popularized anti-Semitism and linked it first with British-Israelism, it took a former Methodist preacher to turn it into Christian Identity. In twenty-five years of preaching, the Reverend Wesley Swift (1913–1970) propagated most of the principle anti-Semitic doctrines embraced by white supremacists in North America. As Warren Kinsella notes: "Jews were responsible for international communism, the two world wars, the U.S. Federal Reserve banking system, homosexuality, abortion, race-mixing, One World Government, Freemasonry, the United Nations, and fluoridation."[4] More than that, Swift both invoked the blessing of God on his campaign of hatred, and moved to make that campaign proactive, lobbying for the complete removal of all Jews from society. In

1946, he founded the original Church of Jesus Christ Christian in Lancaster, California. The name of the church is not redundant by accident, but comes from what is arguably Swift's most notorious speech: "Was Jesus Christ a Jew?"[5] Through the kind of contorted biblical interpretations common among Identity Christians, quite predictably Swift argued that Jesus Christ was *not* a Jew. Rather, he was the incarnation of a God whose face was resolutely set *against* the Jews. "Take your choice," Swift thundered, "Christ or the jews, Christianity or jewry, the kingdom of Yahweh or world government that leads down to socialist and communist slavery." Lest anyone misunderstand his message, Swift concluded:

> You are members of the Church of Christ, you are citizens of a great nation of Yahweh's Kingdom. You are to lift up the standards of the cross and the flag; you are to carry forward the blueprint of Yahweh's Kingdom; you are to resist the very enemy. You are to cleanse your Christian society of the enemies of Christ that seek to pervert your doctrines, your philosophies, your religion, and your nation by destroying your identity and your faith.[6]

Children of God/Children of Satan: The Mythological Construction of Race and Ethnicity

Of those who claimed to be Swift's designated successor, "Pastor" Richard Girnt Butler (b. 1918) is arguably the most well known. While others may challenge his pedigree, Butler is clear that he was Swift's favored disciple, having spent years of study "under Dr. Swift in his magnificent library," learning the doctrine of Christian Identity "line upon line, precept upon precept."[7] Before retiring to devote himself fully to his Christian Identity activities, Butler was an engineer for Lockheed Aircraft and one of the patent holders for the rapid repair of tubeless tires. Eventually, the royalties from this venture allowed him to pursue his racialist ideals relatively unencumbered by the need to raise money that plagued other, less well heeled supremacist groups. From his twenty-acre compound just outside of Hayden Lake, Idaho, he leads not only the Church of Jesus Christ Christian, but also its political and paramilitary arm, the Aryan Nations. Taking the anti-Semitic British-Israelism of William Cameron, as it had been mediated to him through Wesley Swift, Butler organized Christian Identity into a more coherent, comprehensive mythology, one finally capable of answering white supremacist questions of racial origin, difference, and destiny.

Rather than deal with issues of either belief or ethnicity as the determining factors in the divine plan, Butler's version of Christian Identity located the distinction squarely with race and expressed that distinction in unrelentingly religious language. Butler's Identity Christians see both the Church of Jesus Christ Christian and the Aryan Nations as the essential continuation of Jesus' ministry on Earth. Salvation in Jesus, whom Identity Christians call "Yahshua," was no longer linked to correct belief, as traditional Protestant churches taught; for Identity Christians racial purity became the essence of salvation. "True Christianity," writes Butler in "Christianity and the Aryan Vision of God," "seeks above all the preservation and increase of Aryan man, a noble and unique creature which, by God's Grace, has been given to the earth."[8] This, then, is the mission for which Identity Christians are born, and "We hail Christ's victory!" is a constant refrain in Identity rallies and publications. In the nine articles of the Aryan Nations Platform, most of the Identity mythology is laid bare.

The "preservation of our Race, individually and collectively" is the fundamental principle upon which all Identity mythology rests. Viewed as the direct commandment of God, this preservation demands both the separation of whites from other races as well as the eventual removal or destruction of those races. Key to this is the belief that not all races descend from Adam. "Adam is the father of the White race only,"[9] Identity mythology contends, arguing that the real translation of the Hebrew "adam" in Genesis 5:1 means "to show blood in the face." Since Identity Christians allege that only whites have the ability to blush ("to show blood in the face"), only they are the true descendants of Adam; therefore, only they are made in the image and likeness of God. "We believe that the true, literal children of the Bible are the twelve tribes of Israel, now scattered throughout the world and now known as the Anglo-Saxon, Germanic, Teutonic, Scandinavian, Celtic peoples of the earth."[10]

If that is so, then where did the other races come from? "We believe that there are literal children of Satan in the world today," states Article 4. "These children are the descendants of Cain, who was a result of Eve's original sin, her physical seduction by Satan."[11] Not surprisingly, these "literal children of Satan" are the Jews, and there is an eternal conflict between them and the true descendants of Adam. Worth quoting at length, the nature of this mythological battle is articulated in Articles 5 and 6:

> We believe that the Cananite Jew [*sic*] is the natural enemy of our Aryan
> (White) Race. This is attested by scripture and all secular history. The Jew
> is like a destroying virus that attacks our racial body to destroy our Aryan
> culture and the purity of our Race. Those of our Race who resist these at-
> tacks are called "chosen and faithful." . . . We believe that there is a battle
> being fought this day between the children of darkness (today known as
> Jews) and the children of light (Yahweh, The Ever living God), the Aryan
> race, the true Israel of the bible [*sic*]."[12]

This revision of the biblical creation myth is the origin of Christian Identity's "two-seed theory." While both Cain and Abel had the same mother
(Eve), each had different fathers, "two seeds." Abel's father was Adam, but
Cain's was the serpent (i.e., Satan). And it is this transgression that Christian Identity believes constitutes the original sin of humankind. According to the Identity revision, after Cain murdered Abel and was expelled by
God from the Garden of Eden (Genesis 4:1–16), he wandered the land
and fathered the Jewish race, the "literal children of Satan."

One of the problems biblical literalists have long encountered with the
creation story is the question of where Cain's wife came from if Adam
and Eve were the first human beings created on Earth. The biblical witness says merely that Cain "settled in the land of Nod, east of Eden"; there
he married and had children. Who then were these other people among
whom Cain lived? Once again, the Identity revision of biblical mythology
provides the answer. They belonged to a pre-Adamic race, known variously in Identity discourse as "mud people" or "beasts of the field." All
other races but white descend from these "mud people," in which Identity
hatred of both "race mixing" and the Jews converges. Even the Noahic
flood is given a racialist interpretation in Identity mythology. The evil
that was rampant in the world prior to the flood was, again not surprisingly, "race mixing": the illicit commingling of Adamite women with
nonwhite, pre-Adamite men. "Race mixing," often called "mongreliza-
tion" in white supremacist discourse, remains Christian Identity's most
enduring fear and most hated sin. In *Tolerance*, a virulent Identity tract,
James Combs summarizes Identity's horror at the prospect:

> "New blood" being injected into our country, via integration, can only re-
> sult in what has occurred to every other White nation which has received
> the colored as equals. There is NO example in history of a White people
> surviving racial merger; both their genetic stock and culture are destroyed.

An infusion of colored "blood" most definitely does not result in anything other than social decline.[13]

From the Garden of Eden to Hayden Lake: Identity Resistance to the Emerging Multiculture

The convergence of Christian Identity's racialist mythology, its paranoid fear of "race mixing," and its certainty that the Jewish people are behind a vast conspiracy to rid the world of whites has resulted in overt violence against both Jews and nonwhites, a growing network of loosely affiliated supremacist organizations, and an intentional plan to put the world back onto the footing intended for it by God. Like all conspiracy theories, Christian Identity responds to its perception of real events in the world and then interprets them according to its own discursive framework. The success of any conspiracy theory is directly related to its ability to explain experiences and phenomena in terms of that conspiracy. Thus, the growing gap between the rich and the poor becomes a result of Jewish control over the banking industry. The gradual breakdown of racial segregation, which is epitomized most prominently for white supremacists in rising rates of intermarriage, is interpreted as the product of a deliberate Jewish program of miscegenation that is designed to breed the white race out of existence. "The United non-White races of the world under the guidance and leadership of Jewry," writes Richard Butler in the Aryan Nations statement of purpose, "an international mongrelized mixture, are in the process of culminating their ancient war for the total extinction of our racial seedline."[14] The "ancient war," of course, is the battle that began in the Garden of Eden between the children of light (Aryans) and the children of darkness (Jews), and which continues in the world today.

According to Identity conspiracy theories, because these processes are already well underway they must be met with determined and inflexible resistance. In Identity discourse, this resistance will take two practical forms: first, an initial regional separation based on race; and, second, the eventual racial cleansing of North America and its "reclamation" as an exclusively white continent. Butler is clear that both the Church of Jesus Christ Christian and the Aryan Nations are not simply organizations dedicated to protesting what he perceives is wrong with society. Both were organized to bring about these massive social changes explicitly founded on Identity's correlation of its racialist responsibility with God's will as revealed in the Bible.

"We're a dispossessed race now," he says, "If the white race is to fulfill its divine, destined purpose under scripture as God's word, it must have its own territorial imperative a homeland of, by and for its own kind."[15] Those who disagree will be declared the anti-Christ; those who disobey will be killed. "That's what the Bible says," declares Butler. For many Identity Christians "The White Bastion" is to be this new "territorial imperative." In a Pacific Northwest enclave comprising Washington, Oregon, Montana, Wyoming, and Idaho, only white, healthy heterosexuals would be allowed to live there.[16] All others would be relegated to different areas of the country and not permitted to live elsewhere. The Hawaiian Islands, for example, would become "East Mongolia," home to "Orientals." "Alta California," running roughly from Los Angeles east through Phoenix then down the Texas panhandle to Houston, would become home to legal Mexican-American immigrants. It would also provide a northern "buffer zone" against further illegal incursion from either Mexico or the newly created Alta California. According to former Klan Grand Wizard, David Duke, "anyone who crossed into this buffer zone without permission from both countries will be shot on sight."[17] The entire Jewish population of the United States would be confined to "West Israel," to what is currently Long Island and Manhattan.

These relocations would only provide a temporary solution to the problem, however. In an effort to bring about the plan of God—as Identity understands it, that is—the re-creation of the Garden of Eden as a racially pure paradise requires that eventually all nonwhites would have to be eliminated from the continent, except for those kept as slaves to the new master race.[18] For much of this futuristic vision, Identity Christians find inspiration in William L. Pierce's notorious novel, *The Turner Diaries*. Published under the pseudonym, Andrew Macdonald, the book tells the story of the "Great Revolution" from the perspective of Earl Turner, a fictional martyr to the white supremacist cause. White supremacists seize control of the country, eventually returning it to "purity" through a genocidal racial cleansing. Even though Pierce himself rejects Identity beliefs,[19] the racially pure utopia depicted in his novel as well as the appallingly violent manner in which it is brought about is eminently appealing to Identity Christians.

What must be borne in mind at all times, however, is that unlike other supremacist groups whose sociopathic behavior is fueled solely by hatred and bigotry, Identity Christians locate their responsibility to create this racially pure society in the explicit commandment of God. The emerging multiculture is seen as a direct violation of God's laws; according to Identity Christians, while God may love and forgive sinners, for race traitors—the incarnation of the original Edenic sin—there is only damnation. Those who wish to join either the Church of Jesus Christ Christian or the Aryan Nations must sign an oath of "fidelity" that reads: "That for which we fight is to safeguard the existence and reproduction of our Race, by and of our Nations, the sustenance of our children and the purity of our blood; the freedom and independence of our Race; so that we, a kindred people, may mature for fulfillment of the mission allotted us by the Creator of the Universe, our Father and God."

Identity's Appeal: Religious Sanction for a Racist Faith

The very foundation of faith and worship is Racial Truth; for with the Aryan, Christianity and Race are one. On this foundation arises the will to power and world leadership inherent in the soul of the seed of Adam. Through racial purity and an unfettered instinct in procreation, the Aryan goes forward to the repeopling of his world.[20]

Linking religious Christian Identity with secular white supremacism was a very astute move on Butler's part and explains why the Identity movement can function as an umbrella for a much larger constituency than might otherwise be the case. White supremacists who are not religiously inclined, or (like Pierce) for whom the Identity message makes no sense, there is the Aryan Nations. For those, however, who might not be initially attracted by the overtly hateful message of white supremacy but are still convinced of the basic truth of that message, Christian Identity provides a way into the movement that grounds their participation in an act of faith, an important consideration in one of the most religious countries in the world. Identity mythology explains how society came to be the way it is (or at least how it is perceived to be by Identity Christians), and it offers a mythologically sanctioned place in the battle of good against evil. And, in explicitly martial language, Identity mythology assures them that they have chosen wisely their place on that battlefield. Drawing on several biblical allusions, Richard Butler concludes "The Aryan View of Life":

> Therefore, we as kindred warriors, strengthening one another in the true love of our Father's Truth, do fight the good fight to lift His Standard, to make the paths straight, to give knowledge to the ignorant, to expose the lie of darkness, to the light of truth, to slash free the chains of Jewish degradation that hold our brethren in debt to the usury of immorality, depravity, and death.[21]

That the Christian Identity movement does not rely on simple hatred or bigotry, but rather couches its racism in religious mythology, makes it potentially a much more dangerous force in society than those groups that rely simply on the social disaffection of their members and the racialist bombast of their leaders. Committed members are no longer fighting because they do not like desegregation, interracial dating and marriage, or the perceived decline of the power enjoyed by white people in this country. Rather, when committed to the mythology of Christian Identity, their vision of the world had been raised to the level of universality. Through their interpretation of the Bible, Identity Christians can point to a recognized sacred narrative as support for their beliefs, sanctioning racism and sanctifying it with an external religious authority.

NOTES

1. Because of space limitations, I cannot discuss a number of other important figures in the development of Christian Identity. Readers interested in such Identity leaders as William Potter Gale, Gerald L. K. Smith, Bernard Comparet, and Howard Rand are encouraged to consult works noted below.

2. Michael Barkun, *Religion and the Racist Right: The Origins of the Christian Identity Movement* (Chapel Hill: University of North Carolina Press, 1997), 6.

3. Barkun, *Religion and the Racist Right*, 34; on Cameron, see 31–43.

4. Warren Kinsella, *Web of Hate: Inside Canada's Far Right Network* (Toronto: HarperCollins, 1994), 94.

5. While published as a booklet, since it forms a core doctrine of Christian Identity various white supremacist organizations have kept versions of Swift's speech in circulation through the Internet. See, for example, www.aryan-nations.org/jcjew.html.

6. Ibid.

7. Richard G. Butler, "Foundations Biography of Aryan Nations"; available online at www.aryan-nations.org/whoan.html.

8. Richard G. Butler, "Christianity and the Aryan Vision of God"; available online at http://www.aryan-nations.org/1-AryanWarrior.html.

9. Richard G. Butler, "Aryan Nations Platform: Article 2"; available online at www.aryan-nations.org/whoan.html.

10. Butler, "Aryan Nations Platform: Article 3."

11. Butler, "Aryan Nations Platform: Article 4."

12. Butler, "Aryan Nations Platform: Articles 5, 6."

13. James Combs, *Tolerance*; available online at http://www.melvig.org/tol /tolerance-toc.html.

14. Richard G. Butler, "The Goal of Aryan Nations"; available online at http://www.aryan-nations.org/1-AryanWarrior.html.

15. Richard G. Butler, quoted in Doug Vaughan, "Terror on the Right: The Klan and Nazi Resurgence." *Utne Reader* (August/September 1985): 47.

16. For a map of Christian Identity's "The National Premise," taken from Ku Klux Klansman David Duke's *National Association for the Advancement of White People Newsletter*, see James Ridgeway, *Blood in the Face: The Ku Klux Klan, Aryan Nations, Nazi Skinheads, and the Rise of a New White Culture* (New York: Thunder's Mouth Press, 1995), 168–169.

17. David Duke, quoted in Ridgeway, *Blood in the Face*, 168.

18. Butler, quoted in Vaughan, "Terror on the Right," 48.

19. Barkun, *Religion and the Racist Right*, 227.

20. Richard G. Butler, "Population and Race"; available online at http://www .aryan-nations.org/1-AryanWarrior.html.

21. Richard G. Butler, "The Aryan View of Life"; available online at http:// www.aryan-nations.org/1-AryanWarrior.html.

SUGGESTIONS FOR FURTHER READING

Barkun, Michael. *Religion and the Racist Right: The Origins of the Christian Identity Movement*. Chapel Hill: University of North Carolina Press, 1997.

Dobratz, Betty A. and Stephanie L. Shanks-Meile. *The White Separatist Movement in the United States: White Power, White Pride*. Baltimore: Johns Hopkins University Press, 2000.

Kinsella, Warren. *Web of Hate: Inside Canada's Far Right Network*. Toronto: HarperCollins, 1994.

Ridgeway, James. *Blood in the Face: The Ku Klux Klan, Aryan Nations, Nazi Skinheads, and the Rise of a New White Culture*. New York: Thunder's Mouth Press, 1995.

Zeskind, Leonard. *The "Christian Identity" Movement: Analyzing Its Theological Rationalization for Racist and Anti-Semitic Violence*. Division of Church and Society of the National Council of Churches of Christ in the U.S.A., 1987.

Chapter 8

"Loathsome unto Thy People"

The Latter-day Saints and Racial Categorization

Craig R. Prentiss

In 1954, The Church of Jesus Christ of Latter-day Saints (commonly known as the "Mormons"), began placing Native-American Mormon children above the age of eight into the homes of Euro-American, Latter-day Saint (LDS) members for the length of the school year. The program was intended to enhance educational and cultural opportunities for Native American youth by taking them off the reservation to interact with the wider LDS population. At the end of the school year, children returned to their homes on the reservation to share their experiences and re-cultivate bonds with their families and tribal communities. At its peak in the early 1970s, 5000 children were participants in the Indian Placement Services. Though the numbers have dropped into the hundreds, the program continues today.[1]

In 1880, the LDS's principle governing body, the Council of Twelve, rejected Elijah Abel's request for access to the Mormon Temple, as they had done regularly for nearly thirty years. While denying entry to the Temple was not uncommon for the LDS, this case was different. Elijah Abel was ordained an Elder in the priesthood of Melchizedek by the father of the Mormon prophet, Joseph Smith, Sr. Within a year of his ordination, and with the approval of the Prophet Joseph Smith himself, Abel had risen to membership in the Quorum of Seventy, a governing body second only in importance to the Council of Twelve. Moreover, Abel had been a personal friend of Joseph Smith, Jr. and was a pillar of the LDS community. Abel was accused of no wrongdoing and there had been no challenges to his "orthodoxy." But Elijah Abel was an African American, and within two decades of his ordination, higher ranking LDS authorities were saying that "blacks" had no rights to the Temple, nor to the Mormon priesthood. Abel died in Utah on Christmas Day, 1884, as committed to the truth of the Prophet's revelations as he had been nearly half a century earlier.[2]

Neither of the events mentioned above can be understood outside the context of distinctive conceptions of "race" arising from the binding myths of the Church of Jesus Christ of Latter-day Saints. Well before the advent of the LDS movement in the early 1800s, the imagined social boundaries that distinguished between "Euro-American" and "Indian," "black" and "white," had been marked. But like all such "racial" and "ethnic" distinctions, the meanings they encoded were shaped by a collection of socially specific and historically contingent variables. This chapter explores the manner in which *The Book of Mormon, Doctrine and Covenants, The Pearl of Great Price,* the office of the Mormon presidency, and other elements sacred to the LDS have been employed in shaping the Mormon perception of Native Americans, "blackness," and "whiteness." We will see that while LDS myth often overlapped with myths in the wider American culture, they have still provided Mormons with a special system of authorizing the social boundaries they conceived.

LDS Origins

This story must begin with Joseph Smith, Jr. (1805–1844), whose prophecies, revelations, and discoveries lay the foundations for the LDS movement. As a fourteen year-old boy in upstate New York, Joseph Smith had a vision of God and Jesus, both seen as distinct bodies. These divine figures foretold that Smith would be blessed with a new revelation, one that would guide him to a true form of Christianity untainted by the misunderstandings and distortions of the rapidly proliferating Christian denominations in early nineteenth century America. In September 1823, Smith was visited by an angel named Moroni. Moroni told Smith of a hill, not far away, where he would discover a collection of golden plates that would provide him with an additional testament to the teachings of Jesus Christ.

Though Smith found the plates, it was not until 1827 that Moroni deemed him worthy enough to successfully pull them from the ground. And so began the process of translating these plates from the lost language of a distant past—a process aided by special stones invested with a power to render the unintelligible symbols as English. By March 1830, after an arduous translation process, a New York press printed the first edition of what had come to be known as *The Book of Mormon*. While the gold plates and sacred stones have long since disappeared, the fruits of Smith's labor remain the bedrock of the LDS movement today.

The Book of Mormon tells of an ancient people who had populated the Americas since the sixth century B.C.E. Their story began with an Israelite named Lehi, a descendant of the biblical Joseph. Lehi was inspired by God to leave Israel shortly before the Babylonians took over the territory and destroyed Solomon's Temple in the 580s B.C.E. After building a ship, Lehi traveled with his family, including his sons, Laman and Nephi, to "the promised land," a new Zion that came to be known as the Americas.[3] They were not the first to arrive from Israel, according to *The Book of Mormon*. In the second half of the third millennium B.C.E., Jared, the patriarch of the Jaredite people, sailed to the Americas under God's guidance.[4] The Jaredites lived in the land for hundreds of years, but were wiped out after a series of wars.[5] Also, near the time of Lehi's arrival, a band of Israelites known as the Mulekites arrived in the Americas and inhabited a territory called Zarahemla. Eventually, these Mulekites were absorbed by the descendants of Nephi, the Nephites.[6]

Still, the most significant arrivals to the new land were the descendants of Lehi's sons, Laman and Nephi. *The Book of Mormon* is devoted, in large measure, to the saga of these tribes who create a thriving civilization in the Americas. They built cities and temples and followed the Mosaic law of their Hebrew ancestors. While, more often than not, the Nephites were depicted as more obedient to God's laws, the Lamanites too had moments in which they appeared to be in God's favor.

At the pinnacle of *The Book of Mormon*'s tale, America is visited by Jesus himself. In three days, Jesus established his Church through the performance of baptism, the institution of sacraments, and the creation of a priesthood. The Church would serve the people until his second coming which would be marked by the gathering of all of Israel in the Americas.[7] Within a short time, the Nephites and Lamanites were converted to the Church, and with their conversion came peace, prosperity, and tranquility.[8]

But peace was short lived as the Nephites and the Lamanites waged a bloody war, between the fourth and fifth centuries c.e. The Lamanites succeeded in annihilating the Nephites entirely. In the final days of the conflict, the last great Nephite leader, Mormon, was killed, leaving his son, Moroni, to complete Mormon's written account of the Lamanite-Nephite wars.[9] Mormon's dying wish was that his wayward cousins, the Lamanites, would return to their faith in God and Jesus Christ, whom they had abandoned.[10]

Native Americans Explained

For the Latter-day Saints, the aforementioned myth provided an interpretive key for unlocking a mystery that had perplexed Euro-American settlers since their earliest contact with the native people of the "New World": Where did these "Indians" come from? Not surprisingly, most Euro-Americans turned to their own primary mythic resource, the Bible, to answer this question. Perhaps the most popular explanation was that the Native Americans were descendants of the fabled "lost tribes" of Israel, dispersed during the Assyrian invasion of Israel in the eighth century b.c.e. This hypothesis was even posed by such luminaries as William Penn and was popularized by James Adair's 1775 treatise, *History of the American Indians*.[11]

The Book of Mormon provided an amended confirmation of that thesis, though instead of being precipitated by the Assyrian invasion, the impending crisis inspiring Lehi's departure appeared to be the Babylonian invasion nearly two centuries later. As the Bering Strait theory, holding that human beings migrated to the Americas thousands of years earlier, became increasingly accepted, Mormons were quick to point out that their scripture did not contradict the theory, but only explained the origins of a significant percentage of Native peoples. With no way to determine who descends from Lamanites and who does not, Mormons have generally used the term "Lamanite" synonymously with Native Americans.

Mormon myth also explained other key features of indigenous Americans, including their skin color. Lamanites, like the Nephites, were once "fair" skinned. As a punishment for their sinfulness, however, their skin was darkened. "For behold," reads 2 Nephi, "they had hardened their hearts against [the Lord], that they had become like unto flint; wherefore as they were white, and exceedingly fair and delightsome, that they might not be enticing unto my people the Lord God did cause a skin of blackness to come upon them." Until their repentance, they would remain "loathsome unto thy [Nephi's] people." To further reinforce the social divisions between the Lamanites and the Nephites, God cursed Nephites whose "seed" mixed with the "seed" of the Lamanites. Nephites who transgressed would be marked with darker skin.[12]

This passage establishes a hierarchy of pigmentation, with "white" and "fair" skin deigned by God to be superior and preferable to "dark" and "black" skin. As a result of this social division, those at the losing end of this hierarchy, the Lamanites, were said to have become "an idle people, full of mischief and subtlety, and did seek in the wilderness for beasts of prey."[13] It is worth noting that this description reflected Euro-American impressions of Native Americans, particularly their "idleness," a common derogatory term that expressed the colonist's dismay at the apparent ease with which the Native people survived without having to resort to the work schedules and hard manual labor typical of European culture. Rather than viewing this disparity as a mark of Indian cultural superiority, it was seen as evidence of their lack of "civilization."[14]

The curse against the Lamanites was revisited in the Mormon book of Alma. Alma, a high priest among the Nephites, recalled the "dark" skin of the Lamanites as a "mark which was set upon their fathers," intended "so that their seed might be distinguished from the seed of their brethren, that thereby the Lord God might preserve his people, that they do not mix and believe in incorrect traditions which would prove their destruction."[15] The message of Alma clearly communicates that God created different "races," marked by skin color, and that coloration revealed those who were obedient to God and those who were not.

These passages exemplify the role that myth can play in explaining and, in many cases, enforcing a social order. A hierarchy based on color had received divine approval. In a fascinating twist, however, *The Book of Mormon* also provides clues to the possibility that not only could the Lamanites' obedience to God be changed, so too could their relative skin color. The Mormon prophet Jacob warns the Nephites that should they fail to repent for their sins, the skins of the Lamanites "will be whiter than yours." Furthermore, Jacob enjoins the Nephites not to "revile" the Lamanites for the color of their skin or their "filthiness; but ye shall remember your own filthiness, and remember that their filthiness came because of their fathers."[16] In issuing this caution, Jacob reveals that sin, not skin color, is the primary issue, and makes clear that skin color could vary in relationship to devotion. Moreover, *The Book of Mormon* prophesied that ultimately, the Lamanites would return to God, and by the time of that return on the eve of Christ's second coming, their skins would be "white and delightsome." (In the late 1970s, this prophecy [2 Nephi 30:6] raised such an uproar that the Church changed the official translation to read "*pure* and delightsome.")[17]

Mormons had faith in this prophecy. Consider the words of Levi Jackman, one of the original LDS pioneers, whose January 1848 journal entry described his positive encounters with the Native Americans:

> When I reflect and consider that they [the Indians] are of the House of Israel and the children of the covenant seed into whom belongs the priesthood and the oracles of God, and when I think of *what they will be when they become a white and delightsome people*, I say to myself, "O Lord, who can do all this [transform the Lamanties]?" But the decree has gone forth and must be fulfilled.[18]

Well into the twentieth century, belief in the "whitening" of Native American skin prior to the second coming of Christ persisted. "As a child I was taught that if you are good, you will turn white," explained Abby Maestas, a Latin American Mormon of Indian descent, in a 1994 interview. "And that's very confusing for people who are brown."[19]

So, the message of the Latter-day Saints was not one of a static and unchanging social order, but instead anticipated a profound change in a time to come. The LDS church, like much of the Christian tradition, accepts a millennialist theology in which Jesus the Christ will return to usher in a new kingdom of glory on Earth. While the Lamanites may have been castigated and cursed in much of *The Book of Mormon*, the teachings of the LDS Church retain a special role for them in the coming of God's reign. You will recall that Mormon's dying wish was that his Lamanite cousins would return to the fold and subject themselves again to God's will. In keeping with Mormon's hope, in March 1831 the prophet Joseph Smith received a revelation from God that "before the great day of the Lord shall come, Jacob shall flourish in the wilderness, and the Lamanites shall blossom as the rose."[20] This Lamanite destiny ensured that the Saints would devote considerable effort to converting Native Americans in the years to come.

As early as 1830, Joseph Smith sent key members of his infant Church to spread the word of The Book of Mormon to Native Americans, first in New York and Ohio, though soon as far west as Missouri and Kansas.[21] If measured against their initial hopes of gaining massive numbers of Indian converts, their efforts were not successful. Yet the role these missionary efforts played in the development of the LDS movement was profound.

LDS missionary work with Native Americans precipitated a barrage of accusations from non-Mormons that they were conspiring with the Indians to rebel against the U.S. government. Bear in mind that the beginnings of the Mormon movement coincided with the effort to expand the territorial United States from "sea to shining sea." From the perspective of the federal government, this effort required expelling Native Americans from their ancestral homelands. Anything seen as standing in the way of this goal was viewed as a threat to the fortunes of the Nation. As such, the non-Mormon accusation that the Saints were aligning with the Native Americans against the government resonated with U.S. citizens.

The Latter-day Saints were expelled from Missouri in 1839 amid rumblings that they were "keeping a constant communication with the Indian tribes of [the U.S.] frontier, with declaring, even from the pulpit, that the Indians are a part of God's chosen people, and are destined, by heaven, to inherit this land, in common with themselves."[22] This rhetoric obviously ran counter to the burgeoning ideology of a "Manifest Destiny." When the Saints moved west under the leadership of Brigham Young from 1846 to 1847, government fears that the Mormons would align themselves with the Indians of the western territories grew, despite there being little evidence to support the claim.[23] In reality, while the Mormons continued to hold the faith that the Lamanites would "blossom as the rose," and while their relations with the Native Americans were more harmonious than that of a plurality of their Euro-American peers, their interests also conflicted at times with Native Americans and the preservation of indigenous cultures.[24]

The Mormon community in Utah created "tithing houses" in each village where a percentage of the Saints' food and goods were stored for distribution among the Indians. LDS women organized a Relief Society designed specifically to "uplift" the Natives by providing them with access to the trappings of Euro-American life. Furthermore, in an effort to counter a brutal child slave-trading ring that had developed between the Ute Indians and the Mexicans, Brigham Young himself encouraged Saints to purchase Native children and raise them, as sons and daughters, in LDS homes. Several dozen children were brought into the LDS fold in this manner. Finally, Mormons were active in teaching Native Americans about European styles of farming and raising livestock.[25]

With the exception of buying Indian children out of the slave trade, a practice motivated by a genuine horror for their treatment, the LDS conception of what a "blossomed" Lamanite people would resemble differed little from the attitudes of most Euro-Americans who favored "civilizing" the Native population. Being a proper Mormon and a "civilized" member of society appeared to require changes in clothing style, grooming, agricultural techniques, housing methods, gender roles, and economic behavior, to name a few. As with other forms of Christianity, conversion did not involve merely an intellectual or emotional assent to a new set of "truths" and a new mythic framework; conversion was expected to involve a radical transformation in nearly every element of indigenous life. (For more, see Joel Martin's chapter).

By viewing Native Americans through the prism of the Mormon "Lamanite" mythology, a course was charted that continues to mark this distinctive and peculiar relationship between the Latter-day Saints and American Indians. Only in this context does the Indian Placement Services program, described at the beginning of this chapter, make full sense. Not surprisingly, one of the participants in the IPS program came to be at the center of what seemed a high point of Mormon-Indian relations. George Patrick Lee had, at the age of twelve, been sent to live with a Euro-American family of Saints. Twenty years later, in 1975, Lee, a "fullblooded" Navajo, was appointed to the second-highest governing body in the LDS Church, the Quorum of Seventy. It was a momentous occasion and appeared to mark a turning point in the fulfillment of Joseph Smith's prophecy. But by 1989, things had gone awry. Amid allegations of the sexual abuse of a minor, a charge which Lee admitted to years later, he was excommunicated. The story was complicated by his excommunication, which coincided with his accusations that Mormon missionary methods were detrimental to the culture and spirit of Native Americans. The very public proceedings drove a wedge between the two communities.[26]

Still, LDS effort to restore the Lamanites to their former glory in antic-ipation of Christ's second coming continues. A Mormon equivalent of the Peace Corps operates on reservations throughout the United States, as does an Indian Seminary Program that has served tens of thousands of Native American children. Brigham Young University continues to spon-sor scholarships for Native American students, though they currently make up less than one percent of the student body. BYU's curriculum features offerings in a multitude of Native American languages, a minor in Native American studies, and Native American outreach educational programs.[27]

Mormons and "Blackness"

If *The Book of Mormon* associated dark skin with a curse, how influential would the text be in shaping LDS perception of those who came to be identified as "black"? Answering this question is made more difficult upon recognizing that the process of constructing a social hierarchy based on a coloring scheme with "blackness" on one end and "whiteness" on the other had been initiated well before the beginning of the LDS movement. Mormons did not invent social divisions marked by per-ceived coloration. But the mythic resources of the Mormon faith, includ-ing *The Book of Mormon, Doctrine and Covenants*, and *The Pearl of Great Price* (a selection of the prophet's teachings and prophecies), provided a framework through which Saints were able to explain and order social di-visions along "racial" lines.

As the Church was forming, there was a marked ambivalence on the most controversial issue of the day, slavery. Notably, Mormons were ac-cused by their persecutors in Missouri of being abolitionists and trying to promote slave rebellions. While no evidence suggests that the accusations were true, they indicate that, if anything, the Saints were seen by some outsiders as too accommodating to African Americans. Their earliest statements on slavery took the path of least resistance by emphasizing support for upholding the law, whether that law allowed for slavery or not.[28] By 1844, however, the Prophet, in the midst of a presidential run, announced that he favored the abolition of slavery.[29] With Smith's assas-sination later that year, the Church's position was again thrown into con-fusion. In Utah, tolerance developed for southern Mormons who had emigrated to the territory with their slaves in hand, and by 1852 Brigham

Young approved a law that legalized slavery, though few Mormons actually owned them.

While slavery has traditionally been viewed as the benchmark issue for measuring Euro-American attitudes toward race in the 1800s, another issue gained much attention by the 1960s among Mormons and non-Mormons alike: a ban on blacks from the priesthood. While women, both "black" and "white," were (and are) also banned from the LDS priesthood, virtually all Mormon males enter into the priesthood in their youth. The LDS priesthood is divided into the Priesthood of Aaron, traditionally received by nearly all boys at the age of twelve, enabling them to baptize, bless the sacrament, and teach Church doctrine. Then, by age eighteen, most Mormon men in good standing with the Church enter into the priesthood of Melchizedek, enabling them to pass on the priesthood to others, as well as to heal the sick and lead the Church. But until the late 1970s, those boys and men identified as black were prevented from becoming priests. The reasons for this restriction were largely buried in legend and lore, but the work of late twentieth century historians enables us to put the pieces of this restriction together.

In the earliest Church, there was no restriction. In fact, two African Americans are known to have entered into the priesthood during the prophet Joseph Smith Jr.'s lifetime: Walker Lewis, about whom little is known, and Elijah Abel, about whom a great deal is known. Elijah Abel was baptized into the LDS Church in 1832, and by 1836 he had not only been ordained into the priesthood of Melchizedek, but had even been selected to the second-highest governing body in the LDS Church, the Quorum of Seventy.[30] By all accounts, Abel was a friend of Joseph Smith Jr. during the days when the Mormons had settled in Nauvoo, Illinois, and was an active participant in LDS governance until he moved to Cincinnati, Ohio, in 1842, two years before Joseph Smith Jr. was assassinated. Abel maintained his faith and reconnected with the dominant portion of the Saints by moving to Utah in 1853. At that time, Brigham Young had become the president of the Church. Still, the record indicates that Abel continued as a participant in the Quorum of Seventy, and there is no contemporary evidence that his participation was questioned.[31]

But things had changed. We find evidence of resistance to allowing blacks in the priesthood as early as 1849. A journal entry in that year quotes Brigham Young as putting forward this position.[32] By the 1870s, Abel's priesthood had become an embarrassment to the Church leadership. In fact, it wasn't long after his arrival in Utah that he and his family began being denied access to the Temple, making participating in rites that the LDS deemed essential for salvation impossible for them.[33]

What authorized the change? By the 1870s, the policy of denying blacks the priesthood was being attributed to the Prophet Joseph Smith Jr. himself. The assumption that it originated with Smith continued to be promulgated in nearly all Mormon circles until articles by Mormon historian Lester Bush dismantled the tenuous evidence for such a claim in the late 1960s and early 1970s. All signs pointed to the policy originating years after Smith's death.

It appears that three myths buttressed denying the priesthood to blacks, though only one of these had its origins in LDS theology.[34] The first was the widespread belief that African Americans were descendants of Ham's son Canaan, who was cursed to be "the lowest of slaves" to his brothers (Genesis 9:25) (For more, see Paul Harvey's essay). The connection of Canaan's descendants to the African people had ancient roots and was widespread among Euro-Americans as a means of justifying slavery. As early as 1831 evidence illustrates that Joseph Smith Jr. himself believed in the Hamitic origins of the African people.[35] Still, such a belief did not prevent him from ordaining African Americans into the priesthood. The second myth, evident in *The Pearl of Great Price*, was that Africans descended from Cain, the murderous brother of Abel. God punished the "seed of Cain" for sins by making them "black" (Moses 7:22). Again, by the 1840s, Joseph Smith Jr. had come to accept the idea of African descent from Cain. Yet, evidence that Smith rejected the priesthood for black men as a result of this imagined pedigree is lacking. It was not until 1849 that we see the first linkage between the Cain mythology and the denial of the priesthood for blacks, a connection made by Brigham Young himself.[36]

Both of these myths, each dependent upon a combination of creative inference as well as faith that the patriarchs described in the Hebrew Bible were not simply mythic archetypes but real people, were common to Euro-Americans throughout the 1800s and before. But the distinctively Mormon doctrine of the premortal existence opened the door to another authorization for restricting "blacks" from the priesthood.

Based largely upon Jeremiah 1:5 in which God claims to have known us before forming us in the womb, the LDS teaches that souls exist in heaven before birth on Earth. Their narrative of premortal existence reads much like any narrative of earthly existence, filled with struggle, joy, envy, and love. The Book of Revelation 12:7 in the New Testament refers to a war in the heavens. For the Saints, this war in heaven was decisive in determining the earthly social order. The war was fought, according to *The Pearl of Great Price*, over God's decision to appoint Jesus as the Savior (Moses 4:1–4). By the twentieth century, it became common for Mormons to claim that denying blacks the priesthood had resulted from their lack of valor during this heavenly battle. This rationale allowed Saints to claim that blacks were not denied the priesthood because they were black; instead, they were black because they had shown themselves unworthy in their premortal existence, rendering blackness as a mere signifier of a preordained divine decision. While this position began largely as "folklore" (as one Mormon sociologist called it),[37] the appeal to premortal existence became doctrine in a statement of the Mormon First Presidency by 1949, and was reinforced again in 1969.[38]

Lester Bush has argued that invoking the war in Heaven stemmed from the diminished credibility of the Children of Ham and Children of Cain mythologies as a result of the late nineteenth century rise of biblical criticism.[39] As these theories diminished in discursive value, the doctrine of premortal existence took up the slack. But as the strength of any mythic text is its adaptability to changing circumstance, *The Pearl of Great Price* also played an important role in arguing *against* the priesthood ban by the second half of the twentieth century. These "scriptures were actually quite vague in linking the cursed lineages of old to modern blacks," and this vagueness left an opening for those who opposed the ban.[40]

With the rise of the civil rights movement in the 1960s, coupled with the anti-authoritarian ethos of that decade, the LDS ban on the black priesthood became a point of public controversy. At the same time, the LDS was expanding into Africa and South American countries like Brazil, where those who would fall under the ban constituted a majority of the population. As such, the policy was proving an obstacle to growth.

Faithful Mormons who were embarrassed by the policy were at a loss, since it was only through divine revelation through the First President of the Church that doctrine could be overturned. Prophecy and revelation has always played a prominent role in Mormon theology. At times, this feature has enabled the Church to adapt rapidly to changing circumstances, as was the case when the revelation ending the practice of polygamy coincided with the opportunity for Utah to receive statehood. At other times, as in the case of the ban on the black priesthood, popular sentiment could turn well before a revelation had been received. But in 1978, First President Spencer Kimball, the leader of the LDS, recorded a revelation in the *Doctrine and Covenants* that, in answer to his prayers, "confirmed that the long-promised day has come when every faithful, worthy man in the Church may receive his holy priesthood . . . without regard to race or color."[41]

Today, black Mormons in the U.S. remain a small fraction of the total LDS population. Less than one percent of the student body at BYU is African American. But worldwide, since the ban on the priesthood was lifted, black membership in the Church has skyrocketed into the hundreds of thousands.[42] Saints are able to authorize their raceless theology by appealing to statements made by the prophet Joseph Smith Jr. that reflect inclusiveness, or to passages in *The Book of Mormon*, like the one found in 2 Nephi 26:33, that the Lord "inviteth them all to come unto him and partake of his goodness; and he denieth none that come unto him, black and white, bond and free, male and female."

The stories of the Indian Placement Services and Elijah Abel reflect moments in a continually evolving Mormon framework for making sense of Native Americans, "blackness," and "whiteness." While the LDS did not invent these social barriers, their mythic resources gave them a distinctive manner for interpreting, reinforcing, and reformulating social barriers stemming from racial ideology. Color as a boundary marker received divine sanction through a developing mythology grounded in sacred text and revealed authority. Yet faith in continuous revelation opened the possibility for changes in the Mormon understanding of the divine will. As some of the fastest growth in the LDS continues to take place in Africa and Latin America among those whose skin is generally darker than those Euro-Americans who dominate the leadership circles of the Church, one wonders what new readings of the Mormon mythology will develop as the landscape of the LDS's population centers and power structure evolve over time.

NOTES

1. Bruce A. Chadwick and Stan L. Albrecht, "Mormons and Indians: Beliefs, Policies, Programs, and Practices," in *Contemporary Mormonism: Social Science Perspectives*, ed. Marie Cornwall, Tim B. Heaton, and Lawrence A. Young (Urbana: University of Illinois Press, 1994), esp. 287–292.

2. Newell G. Bringhurst, "Elijah Abel and the Changing Status of Blacks

within Mormonism," in *Neither White nor Black: Mormon Scholars Confront the Race Issue in a Universal Church*, ed. Lester E. Bush, Jr., and Armand L. Mauss (Midvale, Utah: Signature Books, 1984), 130–139; Lester E. Bush Jr., "Mormonism's Negro Doctrine: An Historical Overview," also in *Neither White nor Black*, 60, 76–77.

3. 1 Nephi 18:23, *The Book of Mormon* (Salt Lake City: The Church of Jesus Christ of Latter–day Saints, 1981 edition) Cited hereafter as *BOM*.

4. Ether 6:12, *BOM*.

5. Omni 1:21, *BOM*; Ether 15:29–32, *BOM*.

6. Omni 1: 15–19, *BOM*; Mosiah 25:13, *BOM*.

7. 3 Nephi 11–29, *BOM*.

8. 4 Nephi 1:1–1:9, *BOM*.

9. Mormon 2:1 – 9:37, *BOM*.

10. Mormon, chapter 7, *BOM*.

11. See online reproduction of John F. Watson, *Annals of Philadelphia and Pennsylvania: A Collection of Memoirs, Anecdotes, and Incidents of the City and Its Inhabitants and of the Earliest Settlements of the Inland Part of Pennsylvania from the Days of the Founders* (Philadelphia: J. B. Lippincott, 1868), Chap. 3, pt. 1, found at http://ftp.rootsweb.com/pub/usgenweb/pa/philadelphia/areahistory/watson0206.txt, (accessed January 15, 2002).

12. 2 Nephi 5:21–23, *BOM*.

13. Ibid., 5:24.

14. 1 Nephi 12:23, *BOM*; for more on European attitudes toward Native Americans, particularly with respect to "idleness," see James Axtell, "The Invasion Within: The Contest of Cultures in Colonial North America," in *The European and the Indian: Essays in the Ethnohistory of Colonial North America* (New York: Oxford University Press, 1981), esp. 48–52.

15. Alma 3:6–11, *BOM*.

16. Jacob 3:8–9, *BOM*.

17. 2 Nephi 30:6, *BOM*; see also Emily Gurnon, "Minority Mormons," *Christian Century* 111 (February 16, 1994): 158.

18. Emphasis mine; Levi Jackman, *A Short Sketch of the Life of Levi Jackman, 1797–1876*, "January 1848," catalogued by the Book of Abraham Project at Brigham Young University, and available online at http://www.math.byu.edu/~smithw/Lds/LDS/Early-Saints/LJackman.htm 1 (accessed, January 24, 2002).

19. Quoted in Gurnon, "Minority Mormons," *Christian Century*: 158.

20. *The Doctrine and Covenants of the Church of Jesus Christ of Latter-day Saints*, 49:24 (available online at http://www.lds.org/dc/contents).

21. Leonard J. Arrington and Davis Bitton, *The Mormon Experience: A History of the Latter-day Saints*, 2d ed. (Urbana: University of Illinois Press, 1992), 146.

22. Ibid.; citing Sidney Rigdon, Joseph Smith, Jr. et al. in Kirtland, Ohio, to

John Thornton et al. in Liberty, Missouri, 25 July 1836; quoted in *Latter-day Saints' Messenger and Advocate* 2 (August 1936): 357.

23. Norman F. Furniss, *The Mormon Conflict, 1850–1859* (New Haven: Yale University Press, 1960), 33.

24. Ibid., 35; Arrington and Bitton, *The Mormon Experience*, 156.

25. Arrington and Bitton, *The Mormon Experience*, 149–153.

26. Ibid., 160; Gurnon, "Minority Mormons," *Christian Century*, 159; Harrison Lapahie Jr., "George Patrick Lee (1943–): Ashkii Hoyani (Boy Who Is Well Behaved and Good) Tódích'íi'nii—Bitter Water Clan," available online at http://www.lapahie.com/George_Patrick_Lee.cfm (accessed January 10, 2002).

27. For latest information, see Brigham Young University's website at http://www.byu.edu.

28. Dennis L. Lythgoe, "Negro Slavery and the Mormon Doctrine," *Western Humanities Review* 21 (1967): 328–329.

29. Ibid., 330.

30. Lester Bush, "A Commentary on Stephen G. Taggart's *Mormonism's Negro Policy*: Social and Historical Origins," in *Neither White nor Black*, 34, originally published in *Dialogue* 4 (Winter 1969); see also Jessie L. Embry, *Black Saints in a White Church: Contemporary African American Mormons* (Salt Lake City: Signature Books, 1994), 38.

31. Embry, *Black Saints in a White Church*, 38–39; cites Newell G. Bringhurst, "Elijah Abel and the Changing Status of Blacks within Mormonism," in *Neither White nor Black*, 131–137. Bringhurst's article was originally published in *Dialogue* 12 (Summer 1979).

32. Bush, "A Commentary on Stephen G. Taggart's *Mormonism's Negro Policy*," in *Neither White nor Black*, 38, 47 (fn. 45).

33. Bringhurst, "Elijah Abel and the Changing Status of Blacks within Mormonism," in *Neither White nor Black*, 137.

34. Armand L. Mauss, "Mormonism and the Negro: Faith, Folklore, and Civil Rights," in *Neither White nor Black*, 15. Mauss's article was originally published in *Dialogue* 2 (Winter 1967).

35. Bush, "A Commentary of Stephen G. Taggart's *Mormonism's Negro Policy*," in *Neither White nor Black*, 39.

36. Ibid., 47. Bush cites Lorenzo Snow's diaries, entered in *Journal History*, February 13, 1849.

37. Mauss, "Mormonism and the Negro," in *Neither White nor Black*, 12–13.

38. "Appendix: Authoritative Statements on the Status of Blacks," in *Neither White nor Black*, 221–224.

39. Lester Bush Jr., "Whence the Negro Doctrine? A Review of Ten Years of Answers," in *Neither White nor Black*, 208–210; also cited in Mary Lou McNamara, "Secularization or Sacralization: The Change in LDS Church Policy on Blacks," in *Contemporary Mormonism*, 312.

40. McNamara, "Secularization or Sacralization," in *Contemporary Mormonism*, 312–313.

41. "Appendix," in *Neither White nor Black*, 225.

42. "Blacks at Brigham Young University: Objects of Curiosity but No Longer a Breed Apart," *Journal of Blacks in Higher Education*, Issue 10 (Winter 1995–1996): 23.

SUGGESTIONS FOR FURTHER READING

Arrington, Leonard J. and Davis Bitton. *The Mormon Experience: A History of the Latter-day Saints*, 2d ed. Urbana: University of Illinois Press, 1992.

Bringhurst, Newell G. *Saints, Slaves, and Blacks: The Changing Place of Black People within Mormonism*. Westport, CT: Greenwood Press, 1981.

Bush, Lester E. Jr., and Armand Mauss. *Neither White nor Black: Mormon Scholars Confront the Race Issue in a Universal Church*. Midvale, Utah: Signature Books, 1984.

Embry, Jessie L. *Black Saints in a White Church: Contemporary African American Mormons*. Salt Lake City: Signature Books, 1994.

Chapter 9

Our Lady of Guadalupe
The Heart of Mexican Identity

Roberto S. Goizueta

In July 1996 the Reverend Guillermo Schulemburg, the prelate in charge of the Basilica of Our Lady of Guadalupe in Mexico City, offered his resignation to Pope John Paul II. The resignation followed days of nationwide demonstrations, occasioned by a comment Schulemburg had reportedly made in an interview with an Italian journalist. In that interview, he had discussed the Mexican devotion to Our Lady of Guadalupe and Juan Diego, the indigenous man to whom La Morenita had appeared in December 1531. The abbot of the Basilica was quoted as suggesting that Juan Diego was "a symbol, not a reality." This statement was enough to send shock waves throughout Mexico and the Mexican American community in the United States, eventually forcing Schulemburg's resignation.

As this anecdote makes clear, one cannot understand the Mexican people without understanding the central role of Our Lady of Guadalupe (and, thus, Juan Diego) in that people's history. Our Lady of Guadalupe holds a unique place among Latin American popular religious devotions. Indeed, as other Latino and Euro-American communities are introduced to La Morenita through contact with the Mexican American community in the United States, Guadalupan devotion has become a truly Pan-American phenomenon.[1] In this chapter, I will focus on Guadalupe and suggest at least two reasons for her uniqueness and power: first, the intimate, historical connection between Our Lady of Guadalupe and the birth of Mexico as a *mestizo* people; second, Guadalupe's role as liberator of the poor.

La Morenita: Symbol of Mestizaje

The Mexican nation of today was born from the violence of conquest. Mexico is the child of the conquering Spaniards and the violated indigenous Amerindian women whom they raped and, in some cases, married. The offspring are thus a *mestizo* people, a people whose countenances and culture bear the unmistakable imprint of their mixed racial-cultural heritage.

As the child of violence—the child of the European conqueror and the indigenous woman—the mestizo or mestiza has historically suffered scorn and humiliation, which has too often been internalized in the form of self-deprecation and self-hatred. In his classic work *El laberinto de la soledad*, the great Mexican poet and writer Octavio Paz poignantly described this process, whereby the dehumanization suffered at the hands of European conquerors becomes, over generations, a deep-seated self-hatred. The child of the conquistador father and the violated mother is ultimately ashamed of both parents who gave him or her birth through this primordial act of violence.[2] However, the appearance of Our Lady of Guadalupe in December 1531 signals a turning point, or an axial point, in the history of Latin American *mestizaje*; at the very heart of Mexican history stands the figure of Our Lady of Guadalupe.

The popular devotion to Our Lady of Guadalupe is based on the *Nican Mopohua*, a text dating from the 1560s and written in Náhuatl, the language of the indigenous Nahua people. The events recounted take place in 1531, not long after the Nahua defeat at the hands of the invading Spanish *conquistadores*, "ten years after the conquest of Mexico City."[3] The remainder of the narrative, we are told, will tell of a human-divine encounter, a divine revelation through which "the knowledge of Him by Whom we live, the true God [*Dios*], *Téotl*, flowered and burst forth."[4] These events took place "a few days into the month of December," on a Saturday, "while it was still night." In Náhuatl mythology, the creation of the world began *huel oc yohuatzinco*, while it was still night; the act of creation originates in darkness, at night. Thus, the hearers of the story would have understood that the events to be recounted in the narrative would themselves signal a new creation, a new life.[5]

Juan Diego is the first person we encounter in the story; he is described as a *macehual*, a "low-class but dignified Indian."[6] Having left his home during the night, Juan Diego travels to Tlatelolco to attend mass and receive catechetical instruction from the Spanish Christians. On the way, he comes to a hill called Tepeyac: this hill "was well known to the Mexican world as the site where the goddess virgin-mother of the gods [*Tonantzín*] was venerated."[7] There he hears birds singing, a sound so beautiful that he imagines he must be in paradise.

Entranced by the beautiful music, Juan Diego feels compelled to follow the sounds to their origins. As he seeks the source of the music, he hears a soft voice calling to him: "*Quihuia; Iuantzin Iuan Diegotzin.*" These words have been translated into Spanish as "*Juanito, Juan Dieguito*" or "*digno Juan, digno Juan Diego.*" The first translation, using the diminutive form of the name, suggests a special intimacy and affection; the speaker clearly feels a special love toward Juan Diego. The second translation emphasizes the speaker's recognition of Juan Diego's dignity as someone worthy of special respect. In Náhuatl, "*tzin* is a suffix which indicates respect, dignity and also familial affection."[8]

Juan Diego follows the sound of the voice and eventually comes to the top of the hill, where he sees a beautiful "Lady," radiantly dressed. She beckons him and, in an affectionate tone, asks: "Juanito, the dearest of my children, where are you going?"[9] Juan Diego tells the Lady that he is on his way to "her house in Mexico/Tlatelolco to hear about the divine things which are given and taught to us by our priests, the images [or delegates] of Our Lord." She then identifies herself as the Virgin Mary: "Know and rest assured in your heart, my dearest child, that I am the Ever Virgin Mary, Mother of the God of Great Truth, *Téotl*, of Him by Whom we live, of the Creator of Persons, of the Master [literally, Owner] of what is Close and Together, of the Lord of Heaven and Earth."[10] Thus, Mary identifies not only herself but also the Christian God (*Dios*) with the Nahua deity *Téotl*. She then orders Juan Diego to ask the bishop to build a temple on this hill, so that from that place she could "show and give all her love, compassion, assistance, and protection to the people." Although Juan Diego had informed her that he was going to "her house" in Mexico (the seat of the bishop and center of the Spanish evangelizing efforts), she replies that, instead, her house should be built here, at Tepeyac.[11] It is from here that she would evangelize her people.

When he arrives at the bishop's palace, Juan Diego is forced to wait a long time before being allowed to see him. After receiving Juan Diego, the bishop nevertheless asks him to return some other day, when he (the bishop) is less busy. Understandably disappointed, Juan Diego returns to Tepeyac to present his report to the Lady:

My Mistress, my Lady, the dearest of my Daughters, my Girl, I went where you sent me to tell your thoughts and words. Although with great difficulty I entered the place of the Lord of the priests, I saw him, and before him expressed your thoughts and words, just as you ordered. . . . But, I could tell by the way he responded that his heart did not accept it, he did not believe.[12]

Blaming himself for the failed mission, Juan Diego then asks the Lady to send someone else to the bishop, someone worthier, of greater stature: "Because, for sure, I am a meager peasant, a cord, a little ladder, the people's dung, I am a leaf."[13] The Lady rejects his plea. Addressing him again as "the dearest of my children," she insists that Juan Diego will be her chosen envoy and orders him to try again.

Obediently, Juan Diego returns to the bishop's palace the next day. This time the bishop asks Juan Diego many detailed questions about his story but, once again, turns Juan Diego away. The bishop requests from Juan Diego a sign that his story is true, that the Virgin Mary has indeed appeared to him. Yet again, Juan Diego returns to Tepeyac to report on his visit with the bishop: "But even though he [the bishop] was told everything, how she looked, and everything he had seen and admired, through which she was rightly revealed as the beloved, ever Virgin, the wondrous Mother of Our Savior and Our Lord Jesus Christ, yet still he did not believe."[14] The Lady responds by asking the indigenous man to return to Tepeyac the next day, at which time she will give him an appropriate sign for the bishop.

However, Juan Diego does not come back the next day, as the Lady had requested. His uncle, Juan Bernardino, had fallen gravely ill and, as the doctor could do nothing more to help him, the uncle asked Juan Diego to look for a priest who could prepare him for death. As he rushes back to Tlatelolco in search of a priest, Juan Diego sneaks around the back of Mount Tepeyac so that the Lady will not spot him, thereby delaying his important mission on behalf of his uncle. Nevertheless, the Lady sees him trying to avoid her and asks why he is so anxious and hurried. At first, Juan Diego tries to change the subject: "My Girl, my dearest Daughter, Lady, I hope you are happy, how did you sleep?"[15] Then, in a confident manner, he defends his actions, telling the Lady about his uncle's illness and his need to find a priest. He asks her to be patient: "The moment I get back, I will return to take your words and thoughts. My Mistress and Girl, forgive me and, for now, have a little patience, I don't want to deceive you, my dearest Daughter, my Girl. Tomorrow, for sure, I will come in all haste."[16] She tells Juan Diego not to worry; she will cure his uncle. His concerns allayed, Juan Diego then "pleaded very much with her to send him immediately to see the Lord of the priests to take him her sign."[17]

The Lady then asks Juan Diego to go to the top of a nearby hill. There he will find wildflowers, which he should then cut and bring to her. Complying with her order, he is amazed to discover beautiful roses blooming on the hill, a natural impossibility in the middle of December. Honoring the Lady's wishes, he cuts the roses and brings them to her. The Lady then places the flowers in his *tilma*, or mantle, and orders him to take the roses to the bishop as the sign he had demanded. Surely the bishop would acknowledge that only a miracle could make such beautiful flowers bloom in December.

Once again, then, Juan Diego travels to the bishop's palace. Even though the Lady had ordered Juan Diego to open his mantle and show the flowers "only in the presence of the bishop,"[18] the bishop's servants are intensely curious to see what the Indian man is carrying. They insist on seeing what the Indian is carrying in his mantle and convince Juan Diego to give them a peek at the flowers. After entering to see the bishop this third time, Juan Diego unfolds his *tilma*, from which cascade to the floor the many beautiful roses he had picked. At that moment, the "beautiful image of the ever Virgin Mary, Mother of the God *Téotl*" suddenly appears on the *tilma*. Everyone present falls to their knees in wonder and homage. The bishop finally believes; he invites Juan Diego to stay overnight in the palace and orders the construction of the temple on Tepeyac.

Still worried about his uncle, however, Juan Diego first travels to his uncle's house to pay him a visit. Arriving at Juan Bernardino's house with the other co-workers, Juan Diego discovers that his uncle has returned to good health—as the Lady had promised. The narrative describes Juan Bernardino as "very astonished that his nephew would come so well-accompanied and honored; and he asked him why they honored him so much" (in the Spanish translation, the original Náhuatl is rendered as *"muy acompañado y muy honrado,"* which literally means "very accompanied and very honored").[19] Finally, the chapel is constructed on Tepeyac. The image of the Lady is still visible today on Juan Diego's *tilma*, which is on display at the Shrine of Our Lady of Guadalupe, a magnificent modern version of the original church that today stands not far from the hill of Tepeyac.

The image itself is a powerful example of *mestizaje* in that it combines an array of Christian symbols with symbols indigenous to the Amerindian world of Juan Diego. One finds in the image, for example, numerous symbols of new life, a new beginning, and a new birth: the Lady is pictured as pregnant, she is wearing a "maternity band" around her waist, and she bears on her womb the symbol which, for the Nahuas, represented the "reconciliation of opposites."[20] The most obvious symbol, of course, is the very color of the Lady's skin. To Western Christians accustomed to images of a blonde and blue-eyed Mary, this Lady must surely appear incongruous; her olive skin tells the indigenous people of Mexico that she, La Morenita, is one of them. It tells all Mexicans and, indeed, all Latinos that she is one of them. This identity between the Lady and her children is powerfully symbolized by her eyes, in which are reflected the image of Juan Diego himself.[21]

The symbolism and narrative thus reflect the history of Mexico and Latin America as a mestizo people, a rich mixture of different races and cultures. In the figures of La Morenita and Juan Diego, God becomes identified with those peoples, cultures, and races who have been marginalized and rejected. Guadalupe represents God's affirmation of the inherent dignity of the victims of European conquest. If Juan Diego is to be evangelized, it will be through a dark-skinned Lady on Tepeyac, the sacred place of the Nahuas, not through a Spanish bishop in his palace. Indeed, through Guadalupe, the very relationship between evangelizer and evangelized is reversed: the indigenous man, Juan Diego, is sent to evangelize the bishop.

By revealing a Christian God with a special predilection for Juan Diego and his people, Guadalupe thus makes possible the evangelization of America. Without Guadalupe, argues Virgilio Elizondo, there would be no Mexico. Without the hope engendered by La Morenita and her message, Mexico would not have emerged, like the phoenix, from the ashes of the conquest. This direct, historical connection between Guadalupe and Mexican identity is an important source of the passion with which her people celebrate and venerate La Morenita. In Guadalupe, the Mexican people have come to know the reality and power of Christ's Resurrection, not as an abstract belief, but as a historical reality.

Guadalupe and Juan Diego: Liberating Encounter

There is another aspect of the Guadalupan symbols and narrative that also contributes to her particular power and uniqueness. It is important to note, in this regard, that the narrative has *two* main characters, the Lady *and* Juan Diego. As mentioned above, the Guadalupan image itself includes the figure of Juan Diego, who appears reflected in the Lady's eyes. Thus, it should come as no surprise that what provoked the national outcry in 1996 was not a denial of the reality of Guadalupe, but a denial of the reality of Juan Diego. For in the hearts and minds of the Mexican people, the two are inseparable.

This inseparability points to a distinctive aspect of the Guadalupan narrative: this is not the story of an "apparition" so much as it is the story of a true *encounter*. Guadalupe does not merely "appear" to Juan Diego; she invites him into a profound relationship, in and through which he experiences his own humanity and, therefore, his own liberation.

The Guadalupan narrative details the moving process through which Juan Diego evolves from being the passive object of others' actions to the active subject of his own future. In other words, the story begins as an "apparition" but ends as an "encounter." Before he was approached by *La Morenita*, Juan Diego thought of himself as subhuman: "the people's dung."[22] As his relationship with her grows and deepens, however, he gradually claims his own identity and reclaims his dignity as a child of God, a self with intrinsic value, someone whose value is determined not by the Spanish conquerors but by God.

As an indigenous man, Juan Diego internalized the belittling, dehumanizing image of the Amerindians promulgated by the Spaniards; like so many oppressed persons, he had learned self-hatred. He saw himself as, literally, a nobody who, therefore, could never truly "act" but could only be acted *upon* by others: he refers to himself as "a rope" and "a little ladder," two tools that are used by other persons and whose sole value comes from their usefulness.[23] Juan Diego had come to see himself as merely the object or instrument of someone else's actions.

It is this self-deprecation that governs Juan Diego's actions at the outset. When Mary commands him to take her message to the bishop, he feels incapable of doing so: a nobody cannot act. However, at every step, La Morenita refuses to accept his self-deprecation; she will have none of it. Instead, she repeatedly calls him "the dearest of my children," treating him with the utmost respect and love. Gradually, her persistence pays off; Juan Diego begins to accept—indeed, even seek—the responsibility she wants to give him. By the end, he is no longer merely a passive object; he is now a free, active agent in the world. Juan Diego himself becomes an evangelizer, the privileged bearer of the Good News.

Very quickly after the appearance of the Lady, Juan Diego already begins to gain confidence: he "dared to go where he was being called. His heart was not at all disturbed, nor did he have any fear."[24] It is significant that what is undisturbed is Juan Diego's "heart"; for the Nahuas, the heart was the "dynamic and active part of the person," whereas the face or countenance was the "static part of the person" associated with passivity.[25]

Another indication of Juan Diego's newfound sense of dignity is the language he uses in addressing the Lady: he refers to her as "my dearest Girl" and "the most forsaken [or smallest, dearest] of my Daughters." This language reflects a deep intimacy, friendship, and equality between Juan Diego and La Morenita. Indeed, the tables are now turned: if the Lady had referred to him as her child, he now refers to her (the Mother of God!) as his daughter.

Further evidence of Juan Diego's growing stature is provided by a comparison of his different trips to see the bishop on behalf of Mary. Initially, his trips are undertaken out of deference and obedience to her: he considered himself unworthy, unequal to such an important task. By the time of the third trip, however, Juan Diego "pleaded very much with her to send him immediately to see the Lord of the priests to take him her sign."[26] Once again, we see Juan Diego gradually becoming the agent of historical action rather than the instrument of another's activity.

The extent of Juan Diego's transformation is revealed, above all, in his willingness to confront Mary directly when her requests conflict with his priorities. After Mary spies Juan Diego trying to sneak around her, he does not react with embarrassment or fear; instead, he nonchalantly asks Mary: "How did you sleep? Are you feeling well?"[27] And then he asks her to be patient. Thus, out of love for his uncle, he *chooses* to delay his return trip to the bishop's palace, even though in so doing he is disobeying the Lady's express orders. The "old" Juan Diego would never have dared disobey Mary. The surest sign that Juan Diego is now on equal footing with the Lady is his willingness to go against her wishes when those wishes conflict with his own priorities, above all, his familial responsibilities. He is no longer merely acted *upon*; now, he himself *acts*. This new understanding of his ability to act becomes the basis for his relationship with the Lady. Only after the Lady assures Juan Diego that his uncle would recover his health does Juan Diego agree to go immediately to the bishop.

A Freedom Born of Love

Thus, the story of Guadalupe is less an account of an apparition than that of an encounter, which implies an *inter*action *between* two subjects—each of which "appears" to the other. An encounter presupposes free subjects. In the story of Guadalupe, a relationship that begins as the apparition of a subject (the Lady) to an object (Juan Diego) ends, instead, as an encounter between two equal subjects, two full-fledged persons. In the encounter between Juan Diego and *La Morenita*, Juan Diego is literally reborn, or resurrected as a free *person*. The Lady *chooses* him, his identity, and his mission; in so doing, she liberates him to *act* in history. As embodied in La Morenita, God's preferential love for Juan Diego becomes the seedbed of his freedom as a historical subject.

The narrative of Guadalupe thus subverts modern Western preconceptions of human freedom, which equate freedom with autonomy, personhood with in-dependence. In the story of Guadalupe, Juan Diego does not "achieve" his freedom and personhood by extricating himself from his relationships, as if these were limitations or impediments. On the contrary, his relationship with the Lady becomes the precondition of his freedom. His freedom is not "achieved" so much as it is "received" from her; the more he opens himself to her, the more he begins to appreciate his own dignity, freedom, and, indeed, responsibility as a child of God.

Thus, a central theme of the narrative is the affirmation of community (which has its source in God and God's representative, La Morenita) as the birthplace of authentic human personhood and freedom. Indeed, this theme appears explicitly in the narrative's conclusion when, accompanied by the co-workers who will help him build the temple, Juan Diego returns to his uncle's home and discovers that, just as the Lady had promised, his uncle has been cured. Upon seeing the large retinue arrive at his home, the uncle reacts with great surprise. He is astonished, not because his nephew has come to visit, but because his nephew has "come so well-accompanied and honored."[28] Before his encounter with the Lady, Juan Diego had been "the people's dung"; now he is "well-accompanied and honored."

Authentic individuality and authentic community are not contradictory but mutually inherent. As the Lady of Tepeyac affirms Juan Diego's freedom, the true community affirms the freedom and uniqueness of the individual members. Indeed, the true test of an authentic relationship or community is one whose participants are, like Juan Diego, free to disobey, to criticize, and to be different. Juan Diego's newfound freedom is not that of the autonomous individual; it is, rather, a freedom which already presupposes the very relationships that are now freely accepted and appropriated, even if through conscious disobedience or criticism. If, at the outset, Juan Diego was reluctant to accept his mission, by the end, he is eager to carry it out—but he will do it on his own timetable, on his own terms.

To this day, Guadalupe continues to empower her "Juan Dieguitos" in the Mexican and Mexican American communities. Her ubiquitous image, whether on banners carried by striking migrant workers or on the stuccoed walls of a barrio luncheonette, has for centuries been the rallying point of the communities' social and political struggles. Where the Juan Diegos of the world are still marginalized, Guadalupe affirms their fundamental dignity and privileged place among God's children.

In order to fully understand the Mexican (and Latin American) people's passionate love for Our Lady of Guadalupe, therefore, we must appreciate La Morenita *in her relationship with* Juan Diego. For, just as she chooses him and, in so doing, affirms his dignity and freedom, so too does she choose and empower the *mestizo* people of Mexico and Latin America. As the Mexican people demonstrated several years ago, to question the reality of Juan Diego *is* to question the reality of Our Lady of Guadalupe, and to question the reality of Guadalupe is, in turn, to deny the inherent dignity of the Mexican people; the two are inseparable symbols of God's intimate, preferential love for the poor and marginalized peoples of our world.

NOTES

1. For a personal testament to the influence of Our Lady of Guadalupe among U.S. Hispanics beyond the Mexican American community, see especially Jeanette Rodríguez, *Our Lady of Guadalupe: Faith and Empowerment among Mexican American Women* (Austin: University of Texas Press, 1994). "At first," she recalls, "I thought her message was especially and possibly exclusively for Mexicans

and Mexican Americans. My research and personal reflection now tell me that Our Lady of Guadalupe truly comes to show her love, compassion, help, and defense to all the inhabitants of the Americas. . . . Guadalupe again offers God's loving embrace for the rejected people of the Americas," xxii.

2. Octavio Paz, *El Laberinto de la Soledad* (The Labyrinth of Solitude) (México, DF: Fondo de Cultura Económica, 1973).

3. Clodomiro L. Siller Acuña, *Para, comprender el mensaje de María de Guadalupe* (Understanding the Message of Our Lady of Guadalupe) (Buenos Aires: Editorial Guadalupe, 1989), 58. Siller provides the complete text of the story with a commentary. It is important to note that some scholars have raised serious questions about the origins of the Guadalupan narrative, e.g., Stafford Poole, *Our Lady of Guadalupe: The Origins and Sources of a Mexican National Symbol, 1531–1797* (Tucson: University of Arizona Press, 1995). Other scholars have, in turn, raised methodological questions about these revisionist critiques themselves, e.g., Richard Nebel, *Santa María Tonantzín, Virgen de Guadalupe: Continuidad y transformación religiosa en México* (Saint Mary Tonantzín, Virgin of Guadalupe: Religious Continuity and Transformation in Mexico) (Mexico City: Fondo de Cultura Económica, 1995). A serious, systematic analysis of this debate is beyond the scope of this paper. My concern here is to analyze the explicit content of the narrative itself. Thus, for example, I assume the narrative's identification of La Morenita with Mary (though, as mentioned above, with clear allusions to Tonantzín). A provocative, alternative interpretation is currently being developed by Orlando Espín, who suggests that, in the light of popular practice, the Marian language might perhaps be better understood in pneumatological categories; see Orlando Espín, *The Faith of the People: Theological Reflections on Popular Catholicism* (Maryknoll, NY: Orbis Books, 1997), 8–10.

4. Siller, *Para comprender el mensaje de María de Guadalupe*, 59.

5. Ibid., 58–61.

6. Virgilio Elizondo, *Guadalupe: Mother of the New Creation* (Maryknoll, NY: Orbis, 1997), 40.

7. Elizondo, *La Morenita: Evangelizer of the Americas* (San Antonio: Mexican American Cultural Center Press, 1980), 72.

8. Siller, *Para comprender el mensaje de María de Guadalupe*, 63.

9. Ibid.

10. Ibid., 68.

11. Ibid., 68–69.

12. Ibid., 73; Elizondo, *La Morenita*, 77.

13. Siller, *Para comprender el mensaje de María de Guadalupe*, 74.

14. Ibid., 78; Rodríguez, *Our Lady of Guadalupe*, 42.

15. Siller, *Para comprender el mensaje de María de Guadalupe*, 82.

16. Ibid., 83.

17. Elizondo, *La Morenita*, 78; Siller, *Para comprender el mensaje de María de Guadalupe*, 84–85.

18. Ibid., 86.

19. Ibid., 93.

20. Elizondo, *La Morenita*, 83; Rodríguez, *Our Lady of Guadalupe*, 22–30; Espín, "Tradition and Popular Religion," 72–75.

21. Rodríguez, *Our Lady of Guadalupe*, 27.

22. Siller, *Para comprender el mensaje de María de Guadalupe*, 74; Elizondo, *La Morenita*, 77.

23. Siller, *Para comprender a María de Guadalupe*, 74.

24. Ibid., 64.

25. Ibid.

26. Ibid., 84–85; Elizondo, *La Morenita*, 78.

27. Siller, *Para comprender el mensaje de María de Guadalupe*, 82.

28. Ibid., 93.

SUGGESTIONS FOR FURTHER READING

Brading, D. A. *Mexican Phoenix, Our Lady of Guadalupe: Image and Tradition across Five Centuries*. New York: Cambridge University Press, 2001.

Elizondo, Virgilio. *Guadalupe: Mother of the New Creation*. Maryknoll, NY: Orbis Books, 1997.

Stafford Poole, *Our Lady of Guadalupe: The Origins and Sources of a Mexican National Symbol, 1531–1797*. Tucson: University of Arizona Press, 1995.

Portilla, Miguel León. *Tonantzin Guadalupe: Pensamiento náhuatl y mensaje cristiano en el "Nican mopohua."* (Tonantzin Guadalupe: Náhuatl thought and the Christian Message in "Nican Mopohua") Mexico: Fondo de Cultura Económica, 2000.

Jeanette Rodgriguez, *Our Lady of Guadalupe: Faith and Empowerment among Mexican American Women*. Austin: University of Texas Press, 1994.

Chapter 10

Myths, Shinto, and *Matsuri* in the Shaping of Japanese Cultural Identity

John K. Nelson

Imagine an inquisitive child in Japan, fresh from the evening bath, asking for a bedtime story about how the world began. Parents in other cultures with rich mythological foundations, such as Native American, African, or even Judeo-Christian ones, could easily recount these ancient tales without too much editing. But a Japanese parent trying to convey the earliest myths in their original forms would be hard pressed not to inflict a terrifying nightmare. Starting with cosmic incest between deities, then a harrowing escape from hell for one of these divine beings as maggot-infested corpses close in for the kill, followed by an unruly deity flinging excrement upon ritual offerings of freshly harvested rice and vegetables that so shocks a young maiden she hysterically strikes her genitals and dies—well, you get the picture. And this is only the first act of a very long saga.

While sexy, violent, and oftentimes shocking, these stories are part of a mythic heritage that has been promoted at various times by Japan's leaders as the very foundation of the country's culture, civilization, and imperial tradition. Myths of beneficial and destructive deities, of powerful natural forces brought under control, and of heavenly intervention influencing the outcome of numerous internal wars of conquest served in the seventh and eighth centuries to legitimate Japan's emperor as a direct descendant of divine ancestry. In the mid-nineteenth century, the emperor's sanctified lineage was again heavily promoted. But this time the old myths were used to create a sense of shared ancestry and citizenship helping to lay the foundations for the modern nation-state of Japan.

My goal in this chapter is to give you a sense of these myths and how they were used initially for two political ends: first, to establish the rule of a line of emperors; and second, to connect this lineage with the primordial deities that were said to have founded the islands of Japan. However, I also want to make a case for the power of these myths as they continue to influence Japanese cultural identity through the religious institution known as "Shinto." We'll tour a few representative practices and institutions as examples where the old myths are still very much in play. Ranging from solemn rituals to boisterous, colorful, and even sexy public celebrations, Japan's mythic past and its contemporary expressions provide a fascinating story unique among the highly industrialized nations of the world.

Japan's Early Myths and Their Political Utility

What follows is a heavily edited version of the opening passages of Japan's creation myth. While it represents a worldview nearly two thousand years old, its vivid descriptions and situations continue to seize imaginations in profound and sometimes disturbing ways:[1]

> In the beginning, heaven and earth were not divided. Then, a reed rose up from the ocean of chaos, and that was to be the ruler of the eternal land, Kunitokotatchi.
>
> Then came the female deity, Izanami, and the male, Izanagi. They stood on the floating bridge of heaven and stirred the ocean with a jeweled spear. The ocean curdled and so created the first island, Onogoro. They built a house on this island, with a central stone pillar that is the backbone of the world. Izanami walked one way around the pillar, and Izanagi walked the other. When they met face to face, the female deity Izanami spoke first about the attractiveness of Izanagi's body and they united in conjugal intercourse.
>
> Their first child was named Hiruko, but he did not thrive because Izanami had initiated sexual relations. So they placed him in a reed boat and set him adrift, and he became Ebisu, deity of fishermen. They circled the pillar once again and this time Izanagi spoke first and initiated intercourse.
>
> Izanami then gave birth to the eight islands of Japan. And finally she began to give birth to the Gods who would fashion and rule the world—Gods of the sea and of the land, Gods of wind and rain. But when Izanami gave birth to the God of fire, her genitals were burned and she lay down

sick. In her vomit, feces, and urine there came into existence multiple deities, but at last she died. Izanagi crawled around her head and feet, weeping, "Alas, I have given my beloved spouse in exchange for a mere child!"

Izanagi was furious with the fire God and cut him into three pieces. Each of the pieces as well as the drops of dripping blood created more land. Then he set out to search for Izanami who had descended into the Land of Gloom. He called her, saying, "Come back, my beloved spouse. The lands we are making are not yet finished!"

She came to him, saying, "You are too late. I have already eaten the food of this land. But I would like to return. Wait here for me, and I will ask permission from the spirits of the underworld. But do not try to look at me."

At length, Izanagi got tired of waiting, so he broke off a tooth from the comb he wore in his hair to use as a torch and sought her again. When he found her, he saw that she was already rotting and maggots were swarming over her body.

Izanagi drew back, revolted. Izanami screamed after him, "He has shamed me!" She commanded the foul spirit hags of the Land of Gloom to slay him. The hags pursued Izanagi, but he threw down his headdress and it turned into grapes, which the spirits stopped to eat. Then he threw down his comb, which turned into bamboo shoots, and once again the spirits stopped to eat.

By the time Izanagi reached the pass between the land of the dead and the land of the living, Izanami herself had nearly caught up with him. But Izanagi saw her coming and quickly blocked the pass with a huge boulder that would take a thousand men to lift. This created a permanent barrier between the worlds of life and death.

Standing on the other side of the boulder, Izanami raged, "Every day I will kill a thousand people, and bring them to this land!" Izanagi replied, "Every day I will cause one thousand five hundred babies to be born." Then Izanagi left Izanami in the Land of Yomi, and returned to the land of the living, where he purified himself in the waters of a flowing river.

When he washed his left eye, there came into existence a deity named Amaterasu, who would rule the sun. When he washed his right eye, a deity named Tsukiyomi appeared who would rule the night and moon. When he washed his nose, there came into existence a deity named Susano-o, who would rule the ocean. When the last three were born, Izanagi rejoiced greatly, saying: "I have borne child after child, and finally I have obtained three noble children."

Obviously, this creation myth conveys fundamental themes. Among these are the attempt to create order and form out of chaos, a "correct" male/female conjugal relationship, and the random unpredictability (as well as the physical effects) of death. There is also the important matter of the transformation of a male deity so that he continues the birthing process. This adaptation is from the *Kojiki* or "Record of Ancient Matters," a work commissioned in 681 c.e. and then presented to the imperial court in 712. It takes unrelated myths from many regions in Japan and weaves them into a narrative that moves directly from the creation of the Japanese islands to the establishment of the imperial court.

The main purpose of the *Kojiki* was to strengthen and sanctify the imperial clan's control over the regions it had recently conquered. But it was also in the court's interests to claim some of the key symbols of divine rule familiar to the ever-watchful Chinese on the Asian mainland. For example, the primary deity of the Yamato imperial clan, born from the left eye of Izanagi while purifying himself, became that of the sun (Amaterasu). The characters that are used for Japan (in Japanese, "Nippon," or "the source of the sun") also send a message that the land is directly connected to the cosmic life force. The Japanese emperor was said to be a direct descendant of the founding deities and thus his family line could never be deposed. This arrangement was very different from that observed by the Chinese, whereby an emperor could lose the "mandate of heaven" and be replaced by a candidate from another clan with sufficient military and political acumen to rule.

For most of Japanese history, the myths of the *Kojiki* (and its companion, the *Nihonshoki*) were held closely by aristocratic elites able to read and write, but they were also known to the common people through their interaction with local shrines. Priests at these shrines worshiped specific deities mentioned in the *Kojiki* and *Nihonshoki* which had relevance for the dominant clan of the area, for rice agriculture or fishing, or other prime concerns—a topic to which we'll return in a moment.

This arrangement lasted a very long time. However, a political and social revolution in 1867 ended Japan's feudal era of warlords, samurai-led armies, and constant civil war over territory. The new government, called "Meiji" or "Shining Rule," was well aware that other nation-states of the time had religious principles at their core. These ideologies were used to help justify and legitimate territorial expansion (remember the policy of "manifest destiny" in the United States?) and colonization. Rejecting Buddhism as too nihilistic and Christianity as too threatening and Western, the Meiji rulers seized upon the early myths of their culture as resources that could legitimate a revitalized imperial tradition at the center of the "empire of Japan."

With the emperor at the top of society leading his subjects, a rapid program of industrialization and militarism quickly brought a feudal society into the ranks of the world's leading powers by 1890. Through the educational system and a variety of supporting social organizations, the Japanese state convinced its citizens that they and their new nation were embarked upon a unique and sacred mission to liberate Asian countries from the yoke of Western colonialism and oppression. Children learned the early myths as a part of their school curriculum from around 1890 to 1945, especially those parts that linked the emperor to his heavenly forebears.

Japan's modernization as an imperial power in its own right, competing with Russia, England, and the United States for territory and resources, led to military invasions and regional conflicts that exploded into World War II in East and Southeast Asia and the Pacific region. With Japan's devastating defeat by Allied forces in 1945, the orchestrated and sustained use of ancient mythology by a modern state was supposed to have ended.

Looking back on the first half of the twentieth century in Japan, it might seem that its people were victimized and shackled by their mythic past and its political utility. However, I don't think myths work in quite this way. While they may indeed be thought to convey certain "truths" from one generation to another, they also work in the other direction: to anchor the present in the past. Japan's new government of 1867 chose an ancient but interactive tradition to serve as a kind of cultural "software" to run the overall program of modernization. Known as *kokutai*, a word difficult to translate because it implies the essence of the nation, its symbols of imperial rule, affiliated shrines and Buddhist temples, and the nation's foundation in the time of the gods provided a powerful "myth of continuity that signified Japan's national distinctiveness."[2]

But there are a couple more dimensions to myth regarding their operation in Japan. Of course, myths help to educate members of a society about who they are as a people and the way the world is said to work, but these stories project values and themes that mirror both the inner psychology and political tendencies of their anonymous authors.[3] The roles of women and men, their interpersonal relations, what constitutes and maintains a community, what is to be avoided as dangerous, dirty, or chaotic, or worshiped as divine, transcendent, and pure are themes that occur in societies around the world with great regularity, not just in Japan.

Since Japan was defeated so decisively in 1945, we might assume that the myths taught in schools to bolster the imperial and militaristic cause were prohibited and tabooed by the authorities of the Allied occupation. Until recently, this was indeed the case regarding the nationwide school curriculum. However, in 1996, a group of right-wing academics, business executives, comic book artists, journalists, and writers began to advance the idea that Japan's current economic and social problems were due to a lack of pride in being Japanese. Because of the judgments of history and the Tokyo War Crimes' Tribunal concerning Japan's responsibility for waging war, the Japanese people have been "wounded" into believing that their nation's cause from 1935 to 1945 was not only wrong but criminal. To "correct" this version of history, the Japan Society for History Text-book Reform offered its own history textbook, which was approved for possible adoption in middle schools nationwide in 2001 by the Ministry of Education and Science.[4]

The resulting controversy grew quite heated because of the way history was being revised to promote Japan as the liberator of South and East Asia, with little or no mention of the many crimes against humanity committed by Japan's military. But there was also considerable outrage over the way the old myths from the *Kojiki*—about the founding of Japan and the nation's *kokutai* uniqueness—were being introduced to young and impressionable readers. For example, the myth about the first emperor Jimmu—son of a deity, conqueror of rival tribes, and founder of the first imperial court in the Nara region—is presented in a way that blurs the distinction between history and myth. The textbook details and illustrates with a map the full story of Jimmu's journey from southern to central Japan, and reminds the reader that his success in establishing the imperial court is now celebrated every year as a national holiday on February 11, "Founding of the Nation Day."

South Korea and China protested vigorously against the textbook's version of history as well as the government's approval process. This was not surprising considering how terribly their citizens suffered before and during the war at the hands of Japanese administrative and military policies. In light of ideologies about cultural and racial distinctiveness as well as acting in the name of the emperor, Japan's policies further dehumanized the populations its military had conquered. Because the textbook obscured this history, the South Korean government went so far as to break off cultural, educational, and military cooperation with Japan, halting all imports of movies, music, animation, and other forms of entertainment. From their perspective, any school textbook that falsifies history, attempts to use the old myths legitimating imperial ancestry as divine, or advances the idea that Japan is a land founded by the gods is encouraging the same kind of nationalism and ethnic superiority that led to the horrors of World War II in the Pacific.

While this is an extreme example, we can find other mythic associations occurring in more subtle ways. When a politician or business executive is disgraced by scandal, he frequently talks of the need to undergo "purification" for his wrongful deeds. Purification is also required before construction can begin upon a piece of land. According to an architect with Japan's second largest construction firm, nearly 95 percent of all businesses and private individuals conduct this ritual, sometimes at considerable expense. It asks the deity of the land, Okuninushi, for safety at the workplace, for the future inhabitants of the building, and ritually cleanses the land of defilements or impurities that might interfere with the construction process or harmonious existence after completion.[5]

Enhancing Community via the Deities of Myth and Legend

By far the most frequent, visible, and dramatic referencing of the early myths and their deities takes place as festive and often raucous bursts of human energy in honor of a community's local deity, its *kami*.

As a loosely structured and highly-local system of rituals and festivals aimed at ensuring vitality for members of the community, kami worship and veneration is still widespread throughout the Japanese islands. We saw in the creation myth how numerous kami were born to create the lands, natural phenomena, and eventually the people of Japan, and how these accounts were collected into the *Kojiki* and *Nihonshoki*. But just what are the kami and why do they continue to serve as a spiritual and psychic link back to the early myths?

The kami are considered by priests and scholars alike to be a formless power present in everything to some degree but intensified in strength in certain outstanding objects, animals, and individuals. Large, oddly shaped boulders, ancient trees, or waterfalls fit the first category, while the second would include white deer, horses, snakes, or foxes. Individuals can also become deities and range from obvious candidates such as an emperor, a clan's founder or military heroes, or, on rare occasions, exceptional individuals like the court scholar Sugawara Michizane, who died in exile but whose angry spirit was believed to have caused lightning strikes against his persecutors. Some deities are devoted to agricultural concerns, especially the growing and harvesting of rice, while others tend to hunting or fishing. There are also those specializing in defensive and military powers. Finally, the broadest category of all are kami that manifest themselves in lightning, earthquakes, thunder, and typhoons, even in pestilence and epidemics.

The sacred locations and structures that kami are thought to favor and visit during the course of a ritual are today called Shinto shrines. Long before the more doctrinal systems of Daoism, Buddhism, or Confucianism were adopted selectively by imperial elites, the "way of the kami" (which we'll call "Shinto" for the sake of convenience rather than historical accuracy) was the most pervasive religious practice. It blended and reinterpreted ethical, magical, and religious elements from the Asian mainland along with local beliefs, rituals, and the customs of clans and their communities.

While cultural and religious trends come and go, shrine Shinto remains one of the most long lived of all Japan's institutions, predating the imperial court of the sixth century by at least three hundred years.

Although it is rare to find Shinto shrines devoted to the primordial deities Izanami and Izanagi we read about earlier, we do find shrines dedicated to their many offspring, some of which embody the principle of procreation. There is great variety and difference from shrine to shrine, but nearly every one (and there are said to be 80,000 of them in Japan) has deities which promote the restoration of physical and spiritual vitality.

It is probably useful at this point to hit the "pause" button and mention how tricky it is to figure out what a people do or do not "believe." Because of Christianity's influence on Western thought, belief is still seen by many as a requirement for membership and participation in a religious tradition. Terms such as "belief," "faith," or "truth" that may appear obvious to those within a society are actually abstractions that have been shaped and privileged within specific historical contexts. When applied to the religious practices of other sociocultural systems, these same abstractions tend to create artificial categories that are neither shared by nor, in some cases, comprehensible to local peoples. It's as if we asked a congregation assembled for Easter Sunday services how often they offer beer to their ancestors or lit incense at ancestral graves in order to keep those spirits under control.

Likewise, asking whether contemporary Japanese "believe" in Shinto deities and their influence is probably not the right question. It is much more revealing to see how these ancient traditions continue to provide cosmic points of reference and ritual practices for contemporary men and women within Japanese society. Certainly, Shinto's social presence—amplified by its seasonal festivals, the influences they have on fostering a sense of community, as well as the rituals provided by local shrines to mark life transitions—is an institution in Japan that is "culturally loud."[6] With the high visibility of shrines large and small, they are a ubiquitous feature in both urban and rural settings. So too are the numerous festivals they stage throughout the year, requiring significant resources and committed participants. And yet the "volume" of these events might never reach the level of conscious awareness about exactly why these traditions are carried out. In fact, a local festival that an outside observer might interpret as representative of religious devotion or belief might be so taken for granted among its participants that it is not even considered to be a "religious" activity.

Matsuri

To Japanese and foreigners alike, few events compare to the noisy, often raucous atmosphere of a shrine's major festival, when the usually somber businessman, hard-working housewife, or indulgent college student is transformed into a semipossessed servant of the kami, often roaring drunk and careening through the streets as they carry on their shoulders the weight of elaborate portable shrines. Festivals (called *matsuri*) are held at regular intervals to reinforce communal awareness of a reciprocal relationship with those kami protecting their physical, economic, and political well-being. Through its revitalizing energies, the matsuri ensures continued cooperation of humans with divine powers. This is a reciprocal relationship originally benefiting the economic livelihood of fishermen, farmers, merchants, or even political leaders. Today it applies to factory workers, businesspeople, high-tech entrepreneurs, and every other occupational calling. When the kami's golden palanquin comes zigzagging through the streets of one's neighborhood or in front of one's own house or business, few can resist the sensation that a sacred and beneficial energy is being transmitted through the sheer intimacy of the encounter.

While the regenerative aspect of the kami's procession is undoubtedly the oldest and most fundamental characteristic of a major festival, there are other possibilities as well. In Japan's former imperial capital of Kyoto, the Gion matsuri of July 17 commemorates the efforts of an emperor in 869 who successfully petitioned the kami to end a terrible plague. Some five hundred miles to the northeast in Furukawa city, a matsuri that began as a somber, midnight procession has evolved into a kind of class warfare.[7] A huge drum representing the shrine, community authorities, and rich landowners is ambushed on its parade route by platforms of smaller drums carried by young men of the neighborhoods through which the main drum passes. To topple the drum and all those riding upon its supporting scaffold is a great, although short lived, triumph over coercive civic authority for the "little guys." There are also processions because the kami themselves are said to want to "revisit" some particular place that has significance to them, such as a river or the site of a mythological incident.

Usually sponsored by a neighborhood shrine with private and corporate financial backers, matsuri are increasingly promoted by local and often national media as embodying and reinforcing a community's identity. Encoded within this idea are concepts of native and outsider, inclusion and exclusion, and about identifying "Japaneseness" with local cultural events.

It's not surprising that public officials have picked up on the fact that festivals are an effective way to pull people together and provide an occasion for enhancing community. "Citizen festivals" have been encouraged by municipal governments as a way to reclaim the "village within the city," where people can feel some sense of emotional identification with their place of residence—multistory concrete apartment buildings though they may be.[8] Since these festivals are designed and carried out by the "new town" residents and are not affiliated with any established Shinto shrine, the portable shrine, or *mikoshi,* carried by adults and children does not have a kami essence within. While some older people criticize the event as form-without-substance, there is also a certain freedom that more traditional festivals cannot accommodate. While mikoshi are usually elaborately carved and crafted compartments adorned with gold-plated decorations, in a citizens' festival they can be anything from Mickey Mouse or a frilled lizard to pink elephants. But a traditional festival atmosphere does frame the entire event, with hanging lanterns, food stalls, and carnival-type games of chance on the streets. There is also a mustering of team spirit accompanied by choruses of "heave-ho!" (*wasshoi, wasshoi!*)required to pull the mikoshi through the streets. It all combines to encourage a kind of instant community familiar to the vast majority of Japanese, regardless of their ages or the region in which they live.

Perhaps most representative of participation in the cultural foundations of Japan are the New Year visits to shrines large and small (as well as select large temples) across the nation. In 1999, for example, some 74 percent of the entire population of 120 million turned out in the first three days of the new year to petition their local deities and Toshigamisama, the deity of the new year, for a clean slate and a prosperous new year. Additionally, millions of average Japanese continue to visit shrines throughout the year to pray for everything from purifying a new car, to asking for a marriage partner (or a baby, or success in school), or expressing gratitude for *goriyaku*, those benefits received thanks to the intercession of kami.

Rather than overtaxing your patience with more abstract descriptions, let's consider three examples of how Japan's mythic origins and their associations with kami remain "in play" in Japanese society through the medium of Shinto.

First, let's say you are a high school student who desires admission to a brand-name university. In order to pass the university's formidable entrance examination and achieve your goal, for the last three years you have been attending supplementary classes held every evening after the regular school day, and on Saturdays as well. You adopt the motto, "Sleep six hours, fail; sleep five hours, pass," and become obsessed with studying. Wearing a headband proclaiming "victory!," you still have a habit of falling asleep at your desk after midnight before completing that evening's assignments.

As the entrance exam approaches in late January and your anxiety level rockets into the stratosphere, you decide to follow an established custom and visit a nearby Shinto shrine. Its principle kami is Tenjin, who was once a real person renowned for his erudition and calligraphy: the persecuted and exiled scholar Sugawara Michizane of the eighth century. You announce your presence by ringing a large bell, then bow and clap your hands twice. You drop a few coins into a wooden coffer, and then with head lowered and hands clasped, petition fervently for assistance in your struggle. While you don't really believe in deities or magical assistance—you are, after all, a highly educated citizen of one of the world's most technologically advanced societies—the rationale of your parents, friends, and of the society at large is that it surely doesn't hurt to engage in these rituals. After making your request in front of the main shrine, a young priest sells you a small and colorful charm to attach to your bookbag or backpack. Inside the silk casing is a prayer or amulet that has been blessed and purified in a ritual on the shrine's main altar. You promise yourself that should you be successful in gaining admittance to the university, you will return to this same shrine to express your gratitude to Tenjin-sama for giving you that extra edge. And while you may still not believe in the power of deities even after all this, neither do you want to risk the possibility of incurring his wrath for being ungrateful.

Our second example concerns a newlywed couple. Both husband and wife are from established and reputable families, one with a samurai military heritage and the other with roots going back to feudal lords of the fifteenth century. The couple's parents anxiously await the birth of their first grandchild, but for some reason and despite having frequent sex, pregnancy remains only a dream. After a year of trying, the couple begins to visit medical specialists to consider in vitro fertilization. But they also make a pilgrimage to a Shinto shrine noted for its deity of fertility. Located in the farmland outside of Nagoya, the Tagata Shrine's principle kami appears to have been an imperial princess of the eighth century who had many distinguished offspring. Every year during the shrine's major festival in March (which blesses the forthcoming rice planting season), her male consort is brought from an adjacent shrine in a long procession through the community to pay a conjugal visit—a practice common among aristocrats during the *Tale of Genji* period of the tenth to twelfth centuries. Thus, the deity's mythic fertility and productivity, as well as sacred sexual intercourse with her male consort, are linked intimately to the production of rice in particular but also the production of offspring more generally.[9]

Arriving on a non-festival day, the childless couple goes first to the main shrine to petition the deity Tamayorihime. They then proceed to the adjacent shrine to touch a variety of phallic objects that range from graphically shaped stones to tree roots to a massive cedarwood penis weighing some 650 pounds and measuring 12 feet in length. The hope is that coming into contact with these manifestations of divine and mythic symbols of fertility will awaken a spark of new life within the waiting womb. And should a child be born, it will of course be christened at a shrine in their own neighborhood one month after the birth, but an offering of thanks will be sent back to Tagata Shrine.

Our last example shows how the old myths and their deities can still coerce humans, even unruly drunk ones at that, into appropriate behavior. A merchant selling medicinal herbs in Osaka's downtown was faced with an ongoing problem: a tiny parcel of undeveloped land beside his store had become a place for salarymen to relieve themselves while returning from bars and restaurants in the evening. His customers complained of the smell that lingered around the entrance to the store. Despite posting "no trespassing" signs, the problem continued until one day he hit upon a possible solution. After washing down the polluted area completely, he dug a small pond and placed in it two rocks joined by a sacred Shinto rope (*shimenawa*). The inspiration for this idea came from the famous "wedded rocks" on the coast near the Ise Grand Shrine, the tutelary shrine for the emperor of Japan. Almost immediately, people began throwing in coins, asking the store owner for the name of the kami and what benefits it could bestow. Needless to say, the outdoor toilet problem disappeared, replaced with a small shrine whose kami could assist in healing ear problems. You might have guessed already that the store owner offered healing herbs in every way complimentary to the speciality of the kami.[10]

Conclusion

We've just seen how, after nearly sixteen centuries, the respect for and veneration of kami continues to help form, orient, and empower a sense of communal and cultural identity. This is not to imply that the Japanese are one big happy family bound together by observations of deities described in ancient mythic accounts. Like any complex society, there is tremendous variation between geographic regions, social and economic classes, as well as among the people themselves. Korean-Japanese, Chinese-Japanese, Brazilian-Japanese, and Japanese-Americans do not necessarily share or participate in kami-related activities simply because they were born in Japan or because they have Japanese ancestry. The insular outlook of local communities has always discriminated against outsiders as potentially dangerous and disruptive—at least until they demonstrate a willingness to follow established customs or show how they can be of benefit to the community.

Because shrine Shinto rarely follows explicit theological agendas or relies on charismatic leaders, it remains open to a variety of interpretations depending on the needs, expectations, or politics of those coming to a shrine. This flexibility has gotten it into trouble on occasion, as when it allowed itself to be co-opted by Japan's military establishment leading into the Second World War. But by and large Japan's shrines and their deities help to enhance community and remind Japanese of their cultural heritage. Like visitors to an art gallery, a multiplicity of perspectives and meanings are not only possible but essential if a shrine ritual is to hold relevance for both casual and committed visitors.

Based upon ancient mythic encounters with the deities, as well as embellishments of those encounters through the centuries, Japanese society has developed a strong sense of spiritual power: indefinite but always dynamic (the kami). This power is capable of entering virtually any object, influencing any situation, or transforming any person's life. And with the myths from the *Kojiki* and *Nihonshoki* as points of reference for Shinto's many deities, the tradition promotes a situational rather than fixed conception of morality. While there are certain conditions—such as purity, sincerity, and inner harmony—that must be met in order to enhance a ritual or petition's chance of success, Shinto has continually adapted itself to whatever political, social, economic, or religious context it encounters. Its rituals and deities—and the myths that give them cosmic significance—remain one of many resources available to contemporary men and women as they negotiate their identity as Japanese.

NOTES

1. Donald Philippi, *The Kojiki* (Tokyo: Tokyo University Press, 1968), 58. The myth is an abridged version of Philippi's translation.

2. Carol Gluck, *Japan's Modern Myths* (Princeton: Princeton University Press, 1985), 247.

3. Percy Cohen, "Theories of Myth," *Man* 3 (1969): 337–353.

4. John Nelson, "Signs of Recovery for Japanese Nationalism? The 'Reform Society' Movement for Reclaiming Cultural Identity through Educational and Textbook Reform, *Pacific Rim Report* 15 (2000), http://www.pacificrim.usfca.edu/research/pacrimreport/pacrimrepor t15.html

5. John Nelson, *A Year in the Life of a Shinto Shrine* (Seattle: University of Washington Press, 1996), 194.

6. David Parkin, "Ritual as Spatial Direction and Bodily Division," in *Understanding Rituals*, ed. D. Coppett, (London: Routledge, 1992), 15.

7. See Scott Schnell, *The Rousing Drum* (Honolulu: University of Hawaii Press, 1999).

8. Jennifer Robertson, *Native and Newcomer: Making and Remaking a Japanese City* (Berkeley: University of California Press, 1991), 126.

9. See http://www.theony.com/peter/tagata/.

10. Ian Reader, *Religion in Contemporary Japan* (Honolulu: University of Hawaii Press, 1991), 58.

SUGGESTIONS FOR FURTHER READING

Breen, John, and Mark Teeuwen, eds. *Shinto in History.* Honolulu: University of Hawaii Press, 2000.

Brown, Delmer. *The Cambridge History of Japan: Ancient Japan.* Vol. 1. Cambridge, U.K.: Cambridge University Press, 1993.

Nelson, John. *Enduring Identities: The Guise of Shinto in Contemporary Japan.* Honolulu: University of Hawaii Press, 2000.

Nelson, John. *A Year in the Life of a Shinto Shrine.* Seattle: University of Washington Press, 1996.

Schnell, Scott. *The Rousing Drum.* Honolulu: University of Hawaii Press, 1999.

Smyers, Karen. *The Fox and the Jewel.* Honolulu: University of Hawaii Press, 1999.

Chapter 11

Islam, Arabs, and Ethnicity

Azzam Tamimi

When I was commissioned to write this chapter it was suggested to me that my role was to focus on the way in which the binding myths of the Islamic religious tradition have been marshaled in the construction of an "Arab" ethnic identity. The presupposition here was that at the time of the origins of Islam there was nothing comparable to an Arab ethnic (or national) consciousness as there came to be over time, and that Islam itself played a role in the creation of that consciousness.

Three concepts, which are rather difficult to define, especially in relation to the Arabs and Islam, are involved here: ethnicity, race, and myth. The definition of each adopted for the purposes of this volume—that is, by its editors—is quite simple and straightforward. Ethnicity is said to mean a social grouping or form of peoplehood that is marked by traits that are culturally inherited. In contrast, race is said to refer to a social grouping or form of peoplehood that is marked by traits that are biologically inherited. Myth, on the other hand, is said to be a mode of discourse, most commonly in narrative form, which achieves the status of credibility and authority in a given community.

Ethnicity

Political dictionaries tend to have a more cautious approach to defining some of these concepts. The origin of the word "ethnic" is said to be the Greek *ethnos*, meaning a tribe. To be ethnic is, therefore, to belong to a race or kind.[1] It has also been suggested that the origin of "ethnic" is the Greek *ethnikos*, which referred to non-Christian "pagans"; major population groups sharing common cultural and (racial) traits; and groups belonging to primitive cultures.[2]

There is admission, on the other hand, that the term "ethnicity" is a relatively new concept. It first appeared in the *Oxford English Dictionary* in its 1972 *Supplement*. It has since been used to refer to a whole range (and frequently a combination) of communal characteristics: lingual, ancestral, regional, religious, and so on, which are seen to be the basis of distinctive identity.[3] Ethnicity is said to be of particular relevance to nations formed by immigrants. It is in these conditions that the concept refers to a rather complex combination of racial, cultural, and historical characteristics by which societies are occasionally divided into separate, and probably hostile, political families. In this regard almost anything can be used to set up "ethnic" divisions. After skin color, the most common criteria are religion and language.[4] Some contend that definitions of ethnicity in the human sciences have been influenced by a variety of factors that intersect with one another. These include:

1. The impact of different theoretical and disciplinary traditions (such as neo-Marxism or phenomenology, psychology or anthropology).
2. The particular aspects of ethnicity being researched (ranging from the sociostructural dimensions of ethnicity in a plural society, to the cultural individual performance in education, and so on).
3. The region of the world where research is being conducted (e.g., the highlands of Papua New Guinea, American inner cities, and the former Soviet Union).
4. The particular group that is the subject of research (e.g., the Australian Aborigines, migrant Turkish workers in Europe, or the Jewish people).[5]

This term becomes all the more difficult to define in the cast of the Arabs because of the difficulty in defining an Arab. According to an Islamic (Prophetic) tradition, an Arab is one who speaks Arabic. But as Bernard Lewis rightly questions: Is the Arabic-speaking Jew from Iraq or Yemen or the Arabic-speaking Christian of Egypt or Lebanon an Arab?[6]

I recall as a young student in 1976 in the north of England being asked by a fellow Muslim student from Malaysia why an Arab by the name of Marwan at our University did not attend Friday prayer with us. I answered explaining that Marwan was a Christian. The Muslim Malay just could not believe what he heard and hurriedly asked with astonishment: "Can an Arab be Christian?" To many non-Arab Muslims, especially those who never had the opportunity of visiting countries such as Palestine, Egypt, Jordan, Lebanon, Syria or Iraq, where large Christian communities have been living for many centuries and where churches exist next to the mosques, an Arab is assumed to be a Muslim by definition. However, at the same time a visitor of Jeddah, Mecca, or Medina in Saudi Arabia will meet Chinese, Malay, European, or Indian-looking people who may know no other language than Arabic and whose style of living boasts of a mixture of Arab and Chinese or Malay or European or Indian eating, dressing, and other habits. Perhaps it is common knowledge to Bernard Lewis that other Arab fellow countrymen saw Arabic-speaking Jews, irrespective of how they viewed themselves or how other world Jews viewed them, as Arab Jews. In much of the literature in Arabic that addresses the events leading to the migration of Iraqi or Yemeni Jews to the newly established Jewish state in Palestine, such Jews are referred to as Arabs of Jewish creed who were driven out of their homes by intimidating Zionist attacks and propaganda to meet the requirements of the newly founded Jewish state for a larger population.

The case of Arab Christians is much more clear-cut. They themselves identify themselves as Arab. Not only do they have the Arabic language in common but also many customs and practices. Studying at a college in Cornwall, southwest England, between 1974 and 1976, I had an unforgettable experience. I shared accommodations at a Cornish family's residence with two Jordanian students who happened to be Christian. The two landladies, middle-aged sisters, were kind and most compassionate, treating us like their own children. One day they wanted to throw a party for us and decided to feed us a rabbit. They invited us to witness the slaughtering of the rabbit, a mission for which the neighbor was summoned to help. There were no knives or any such tools. The man held the rabbit from its hind legs and stuck its head against the wall. Our jubilant landladies were deeply disappointed as the three of us objected and refused to eat the rabbit's meat. We insisted that since the rabbit had not been properly slaughtered we just could not touch the food. The two landladies accepted my explanation that as a Muslim I just could not eat the meat of an animal not properly slaughtered, but they could not understand why my two Christian fellow countrymen refrained as well. The two young men insisted that they too never eat the meat of an animal not properly slaughtered. Simply, this is the way they had been brought up. This was the culture of their people back home.

Myth

The difficulty with the concept of ethnicity is paralleled by another difficulty with regard to the term "myth." It is not a term that Muslims find comfort in applying to Islamic theology and related sciences. The discomfort is relatively a great deal less when the topic is Islamic history. Myth is problematic because on the one hand it can mean an untrue story, while on the other it can refer to a story that contains religious truth. In other words, religious truth, as is assumed in secularist thought, is questionable. Myth may be of relevance to the Greek and medieval European experience where its subject matter is either the gods and their relations with humans or other beings, or the complex explanations of physical phenomena. As far as Muslims are concerned, there is nothing mythical about the fact that Muhammad was the messenger of God and that the Qur'an is God's revealed message to him to convey to humanity.

The problem here is that accepting that the Qur'an is a divine revelation and that Muhammad was a messenger of God will have one consequence, namely becoming a Muslim. It is the reluctance on the part of non-Muslim scholars of Islam to reach that consequence that prompts them to place the Islamic scripture in the category of "myth," casting doubt on its authenticity even as some of them cannot conceal their admiration for it. Albert Hourani brilliantly summarizes the way in which such scholars view this matter. Addressing the question of the originality of the Qur'an, he wrote:

> Scholars have tried to place [the Qur'an] in the context of ideas current in its time and place. Undoubtedly there are echoes in it of the teaching of earlier religions: Jewish ideas in its doctrines; some reflections of eastern Christian monastic piety in the brooding on the terrors of judgment and the descriptions of Heaven and Hell (but few references to Christian doctrine or liturgy); Biblical stories in forms different from those of the Old and New Testaments; an echo of the Manichaean idea of a succession of revelations given to different peoples. There are also traces of an indigenous tradition: the moral ideas in some ways continue those prevalent in Arabia, although in others they break with them; in the early revelations

the tone is that of the Arabian soothsayer, stammering out his sense of an encounter with the supernatural.[7]

He goes on to say:

> Such traces of the past need cause no anxiety to a Muslim, who can regard them as signs that Muhammad came at the end of a line of prophets who all taught the same truth; to be effective, the final revelation might use words and images already known and understood, and if ideas or stories took a different form in the *Qur'an*, that might be because adherents of earlier prophets had distorted the message received through them. Some non-Muslim scholars, however, have drawn a different conclusion: that the *Qur'an* contains little more than borrowings from what was already available to Muhammad in that time and place. To say this, however, is to misunderstand what it is to be original: whatever was taken over from the religious culture of the age was so rearranged and transmuted that, for those who accepted the message, the familiar world was made anew.[8]

There are, therefore, strong grounds for questioning the assumption that the Arabs constitute an ethnic group and the categorization of Islamic religious facts as myths. However, it would still be of great relevance to this work to illustrate the profound influence that Islam, as a religion, had on the Arabs. For had it not been for the impact Islam had on them, the Arabs would never have had the power or the will to influence other communities that converted to Islam or that were conquered by its adherents. But first, who are the Arabs?

The Arabs

Until the advent of Islam, the Arabs might, for the sake of argument, be said to have represented more a race than an ethnicity, although it could be argued that both definitions applied equally to them. Upon embracing Islam, the Arabs took upon themselves the mission of carrying it to the world, consequently Arabizing both those who accepted their message as well as those who accepted their authority.

The Arabs as a people, both in terms of race and ethnic category, predate Islam. The name is derived from the word *'arab*, meaning desert or wilderness, or a land with no water or vegetation. The peninsula in West

Asia known as Arabia has since ancient times derived its name from this basic linguistic root because of its dry climate and arduous terrain. The location, climate, and terrain of Arabia have always had a marked influence on its inhabitants, molding their traits and shaping their attitudes. Of an area of approximately 1.3 million square miles, Arabia posed a formidable challenge to invaders throughout history. Surrounded by impenetrable deserts, the Arab inhabitants of deeper centers within the peninsula remained relatively free of foreign invasion or intervention until quite recently.

Up to the advent of Islam, a little over fourteen centuries ago, the two prevailing superpowers of the day, Persia and Byzantium, were content with extending their influence to the reachable peripheries of Arabia, leaving the interior bulk of the peninsula unadulterated. Such equilibrium provided the central tribes of the Arabs with autonomy and a freedom not enjoyed by their brethren farther to the north, to the east, or to the south where Arab tribes organized themselves into tribal monarchies that paid allegiance to adjacent empires, providing them with security in exchange for protection and material rewards. Their only tangible link between the more central parts of Arabia and the outside world existed through the north-south trade trail that crossed their homeland and provided passage for trade caravans between the demanding markets of both Byzantium and Persia and the ports of Hadramawt and Yemen through which communications with the commercial ports of China, India, and Eastern Africa were maintained. It is no wonder that the southern and northern precincts of pre-Islam Arabia, unlike its more central parts, witnessed the emergence of cosmopolitan centers boasting of religious and cultural plurality and high-level commercial activity.

Historians divide the Arabs into three categories, depending on their ancestral origin. The first category is that of al-'Arab al-Ba'idah, the most ancient of all the Arabs, whose history is only sketchily known. The word *al-Ba'idah* means the perished ones, and they are known as such because they are believed to be entirely extinct. The Qur'an refers to some of them while others are referred to in some pre-Islamic Arabic poetry. They include the peoples of 'Add, Thamud, Tasam, Jadis, and 'Imlaq.

The second category of Arabs is known as al-'Arab al-'Aribah. These are the descendants of Ya'rub bin Yashjub bin Qahtan and are also known as al-Arab al-Qahtaniyah. The *Qahtaniyah* Arabs are known to have inhabited the southwest of Arabia in the region of Yemen. The two main tribes comprising the *Qahtaniyah* are Himyar and Kahlan. While the former remained in Yemen, the latter were forced out of their ancestral homeland in the aftermath of the destruction of the Ma'rib Dam and the consequent flood that destroyed their homes and threatened their very existence. They migrated northward and settled in various parts of Arabia. Their two most famous divisions, and relevant to Islam, had been al-Aws and al-Khazraj, whose ancestral father Tha'labah bin 'Amr resided in Yathrib, which was later renamed by Prophet Muhammad, upon his migration to it, as al-Madinah. The descendants of al-Aws and al-Khazraj became known as al-Ansar (the supporters) after they embraced Islam and pledged support for Prophet Muhammad and his Meccan followers who abandoned their own hometown and sought refuge in Yathrib. They pursued a safe haven after thirteen years of persecution at the hands of their own pagan fellow tribesmen in Mecca.

The third category of Arabs is known as al-Arab al-Musta'ribah (or the Arabized Arabs). These are the descendants of Ishmael, son of Abraham, and are also known as al-'Adnaniyah, where 'Adnan is the twenty-first grandfather of Prophet Muhammad. These Arabs are described as Arabized because Ishmael, who had been brought from Palestine, together with his mother Hagar, to Mecca, the dry treeless valley, by his father Abraham, acquired his Arab identity from the originally Yemeni Arab tribe of Jurhum among whom he grew up, learned Arabic, and was married into.[9]

The most powerful as well as most ancient and persistent characteristic feature of the Arabs has been their language. Arabic, like the Arabs, existed long before the inception of Islam in the seventh century. However, since Islam's scripture, the Qur'an, is in Arabic, the language has been closely associated with the religion since its inception in around 612 C.E. The Arabs, whose country provided the birthplace of Islam, were radically changed by the new religion. In addition to renouncing polytheism and embracing monotheism, numerous practices and attitudes, especially in the fields of morality, social relations, and economic transactions, were radically changed so as to conform to the principles of justice and human dignity, which the Qur'an emphasizes repeatedly. However, not all aspects of Arab pre-Islamic life were condemned. The practices that did not infringe on the values of justice and equality of human dignity remained unchanged, having been condoned or even praised by the Prophet. Meccan Qur'an, that is, the Qur'anic text that was revealed prior to the migration of the Prophet from Mecca to Medina in 622 C.E., when the Muslim community was still stateless and oppressed by the powerful opponents of the new creed, contains clear indications of what was required of the Arabs. Three main targets can be discerned: the introduction of a new frame of reference, the establishment of a new scale of preference, and the establishment of a well-defined code of morality.

Frame of Reference

The primary focus during this formative period was on replacing the tribal and ancestral frame of reference with a divine frame of reference. The Arabs were very proud of their ancestors and of the way of life they inherited from them. The Qur'an sought to discredit such a frame of reference by calling on the Arabs to judge on the basis of pure logic the validity of the modes of behavior they boasted about. Time after time throughout the Meccan Qur'an, the Arabs are hammered to rethink their tribal ancestry. Such a challenge was put to them in response to their proclamation, whenever told to worship God alone or to refrain from committing certain evil acts, that their faith and their social habits were derived from their forefathers, who could not have been at fault.

Consider the following examples of Qur'anic discourse:

When they commit an indecency, they say: "We found our fathers doing so"; and "Allah commands us this." Say: "Nay, Allah never commands what is indecent. Do you say of Allah what you know not?" Say: "My Lord has commanded justice; and that you set your whole selves (to Him) at every time and place of prayer, and call upon Him, making your devotion sincere such as He created you in the begging, so shall you return." (7:28–29)

They say: "We found our fathers following a certain religion, and we do guide ourselves by their footsteps." Just in the same way, whenever We sent a warner before you to any people, the wealthy ones among them said: "We found our fathers following a certain religion, and we will certainly follow in their footsteps." He said: "What! Even if I brought you better guidance than that which you found your fathers following?" They said: "For us, we deny that which you (prophets) are sent with." (43:22–24)

When the female (infant), buried alive, is questioned for what crime she was killed. (81:8–9)

The discrediting of the Arabs' inherited frame of reference amounted to a revolution, a coup that threatened to change the lives of the Arabs radically and forever. Horrified by this prospect, the leading families of Quraysh, the Arab tribe to which Prophet Muhammad belonged, approached his uncle Abu Talib, who shielded him from those adversaries who did not accept his claim to be a messenger of God and saw him as one who attacked their way of life. They said: "O Abu Talib, your nephew has cursed our gods, insulted our religion, mocked our way of life, and accused our forefathers of error."[10] Confident of the appeal and credibility of his message, the Prophet challenged the elders of Quraysh to give the people of Mecca the freedom of choice. He said to them, "*khallu bayni wa bayna al-nas*," literally meaning: vacate the space between the people and me. What he actually meant was that he was prepared to accept the verdict of the people provided the elders of Quraysh did not impose themselves, as they did, on people by barring them from meeting the Prophet and his followers or even by going as far as torturing those who converted or contemplated doing so.

Standard of Preference

In addition to establishing a new frame of reference, which affirmed the oneness of the Creator, the Qur'anic discourse to the Arabs in Mecca heralded a new standard of reference that emphasized the oneness of the origin of mankind. When on the one hand God alone deserves to be worshiped, on the other hand all humans are equal in the eyes of their Creator, the only criterion of preference is piety. Until this new standard of preference was installed, the Arabs had been discriminating against non-Arabs, against women and against the colored, and had been looking down upon the poor and indulging in a prevalent slavery trade, which treated enslaved humans as commodities. In place of a standard of preference based on their own whims and desires, the new standard of preference derives from the fact that humans are brothers and sisters and that they originate from Adam, who was made by the Creator out of clay, as Prophet Muhammad is quoted as saying in a famous tradition. Hence, the Qur'an repeatedly reminds the Arabs, and for that matter humanity as a whole, of the humble origin of humanity and of the insignificance of any racial, linguistic, or other human-made distinctions. Consider the following Qur'anic narratives:

O mankind! Fear your Guardian Lord, who created you from a single person, created, out of it, his mate, and from them twain scattered (like seeds) countless men and women. Fear Allah, through whom you demand your mutual rights and be heedful of the wombs (that bore you), for Allah ever watches over you. (4:1)

It is He who created you from clay, and then decreed a stated term (for you). And there is with Him another determined term; yet you doubt within yourselves. (6:2)

We have honored the children of Adam; provided them with transport on land and sea; given them for sustenance things good and pure; and conferred on them special favors, above a great part of Our Creation. (17:70)

The Prophet himself is quoted to have warned his relatives, including his own daughter Fatimah, on more than one occasion that he would be of no benefit to them should they fail to please God. To the Arabs, whose tribal and familial associations provided them with both pride and security, this was quite a departure. On the one hand, the Arabs did not believe in a Day of Reckoning, when humans are called to account and accordingly punished or rewarded for their endeavors in this life. On the other hand, they grew accustomed to counting on the help of a brother or a cousin in challenging any adversary. Their famous *jahili* (pre-Islamic) slogan used to be "support your brother whether he is right or wrong." The Prophet corrected the principle by adding the qualification that if your brother is wronged, rush to his aid; but if he is wrong, stop him from being wrong. "An Arab is no better than a non-Arab, a white is no better than a black and a red is no better than a yellow."[11]

Code of Morality

Finally, from cover to cover, both in the Meccan as well as Medinan verses of the Qur'an, one can see a great emphasis on the code of morality the Arabs, and all newcomers to Islam, were enjoined to observe. It is a code of morality that in some important ways totally abolishes and replaces a pre-Islamic code of behaviour that is strongly condemned and often ridiculed by the Qur'an.

Consider the following examples:

The narrative in *Surat al-An'am* (Chapter Six), verses 151–153:

> Say: Come, I will rehearse what Allah has prohibited you from: join not anything with Him; be good to your parents; kill not your children on a plea of want, We provide sustenance for you and for them; come not nigh to indecent deeds, whether open or secret; take not life, which Allah has made sacred, except by way of justice and law: thus does He command you, that you may learn wisdom.
>
> And come not nigh to the orphan's property, except to improve it, until he (or she) attain the age of full strength; give measure and weight with (full) justice, no burden do We place on any soul but that which it can bear; whenever you speak, speak justly, even if a close relative is concerned; and fulfill the Covenant of Allah, thus does He command you that you may remember.
>
> Verily this is My Way leading straight. Follow it and follow not (other) paths that will scatter you about from His Path. Thus does He command you that you may be righteous.

The narrative in *Surat al-A'raf* (Chapter Seven), verses 31–33:

> O Children of Adam! Wear your beautiful apparel at every time and place of prayer, eat and drink but waste not by excess, for Allah loves not the wasters.
>
> Say: Who has forbidden the beautiful (gifts) of Allah, which He has produced for His servants, and the things, clean and pure (which He has provided) for sustenance? Say: They are, in the life of this world, for those who believe, [and] purely for them on the Day of Judgment. Thus do We explain the Signs in detail for those who know.
>
> Say: The things that my Lord has indeed forbidden are: Indecent deeds, whether open or secret; sins and trespasses against truth or reason; assigning of partners to Allah, for which He has given no authority; and saying things about Allah of which you have no knowledge.

The narrative in *Surat al-Nahl* (Chapter Sixteen), verses 90–91:

> Allah commands justice, the doing of good, and giving to kith and kin, and He forbids all indecent deeds, and evil and rebellion: He instructs you, that you may receive admonition.

•

Fulfill the Covenant of Allah when you have entered into it, and break not your oaths after you have confirmed them: indeed you have made Allah your surety; for Allah knows all that you do.

In *Surat al-Isra'* (Chapter Seventeen), verses 22–39:

Take not with Allah another god, or you (O man) will sit in disgrace and destitution.

Your Lord has decreed that you worship none but Him, and that you be kind to [your] parents. Whether one or both of them attain old age in your life, say not to them a word of contempt, nor repel them but address them in terms of honor. And out of kindness, lower to them the wing of humility, and say: "My Lord! Bestow on them Your Mercy even as they cherished me in childhood." Your Lord knows best what is in your hearts. If you do deeds of righteousness, verily He is Most Forgiving to those who turn to him again and again (in true penitence).

And render to the kindred their due rights, as (also) to those in want, and to the wayfarer. But squander not (your wealth) in the manner of a spendthrift. Verily, spendthrifts are brothers of the Satans. And the Satan is to his Lord (Himself) ungrateful. And even if you have to turn away from them in pursuit of the Mercy from your Lord which you do expect, yet speak to them a word of easy kindness.

Make not your hand tied (like a niggard's) to your neck, nor stretch it forth to its utmost reach, so that you become blameworthy and destitute. Verily, your Lord does provide sustenance in abundance for whom He pleases, and He straightens it for He does know and regard all His servants.

Kill not your children for fear of want: We shall provide sustenance for them as well as for you. Verily the killing of them is a great sin.

Nor come nigh to adultery: for it is an indecent (deed) and an evil way.

Nor take life, which Allah has made sacred, except for just cause. And if anyone is slain wrongfully, we have given his (or her) heirs authority (to demand *qisas* or to forgive), but let him (or her) not exceed bounds in the matter of taking life, for he (or she) is helped (by the Law).

Nor come nigh to the orphan's property except to improve it, until he (or she) attain the age of full strength.

And fulfill (every) engagement for (every) engagement will be inquired into (on the Day of Reckoning).

Give full measure when you measure, and weigh with a balance that is straight. That is better and fairer in the final determination.

And pursue not that of which you have no knowledge, for surely the hearing, the sight and the heart, all of those shall be questioned of.

Nor walk on the earth with insolence, for you cannot rend the earth asunder nor reach the mountains in eight. Of all such things, the evil is hateful in the sight of your Lord.

These are among the (precepts of) wisdom, which your Lord Has revealed to you. (Above all) take not, with Allah, another object of worship, lest you should be thrown into Hell, blameworthy and rejected.

The first generation of transformed Arabs embodied the values of Islam and carried them to the nations surrounding them and to those beyond them. For the first time in their entire history, the Arabs had become actors influencing others rather than passive subjects under the influence of others. It was the example they provided to those whom they invited to the new religion that impressed and attracted new converts. The most attractive thing about their message was its ability to address the major grievances that were common to all humans of the time, Arab and non-Arab alike. Nations everywhere had been longing for freedom from servitude and thirsty for justice and dignity. Rather than turn the Arabs into an exclusive inward-looking community, Islam did exactly the opposite simply because it introduced itself as a message from God to all of humanity. Yes, it did start with the Arabs, for it had to start somewhere, but its vision was, and continues to be, global.

NOTES

1. Roger Scruton, *A Dictionary of Political Thought* (San Francisco: Harper-Collins, 1983).

2. *The Harper Dictionary of Modern Thought* quoted in Iftikhar Malik, *State and Civil Society in Pakistan—Politics of Authority, Ideology and Ethnicity* (New York: St. Martin's Press, 1997), 172.

3. *The Fontana Dictionary of Modern Thought* (San Francisco: HarperCollins, 1988).

4. *Penguin Dictionary of Politics*, ed. David Robertson (New York: Penguin, 1993).

5. Sian Jones, *The Archeology of Ethnicity: Constructing Identities in the Past and Present* (London and New York: Routledge, 1997), 56.

6. Bernard Lewis, *The Arabs in History* (London: Hutchinson, 1977), 9.

7. Albert Hourani, *A History of the Arab Peoples* (London: Faber and Faber, 1991), 21.

8. Ibid.

9. S. Al-Mubarakfuri, *Al-Rahiq al-Makhtum* (The Pure Nectar) (Mecca, 1980), 19–27.

10. Hourani, *A History of the Arab Peoples*, 17.

11. Prophetic tradition.

SUGGESTIONS FOR FURTHER READING

Al-Ghazali, Shaykh Muhammad. *A Thematic Commentary on the Qur'an.* Herndon, VA: IIIT, 1995.

Bashir, Zakaria. *Life of the Prophet in Makkah.* Leicester, U.K.: Islamic Foundation, 1990.

Hitti, Philip. *The Arabs: A Short History.* London: Macmillan, 1948.

Hourani, Albert. *A History of the Arab Peoples.* London: Faber and Faber, 1991.

Jones, Sian. *The Archeology of Ethnicity: Constructing Identities in the Past and Present.* London and New York: Routledge, 1997.

Malik, Iftikhar. *State and Civil Society in Pakistan: Politics of Authority, Ideology and Ethnicity.* Wiltshire, U.K.: Antony Rowe, 1997.

Chapter 12

Cosmic Men and Fluid Exchanges

*Myths of Ārya, Varṇa, and Jāti
in the Hindu Tradition*

Laurie L. Patton

Mythic narrative and ideas about ethnicity in Hinduism are as intertwined as, to use an ancient Indian metaphor, a creeper hugs a pole (Ṛgveda 10.33). For the purposes of this chapter we will define myth and ethnicity along the lines outlined in this book. We will assume that the relationship between myth and ethnicity can work in different directions. A myth can bolster ideas about ethnic identity or a sense of belonging to a particular ethnic group; it can also be used to resist ideas about social divisions. Members of an ethnic group can take up a myth and analyze it critically or appropriate it in new ways that serve their interests and imaginations.

First, ethnicity is not an easily translatable term in India, and thus we will ask a different kind of question: What did people think about ideas analogous to ethnicity in early India, and how did myths support and subvert such ideas? The indigenous categories for such ideas are complex ones. This article will focus on three concepts of social boundaries between people and the myths related to them: *Ārya*, or nobility; *varṇa*, or "social role," and *jāti*, or birth.

The Ārya: Fragmentary Myths of Light and Dark

The term Ārya arrives on the early Indian scene as a complex notion. The sources of the words are texts called the Vedas, the oral compositions concerning a set of sacrifices involving fire. While oral texts and the practice of fire sacrifice probably existed for several centuries, if not millennia, before 1500 B.C.E., the scholarly consensus is that the Vedic practices emerged as we know them around this time in western India and moved eastward along the Gangetic plain. They were the property of people who called themselves ārya, or nobility, and distinguished themselves linguistically from the *dāsa*, or enslaved ones, and the *mleccha*, or "those who speak indistinctly," that is foreigners. The English word "Aryan" is a translation of that term but has its own mythic history in English as well.

At present much debate exists about the origins of the Aryans themselves. While the debate is still raging,[1] suffice it to say that the Vedic world emerged in a complex and gradual way, involving both migration from outside as well as indigenous growth from within. Thus, "ārya" and "dāsa," and "ārya" and "mleccha," may not have only referred to actual invaders and indigenous people, but were a series of words that people who cohabited used to differentiate themselves as they lived together over a period of time. As we shall see, the question of indigenous status is crucial to our discussion.

How would the Aryans have understood themselves as a people? What distinguished the Aryans from other groups, and the Vedas from other texts? First, the Aryans worked with chariots, horses, and weapons of war that included iron. Second, their social organization was broadly tribal in nature and focused on cattle as a form of wealth and status. Third, their method of worship revolved around an elaborate system of sacrifice involving vegetable and animal offerings, in which the power of speech played a central role.

Myths about the ārya-dāsa relationship are piecemeal in the earliest religious compositions of the Aryans, the Ṛgveda (hereafter referred to as RV). They tend to revolve around celebrating the Aryan warrior god Indra's victories over the dāsas, who are considered dark-colored ones (*krsna varṇa*): "You, Indra, subdued Pipru and powerful Mrgayyu for Rjisvan, the son of Vidathin, you smote fifty thousand dark ones, you shattered cities, as old age shatters good looks" (RV 4.16.13). Not only are the dāsas considered lesser because they are darker, but their being conquered actually increases the strength of the conqueror: in one hymn, the Ṛgvedic poet says, "Indra kills dāsas and increases the might of the Aryans" (RV 10.22.8). In this same hymn there are references to the dāsa as nonhuman, or *amanuśya*, and hence related to the idea of mleccha, or those who speak indistinctly.

So, too, fire was used as a means of acquiring lands over the dark ones. A hymn to fire suggests this idea: "O Fire, due to your fear the dark ones fled; scattered abroad and deserting their possessions, when for Puru, glowing Vaiśvanara, you burn up and tear their cities"(RV 7.5.3). Fire also "Drives out dāsas and brings light to the Aryans" (RV 8.5.6).[2] Relatedly, the dāsa seemed enslaved to Indra, or driven out, wandering from place to place. Many hymns refer to the fact that Indra "binds dāsas one hundred and ten dāsas" and "leads away dāsas at his will" (RV 5.34.6). So too "the dark colored dāsas are driven away by Indra from place to place" (RV 4.47.21).

While these references are important in early Indian imagining about social boundaries, other social boundaries also existed. The dāsa is someone who worships the wrong gods, who hoards wealth, who neither conducts Vedic sacrifices nor speaks Sanskrit correctly like the ārya (RV 1.32 and 2.12). Moreover, there is also a sense of nobility to the term ārya, connoting dignity and strength. The ārya is the one who receives the Earth from Indra (4.26) and has superhuman strength.

How might we begin to think about ethnicity from these fragmentary myths about Aryans, and what became of such mythic references over time? We can see that Aryan identity is based on its distinction from the other, darker ones, and exists in relationship to definitions of other peoples. The Aryans' understanding of themselves was based on skin color characteristics as well as their prowess in battle and war. Most importantly, the ārya had control over sacred language.

Do references such as the ones above imply an ethnicity, or perhaps even more importantly, a race—members of a common biological origin? It is not clear; all we can glean from the texts is that an ārya is someone who is to be respected, who is victorious over the dark ones, and who lays hereditary claim to a higher social status by virtue of language.

However, it is just this racial (and by implication, ethnic) connotation that has dominated certain uses of this fragmentary myth. The history of the myth of Aryan racial identity within India is a long and complex one and too detailed to go into at length here. Some important points are worth noting in this basic discussion, however, as we explore the ideas of social boundaries and how such boundaries change over time. The word "ārya" is indeterminate enough in the early texts that it could be used, during the colonial period, to develop a theory of race, both by Europeans and Indians alike. A French thinker, Gobineau, developed the idea of Aryan, non-Aryan, and Semitic in the nineteenth century. A German scholar working in Britain, Max Mueller, expanded and solidified this theory in the mid-1800s. After editing and translating the Vedas, Mueller theorized that there was an invasion of Aryans into northwestern India, who brought with them technologically and culturally superior civilization and imposed it over the more primitive dāsas. For Mueller, linguistic comparisons between Sanskrit and European languages showed that the Aryans were also the font of Indo-European civilization; thus, while more primitive than the Europeans, the Aryans were nonetheless their distant cousins. Europeans, too, theorized about racial origins using the term "ārya," including the idea that the true Aryans must have been indigenous to Europe, and not India. During the period of the Third Reich in Germany, many Indologists were employed to develop the Aryan racial theory based on these earlier sources.

In India, too, the myth of the Aryan was used by Hindu groups who equated ethnic and racial purity with Hindu purity. One such organization is the Arya Samaj. Swami Dayananda (1824–1883), the founder of the Arya Samaj, wanted to spread a reformed view of the Vedic religion, and a view of the Aryan race and religion as the best source for an Indian renaissance. As legend has it, Dayananda became disillusioned with image worship in his childhood after he saw mice eating the images and food that he and his family had just consecrated. Rejecting marriage and adapting an ascetic life of study, in 1875 he established the Arya Samaj. Arguing that other Hindu reform movements were too Western, he taught that the Vedas, and thus, Aryan identity, were original to India, and originally progressive and clear sighted and ethical. The Arya Samaj's main popularity was in northwest India, but it was a major force in the nationalist movements right before independence, and today it is popular in rural India and among Hindu nationalists.

Other Hindu nationalist organizations also felt that racial or ethnic purity of the Aryan race was the only way to resist British colonialism. One such organization is the Rashtriya Svayam Sevak (RSS), or National Volunteers Association, founded in 1925 by Hedgewar. His successor, Madhav Sadashiv Golwalkar, who was anointed head of the RSS by Hedgewar shortly before his death, clarified the idea of the nation, and the Aryan, in his treatise *We, or Our Nationhood Defined*.[3] Based on a racial idea of nation, Golwalkar praises Hitler:

> To keep up the purity of the Race and its culture, Germany shocked the world by her purging the country of the Semitic Races—the Jews. . . . Ger-

many has also shown how well nigh impossible it is for Races and cultures, having differences going to the root, to be assimilated into one united whole, a good lesson for us in Hindustan to learn and profit by.[4]

The above quote reflects Golwalkar's clearly articulated twin-pronged ideology of exclusion (of other races/religions) and supremacy (of Hindus). Thus, in the 1920s and 1930s, an alliance was built between the European myth of the Aryan and the Indian one.

Contemporary debates about the Aryan myth tend to revolve around the question of indigeneity: Were the Aryans outsiders to India or indigenous to India? Some recent archaeological and linguistic evidence shows that Aryans and Indus Valley civilization must have coinhabited and mingled for a much longer period than originally thought. This evidence becomes interpreted to mean that the Aryans were in fact the Indus Valley inhabitants, and thus the ultimate original inhabitants. According to some Hindu nationalist writers, Hindu Aryans spread from their *pitṛbhūmī*, or homeland, to the west, thus reversing the theory of the European scholars. Moreover, they argue that all Hindus are āryas, and thus develop a kind of early, pan-Indian ethnic identity.

Most important for the purposes of this chapter is that the idea of the Aryan as a pan-Indian ethnic identity is resisted in contemporary India by groups who actually use the English term "ethnic." Dravidian activists in south India have resisted this Aryan hegemony and claimed that their ethnicity may have been the original ethnicity of India, and their Dravidian language the substratum the Vedic language subsumed into it. Some have also claimed that Dravidians were the original inhabitants of the Indus Valley and the great cities of Mohenjo Daro and Harrappa, which thrived from 4000 to 1700 B.C.E.[5]

Dalit, or low-caste groups, and tribal movements too have asserted their own ethnicity in resistance to the Aryan myth. It is worth spending some time here discussing the myth of Eklavya, who has been appropriated by some Dalits and those beyond the caste system altogether, formerly called "untouchables." The story is from the Mahābhārata and goes as follows: Eklavya, an untouchable, approached the teacher Drona to learn the arts of war and archery. Drona asks Eklavya to cut off his thumb, and he complies. Eklavya eventually becomes a successful and exemplary warrior. One educational foundation for low-caste people in India called itself Eklavya and built its philosophy around this myth in order to advocate empowerment for low-caste groups. Yet even this myth has been resisted by other Dalit activists, because it is too derivative of Aryan identity and comes from the Sanskritic epic, the Mahābhārata. As one Dalit writer puts it, Eklavya is in fact a false hero who only imitates the upper castes, and who should not have cut off his thumb at their whim.[6]

The Puruṣa Sūkta: Colors in Tandem

Later in the Ṛgveda, however, the ideas about light and dark were systematized a little more thoroughly, in the myth of the Puruṣa Sūkta, or the hymn of the man. In this hymn, the world is created through a sacrifice, which is the dismemberment of the cosmic man. From various parts of his body the four classical *varṇas*, or "colors" are formed. The relevant parts of the hymn go as follows:

> From that sacrifice in which everything was offered, the vedas and chants were born, the meters were born from it, and from it the formulas were born.
>
> Horses were born from it, and those other animals that have two rows of teeth; cows were born from it, and from it goats and sheep were born.
>
> When they divided the Man, into how many parts did they apportion him? What do they call his mouth, his two arms and thighs and feet?
>
> His mouth became the brahmin, his arms were made into the warrior, his thighs the people, and from his feet the servants were born.
>
> The moon was born from his mind; from his eye the sun was born. Indra and Agni came from his mouth, and from his vital breath the Wind was born.
>
> From his navel the middle realm of space arose; from his head the sky arose. From his two feet came the earth, and the quarters of the sky from his ear. Thus they set the worlds in order.

How might we interpret this hymn in terms of its approach to ethnicity? First and foremost, the source of all food, and both immortality and moral creatures, the one who ranges behind and before, is the sacrificed Man. Not only is he the source of the cosmos, he is the origination of the natural world—the seasons, the birds who live in the area, the forest and the villages. Yet he is also the originator of the social world, and thus the social world is seen as having the same transcendent referent as the natural world. Put even more simply, the social divisions are also cosmic divisions, and thus social hierarchy is presented as a natural thing. He donates his mouth to create the sacred priesthood or brahmin, his arms the warrior class, his thighs the *vaiśya*, or cultivator class, and his feet the *śūdras*, or servants of the world. Notice that in the next verse, the great gods of the sacrifice are also born, as well as the realms of space in the verse following that.

Many scholars have remarked upon the ways in which this social hierarchy is naturalized in both this creation myth and in later texts from the early Indian period.[7] This means that one's varṇa (meaning both "color" and "social role") is therefore sanctioned at the beginning of time, has a sacred origin, and should be treated as inviolable. Human, historical creation becomes a sacred pattern and of suprahuman origin. This move is the essence of myth making, according to Roland Barthes and others, whereby what is historical is represented as natural.[8] And according to others, this kind of thinking is essential to early Indian mapping of natural elements of the universe to the varṇa system.[9]

The Puruṣa Sūkta has been used in many different contexts, not all of them specifically ethnic. It was used in sacrificial rituals during the Vedic and classical periods and forms the basis of conceptual discussions on the nature of the universe in Vedānta philosophy in the medieval and colonial periods. However, even in the discourses which are less explicit in the imagining of social boundaries, authors still have a basic view of the dharmic boundaries between brahmins or priests, kṣatriyas, vaiśyas, and śūdras.

Around the second century C.E., legal texts called the Manava Dharma Śāstra and the Yajñavalkya Smṛti laid out a more strict view of the varṇa/color systems. They put forward a series of rules that guided interaction between varṇas, as well as interaction within them (i.e., how Brahmins interact with other varṇas as well as how they interact with one another). In these texts, the purity of the Brahmin caste is equated with the head as "high status," the kṣatriya with the torso as strength, the vaiśya with the thighs as fertility, the śūdra with the feet or servitude. This view might be implied in the hymn itself, but the explicit hierarchy is confirmed in the Laws of Manu, an ancient Hindu legal code. As the hierarchy of society is analogized with the hierarchy of the body, movement between the varṇas is highly regulated on the basis of purity. This is not to say that there was no movement between varṇas, but rather, that ideas about purity now defined how people imagined social boundaries.

In the colonial period, the myth of the Puruṣa Sūkta emerged as both a critique and a defense of Hinduism. The Laws of Manu and other texts were criticized by British administrators and Western missionaries as the source of the pernicious caste system in which there was no social mobility, and in which śūdras in particular suffered greatly. While the literature is voluminous, suffice it to say that as the British learned the myth of the Puruṣa Sūkta, it was interpreted as the sanction of all social cruelties. We see this particularly in the interreligious polemics of the colonial period. Some have even argued that, for all their critique, the British replaced an indigenous definition of varṇas with a pseudoscientific one of race, which was equally damaging. Even Gandhi used arguments about a spiritually functioning harmony to defend a certain version of the accepted Hindu social order.[10]

The Hindu response, both in the colonial and the postcolonial periods, involved arguing, as Gandhi did, that the Puruṣa Sūkta is a kind of spiritual ecology. Just as the body parts mentioned in the hymn are interdependent, so too are the varṇas interdependent. And, as for the terrible treatment of the śūdras, how could a body possibly exist without the feet? A footless body cannot move. The Hindus argue that, while the human interpretation of this hymn has been a major travesty, the hymn per se does not sanction cruelty and social segregation. Rather, it describes the harmony of the whole. A recent pamphlet of the Divine Life Society, a society following the Indian philosophy of nondualism, discusses the view of the Puruṣa Sūkta at length:

> [W]e do not see many things, bodies, objects, persons, forms, colours or hear sounds, but only the limbs of the One Purusha [sic]. And, just as, when we behold the hand, leg, ear, eye or nose of a person differently, we do not think that we are seeing many things, but only a single person in front of us, and we develop no separate attitude whatsoever in regard to these parts of the body of the person, because here our attitude is one of a single whole of consciousness beholding one complete person irrespective of the limbs or the parts of which the person may be the composite, we are to behold creation not as a conglomeration of discrete persons and things, with each one of whom we have to develop a different attitude or conduct,

but as a single Universal Person who gloriously shines before us and gazes at us through all the eyes, nods before us through all the heads, smiles through all lips and speaks through all tongues. This is the Purusha of the Purusha-Sukta. . . . This is not the god of any religion and this is not one among many gods. This is the only God who can possibly be anywhere, at any time.[11]

In a recent issue of *Dharma* magazine, we see a more social kind of "spiritual economics" defining the Puruṣa Sūkta as wholistic division of labor in the service of the nation:

In Purusha-Sukta [sic] of the Rg-Veda, there is reference to the division of Hindu society into the classes. It is described there that the Brahmanas came out of the face of the Lord the Creator, Kshatriyas from His arms, Vaisyas from His thighs, and the Sudras from His feet. [This is] the Law of Spiritual Economics. The underlying principle of caste system or Varna Dharma is division of labour. Rishis studied human nature carefully. They came to the conclusion that all men were not equally fit for all kinds of work. Hence, they found it necessary to allocate different kinds of duties to different classes of people, according to their aptitude, capacity or quality. The Brahmanas were in charge of spiritual and intellectual affairs. The work of political administration and defense was given to the Kshatriyas. The Vaisyas were entrusted with the duty of supplying food for the nation and administering its economic welfare. The Sudras did menial work. The Rishis felt all these needs of the Hindu nation and implemented the system of Varna and Asramas. This division of labour began in Vedic times The Vedas taught that the Brahmana was the brain of the society, the Kshatriya its arms, the Vaisya its stomach, and the Sudra its feet.[12]

In both of these treatments, the law of spiritual economics applies; in the first, social boundary is imagined as a way to access a higher state of consciousness. In the second, social boundary is the divinely sanctioned labor whereby each labors according to his own gifts, thus contributing to the universe as a whole. While space does not permit a long discussion of the theme, it should be noted here that many of these ideas have emerged in the Hindu diaspora, where Hinduism has become a minority tradition in need of rearticulating itself in a number of different kinds of contexts.

Finally, in postcolonial India, the myth of the Puruṣa Sūkta has been the object of great critique by Dalits. Dr. B. R. Ambedkar, called the father of the Dalit resistance movement, converted to Buddhism as a critique of the codes of Hinduism. He focused on the Puruṣa Sūkta as the center of Hinduism's caste system:

> The social order prescribed by the 'Purusha Sukta' has never been questioned by anyone except Buddha. Even Buddha was not able to shake it, for the simple reason that both after the fall of Buddhism and even during the period of Buddhism there were enough law givers, who made it their business not only to defend the ideal of the 'Purusha Sukta' but to propagate it and to elaborate it.[13]

In sum, the history of the myth of the Puruṣa Sūkta revolves around the question of whether social boundaries called varṇa are at the heart of the religious practices we now call Hinduism, or whether they are accidental to it. Is Hinduism about hierarchy or interdependence? Like the term ārya, the Puruṣa Sūkta seems not to answer definitively, and its indeterminate nature will continue to provide rich fodder for social speculation and imagination for Hindus and critics of Hinduism for centuries to come.

Jāti: A Myth of Various Callings and Fluid Exchanges

Our final category, jāti, is frequently associated with varṇa, and is called a "subcaste." Coming from the Sanskrit root "jā", to be born, "jāti" tends to be associated with traditional occupations and families associated by birth and trade, as well as identities defined by regional affiliations. The traditional concept of jāti comes closest to the contemporary idea of "ethnicity."

One early description of the idea of jāti is in the Ṛgveda and suggests the fluidity of social boundaries. The Ṛgvedic hymn to the sacred drink, Soma (RV 9.112), celebrates the various means of producing Vedic wealth. The hymn is from the ninth book of the Ṛgveda, thought by most scholars to have been gathered for ritual reasons at a time when the sacrificial cult was well solidified. Its verses compare the brahmin priest who crushes the Soma, the intoxicating source of wisdom and eloquence in the Vedic sacrifice, to a number of other kinds of wealth seekers, and thus, various kinds of jāti.[14]

> Our thoughts bring us to various callings, setting people apart: the carpenter seeks what is broken, the physician a fracture; and the Brahmin priest seeks one who presses Soma. O, Drop of Soma, flow for Indra. With his dried twigs, with feathers of large birds, and with stones, the smith seeks all his days a man with gold. O drop of Soma, flow for Indra. I am a poet; my Dad is a physician and Mom a miller with grinding stones. With diverse thoughts, we all strive for wealth, pursuing it like cattle. O drop of Soma, flow for Indra. The harnessed horse longs for a light cart; seducers long for a woman's smile; the penis for two hairy lips, and the frog for water. O drop of Soma, flow for Indra.

As many scholars have remarked, the hymn is both worldly and ironic, suggesting that among all the diverse occupations in early India, wealth is always the object. Just as the harnessed horse longs for a light cart and the frog for water, so too the smith seeks all his days for a man with gold and the sacrificer longs for a generous patron. Some have interpreted the hymn as a "working song" for those who are pressing the Soma to prepare it.

The hymn also suggests a kind of rudimentary theory of jāti: the carpenter looking for what is broken, the physician looking for a fracture, and even the seducer seeking a woman's smile are all forms of work. On at least one level, the hymn seems to celebrate all forms of human labor, not ranking them in a hierarchical fashion but juxtaposing them creatively. Indeed, in much of early Vedic literature the practice of the poets is compared to the specialized skill of the artisans or manual laborers, such as cartwrights, weavers, and carpenters.

But social boundaries are still being imagined here: while *Rgveda* 9.112 explicitly celebrates the fact that the crushing of Soma promises a perfect abundance of wealth, the first verse is equally unambiguous: the various means of producing wealth "set people apart" (*nananam jananam*). Implicitly, the priests' crushing of Soma is seen to be the most appropriate and effective means of gaining gold and cattle, "set apart" from other means. The implication is that the priestly varṇa (social class) produces more and better abundance. While the hymn ostensibly relativizes social hierarchy by comparing forms of labor, the priestly sacrificial system is still in place.

Later commentaries on the hymn RV 9.112 from the late Vedic and early classical periods are revealing. In these texts (Nirukta 5.2 and Brhaddevatā 6.137–46), these diverse forms of labor are named, but they are treated as possible only in the case of distress, such as a drought or an emergency (*apad dharma*). A Brahmin can be a carpenter or miller or an agriculturalist only when he is forced to. The Laws of Manu (10:116) go even further and codify exactly what a Brahmin can do in the time of distress and what he cannot do. Brahmins have become eternally pure, their speculative musings replaced by strict rules of exigency. As it did with the term varṇa, The Laws of Manu make practical theories of jāti into an elaborate science.

Other narratives of jāti, however, focus on the resistance to social division through occupation. Imagined boundaries are overcome through the mediation of a god or the wiliness of a human. One South Indian narrative, collected by Dianne Mines, tells "the origin of a relation among a lineage of a middle-ranking jāti (Muppanar)—one of Yanaimangalam's three politically and economically dominant jātis—and a low-ranking, blood-eating, fierce god named Mundacami who lives out beyond the edge of village fields at the cremation ground with his brother, the god Cutalaimatan ("Fierce god of the Cremation Ground")."[15]

One day, about a hundred years ago, the story goes, a man of the relatively high Muppanar caste was out working in his field by the river bank. He saw something floating down the river towards him. He fished it out, and found it was a banana *kanru* (shoot). He planted it on the edge of his field.

Now, it just so happened that his field lay in the line of sight of a god named Cutalaimatan, whose stone power-filled image stood nearby positioned to look across this field. Cutalaimatan is the god of the cremation ground and he is known as a fierce god (*matan*) who has a propensity to attack—sometimes quite violently—passersby who displease him or who make him jealous. So, people tend to avoid him, to tiptoe around him. But if your field lies right in the god's line of sight, there's not much you can do about it other than defer to him, soften him up, and hope for the best.

The Muppanar farmer did just that. He tried to win over the god by making a vow. He promised Cutalaimatan that he would give him the first stalk of bananas that his new tree produced, in return for the god's protecting the plant and field.

Well, a year passed and the banana plant flourished and produced a big stalk of bananas. The owner came out and cut the stalk and took it home, forgetting his vow to Cutalaimatan. He took one banana from the stalk, peeled it, and took a big bite. Immediately he choked, spat out the banana, and could eat nothing from then on.

He realized that the fault was his for forgetting his vow and so this higher caste man went to see a local man favored by Cutalaimatan, a lower-ranking Dhobi (Washerman) named Mukkan, to enlist his aid and find a solution. He went to Mukkan because he and his entire lineage were the special devotees of Cutalaimatan. They took care of him and he took care of them. Mukkan was the one whose connection to the god was closest: Cutalaimatan regularly possessed him and communicated his needs through this human host (*camiyati*, lit. "god dancer"). The solution that the Dhobi and the god offered was that the Muppanar man and his whole lineage should adopt Cutalaimatan's younger brother, Mundacami, as their own special god. They should construct a shrine to Mundacami opposite Cutalaimatan's shrine, and worship there from now on, side by side with the low-ranking Dhobis, as equals. So, to this day the Muppanar and Dhobis are equals in that temple.

As Mines discusses this story, she focuses on the substantive relationships that are established as new jāti alliances are formed: "A chance event (a banana shoot floating down the river) led to a vow made, and then a vow broken. A vow broken established a permanent relation between a low-ranking, peripheral god and a relatively high-ranking, central jāti."[16] There is an eternality to this new relationship, even though it emerged in a contingent situation in which social boundaries were relatively fluid. Mines goes on:

This relation between Mundacami and the Muppanar lineage is understood as an enduring, substantial, bodily relation between the god and lineage members and it cannot be attenuated at will. The Muppanar lineage (which corresponds roughly to the local Muppanar *jāti* grouping) is forever more substantially connected (*cerntatu*) with their new god. The god inhabits their houses, bodies and lives. The god eats what they eat, the god possesses them, the god fills them with energy and can also cause them illness if weak or displeased.[17]

Thus, according to this myth, jātis are renegotiated even as they are reestablished, and so too are the bodily and geographical relationships inherent in them.

These two tiny examples of myths about jāti show us that "belonging" and social groupings in occupational and "ethnic" exchanges are fluid. This fluidity can be taken up in myth in two ways: fluidity of jāti can be frozen through reinterpretation, as we saw in the case of *Ṛgveda* 9.112. Alternatively, fluidity of jāti can be renegotiated through new relationships with divinity, as we saw in the south Indian myth.

Concluding Remarks

With all three of our terms, then, we have discovered that a myth's indeterminate nature and meaning can lend itself to new imaginings of social boundaries. In the case of the ārya, we saw the very idea of race, ethnicity, and indigeneity come into play in new ways throughout colonial and postcolonial debate. In the case of varṇa, a more explicit myth of social division becomes reinterpreted as either pernicious hierarchy or social ecology. In the case of jāti, occupations and "birth groups" become fixed and renegotiated through myth. With the hints given by Hindu myths, Hindu and Western imaginations have created social boundaries of clear and distinct order, only to be confronted with yet another possible ethnic configuration in a moment's time.

NOTES

1. Much of nineteenth-century European scholarship posited an "invasion" of an early group, springing from an Indo-European homeland and migrating through the Caucasus, Iran, and into the Hindu Kush, around 2000–1500 B.C.E. However, recent archaeological evidence suggests that the story is more complex and does not involve invasion at all. Rather, the Aryans might have cohabited or mingled with their counterparts, the inhabitants of the Indus Valley civilization (covering what is now present-day Pakistan and parts of western India), for several centuries, before the towns and cities of the Indus Valley civilization fell into decay around 1700 B.C.E.

Archaeological evidence also suggests that Indus Valley towns and ways of life lasted in smaller scale after the demise of its great cities, and that the Aryans were present in the more central parts of India far earlier than previously thought. In light of this picture of ancient developments, some scholars argue that the Indus Valley and the Vedic civilizations were a single civilization. See, for example,

Edwin Bryant's *The Quest for the Origins of Vedic Culture: The Indo-Aryan Migration Debate* (New York: Oxford University Press, 2001).

2. So, too, fire is used to root out the treasure of another wealthy group, the Panis, whose myth is that they have stored their wealth in a cave, and fire itself has routed it out. "Agni, the hero, kills his enemy. The poet takes away the riches of Pani" (RV 6.13.3). In another, Agni is described as "the wisest god who opens the doors of the Panis forcefully"(RV 7.9.2).

3. Madhav Sadashiv Golwalkar, *We, or Our Nationhood Defined* (Nagpur: Bharat Publications, 1939), 21.

4. Ibid., 35.

5. See Asko Parpola's work, *Deciphering the Indus Script* (Cambridge, U.K.: Cambridge University Press, 1993).

6. In a review of Malavi's book *Patana*, R. K. Jamanadas writes:

A special mention must be made about his denial of Ekalavya as a hero. A powerful consent system has been built by Brahmanic scholars in the name of Ekalavya. All the text books since my childhood mention Ekalavya as the "Ideal sishya" by cutting his thumb away at the orders of Drona as a Guru Dakshina, for the education NOT imparted by him. And Drona is depicted as ideal "Guru" as prestigious Awards in Sports are named after him. "Patana" condemns this story and declares that such Adivasis can not be our leaders and heroes.

7. For a paradigmatic treatment, see Bruce Lincoln's *Myth, Cosmos, and Society: Indo-European Myths of Creation and Destruction* (Cambridge, Mass.: Harvard University Press, 1985), which deals with this myth from a comparative Indo-European perspective.

8. Roland Barthes, *Mythologies*, translated by Annette Lavers (London: Vintage, 1993).

9. See Brian Smith, *Classifying of the Universe: The Ancient Indian Varna System and the Origins of Caste* (New York: Oxford University Press, 1994), for a systematic presentation of this controversial thesis.

10. Gail Omvedt, "The UN, Racism and Caste," *The Hindu*, April 10, 2001.

11. Swami Krishananda, *Divine Light Society* (Rishikesh, 2000).

12. *Dharma Magazine*, February 2001, 34.

13. Dr. B. R. Ambedkar, *Who Were the Sudras?* Cited in *Dalit Forum*, November 9, 2000.

14. A version of this section appears in a previous article, "A Practical Theory of Myth with a Case Study of RV 9.122" in Frank Reynolds and David Tracy, eds., *Religion and Practical Reason* (Albany: State University of New York Press, 1995).

15. Dianne Mines, "From Homo Hierarchicus to Homo Faber: Breaking

Convention through Semeiosis," in *Irish Journal of Anthropology* 2 (1997): 33–44.

16. Ibid., 39.

17. Ibid.

SUGGESTIONS FOR FURTHER READING

Bayly, Susan. *Caste, Society and Politics in India: From the Eighteenth Century to the Modern Age.* Cambridge, U.K.: Cambridge University Press, 1999.

Bryant, Edwin. *The Quest for the Origins of Vedic Culture: The Indo-Aryan Migration Debate.* New York: Oxford University Press, 2001.

Dumont, Louis. *Homo Hierarchicus: The Caste System and Its Implications,* translated [from the French] by Mark Sainsbury, Louis Dumont, and Basia Gulati. Delhi: Oxford University Press, 1988.

Hutchinson, John, and Anthony D. Smith. *Ethnicity.* New York: Oxford University Press, 1996.

Lincoln, Bruce. *Myth, Cosmos, and Society: Indo-European Myths of Creation and Destruction.* Cambridge, Mass.: Harvard University Press, 1985.

Sharma, K. L., ed. *Social Stratification in India.* New Delhi: Manohar, 1986.

Smith, Brian. *Classifying of the Universe: The Ancient Indian Varna System and the Origins of Caste.* New York: Oxford University Press, 1994.

Srinivas, M. N.. ed. *Caste: Its Twentieth Century Avatar.* New Delhi: Oxford University Press, 1996.

Trautmann, Thomas R. *The Aryans in British India.* Berkeley: University of California Press, 1997.

Chapter 13

Religious Myth and the Construction of Shona Identity

Chirevo V. Kwenda

This chapter attempts to show how clan and superclan Shona identities were forged around the ancestress Nehanda, the Mwari cult, and the linguistic and educational enterprises of various missionary bodies. Of special interest is the role played by the religious myth about Nehanda in the Chimurenga I and Chimurenga II,* as well as in the postindependence nation-building efforts of the Zimbabwean government.[1]

Nehanda is the most important ancestress and powerful *mhondoro* (lion spirit) of Zimbabwe. The name of Nehanda surfaces in the oral traditions and myths of origin of the various clans of the Shona people. That there are many versions of these traditions is a reflection of the multiplicity of clan histories as well as the nature of the narrative genre in which they are expressed. Calling her a *mhondoro* identifies Nehanda as a very powerful spirit. The Shona, as many other African people, believe that when an adult man or woman dies, he or she becomes a spirit being, ideally a *mudzimu* (ancestor). Though if the person was bad in earthly

---

* "Chimurenga I" refers to the 1896–1897 risings by the indigenous Shona people of Zimbabwe against the forces of the British South Africa Company, which since 1893 had begun to colonize their country. Near the same time, the more recently arrived Ndebele who had exercised over-lordship on the Shona until their crushing defeat by Company forces in 1893, made a last-ditch effort to reverse their fortunes. Seventy years later (1966–1980) the Ndebele and Shona, under the aegis of the armed wings of the Zimbabwe African People's Union (ZAPU) and the Zimbabwe African National Union (ZANU) waged a guerrilla war on the white minority state, the colonial legacy of the British South Africa Company. Seen as a continuation of the earlier resistance wars of the 1890s but fought on modern terms with sophisticated weaponry, this war was named Chimurenga II.

life or disqualified by any number of reasons including dying a bad death (through violence or being struck by lightning, for instance), or dying without a child, that individual might be consigned to being a kind of wandering ghost. Family ancestors care for and protect their living family members. But it is held that chiefs and founders of clans become powerful ancestors whose moral jurisdiction extends beyond their immediate descendants. Just as they ruled over their chiefdoms in this life, they have oversight of a wide spiritual realm as ancestors. It is believed that these powerful spirits make their wishes known by periodically and temporarily possessing human mediums. When not possessing their mediums, these spirits are thought to reside in and manifest themselves as friendly lions. Hence the name *mhondoro* (lion).[2]

It is necessary here to explain the concept of a clan. A clan is a group made up of families or lineages (groups of interlinked families) descended from a known or theoretical common ancestor. Among the Shona, members of a clan normally share all three of the recognized identity markers: *dzinza* (clan name), *mutupo* (totem), and *chidao* (praise name). They marry outside the clan. In religious terms, a clan forms a worshiping unit, since it invokes and venerates the same common ancestor in its rituals. We have used the term "superclan" here as the equivalent of "tribe."

Now, to come back to the myth of Nehanda, the celebration of her in postindependence Zimbabwe seems to endorse the view of those who think that she is the most important figure in Zimbabwean history. The celebratory register includes the biggest maternity hospital in Zimbabwe, the Mbuya (grandmother) Nehanda Maternity Hospital in the capital, Harare. It also includes the renaming of Victoria Street in Harare as Mbuya Nehanda Street. The midlands capital of Gweru put the head of Nehanda together with that of Josiah Tongogara, a hero of Chimurenga II, on its coat of arms. There is a Nehanda Children's Fund and a Nehanda Children's Centre, which cares for street children and AIDS orphans. Poignantly, Mbuya Nehanda Street is the home of many non-governmental organizations (NGOs). Of special note among these, in gender terms, is the headquarters of the Zimbabwe Women's Organizations. The Reserve Bank of Zimbabwe has not been renamed, but it is said that it stands on sacred ground—the site where Mbuya Nehanda and Sekuru (grandfather) Kaguvi were executed by the British Colonial administration at the close of Chimurenga I. No coincidence could more fittingly sum up the meaning of the clash between the violent exchanges that drove colonialism, leading to Chimurenga I and II and the death of thousands of people, and the forces of resistance that are so powerfully represented in Nehanda and Kaguvi's execution.[3] It is also impossible to miss the powerful symbolism entailed by associating the Nehanda memory with a maternity home. What better place to celebrate the founding fertility and ethos of an ancestress than a major maternity home, the dispenser of life par excellence?

These examples accord with the view that political legitimacy derives not from observing the rule of law as defined by the Western liberal tradition,[4] but from the *endorsement of the ancestors*. David Lan underscores this point with respect to the present Zimbabwean government: "Since the achievement of independence the state of Zimbabwe has acquired legitimacy from the endorsement it has received from Nehanda and other senior mondoro."[5] This system of legitimation of political power goes back to precolonial days and deeper in time to the days of the founders of Shona polities. Acquiring and holding political power then involved gaining the nod of approval not only from the people concerned, but from the blessing of other forces as well. Among these forces was the land and the spirits of those who had worked it before (the founding ancestors, culture heroes, and past rulers), even if these were the forebears of those who were later vanquished in war. Political legitimacy involved processes of taming the land. This meant not so much subjugating it as tuning into the spiritual ways and forces of that particular land. This sentiment is illustrated by the current practice of some people in southern Africa to lick the earth when arriving at a new place.

An important principle was being recognized in all these ways, namely, that ruling was much more than conquest and subjugation of peoples. It had to do with creating the conditions within which life could be generated, sustained, and transmitted. Rulers had to have the ability to control and manipulate the forces of fertility in the land and ensure reliable rainfall, and to overcome the perils of diseases and pests. Thus, the successful ruler was not necessarily the one who commanded the leanest and meanest war machine, but the one who could enhance the total well-being of life in the realm.

Taming the land was a religious operation that brought together king and priest or diviner in the performance of elaborate rituals. An important aspect of some of these rituals was cleansing the land after a war, especially the most polluting wars of conquest and occupation. Peace had to be made not only with the vanquished, but with their ancestors as well.

Of crucial importance too was what the rulers did with the many alien subject peoples. Simple enslavement, though clearly one of the options open to victors, was not practiced on a large scale. The most popular strategy was absorption of these subject elements into the nation. Great ingenuity was exercised in these endeavors as rituals of incorporation were concocted and mythologies of identity were woven in the invention and reinvention of peoplehoods. There is ample evidence of the proliferation of this kind of activity of statecraft in the southern African region from the mid-nineteenth century up to the eve of the colonial era in response to the rise of Shaka, the warrior founder of the mighty Zulu kingdom in what is now South Africa.

Incorporation was possible in the first place because of the kind of philosophy of war held by many African polities. Scorched-earth or total-war policy was rarely, if ever, resorted to. The usual thing was for war to be waged to secure much needed resources, both material and human. But with the arrival of European conquerors and civilizations we see a different philosophy of conquest and statecraft. Although initially colonial conquest in southern Africa was not for purposes of extermination (in contrast to, say, Australia and North America) it certainly was not motivated by a desire to augment resources, with the exception of land, of course. Autochthons (indigenous people) were generally perceived as liabilities, necessary evils to be tolerated or endured. Like all conquerors, the Europeans did engage in exercises of reinvention of both self and other. But in sharp contrast with similar projects of African conquerors, the new myths they created were for purposes of segregation and denial of the humanity of Africans. They did not need the Africans except as laborers; they had no use for indigenous wisdom regarding the manipulation of the region's forces of fertility; much less did they see any need for legitimation of their political power by the indigenous religious and legal systems.

It is against this background, and in some ways in response to it, that the forging of a long-emerging Shona identity continued to take place. And it is in this melee that the mediums of such founding ancestors as Nehanda and Kaguvi rose to prominence consciously as resistance leaders, and perhaps less consciously as molders of discrete ethnic identities. It is significant that Nehanda is specifically mentioned in relation to the ancestral role of authenticating political power in modern Zimbabwe. This recognition of an ancestress and one of her female mediums makes a statement about gender flexibility, if not equity, in the unfolding both of

Shona identity and history. But in order to catch the full significance of this political role of the ancestress, we need to understand the Nehanda myth and the historical events it unleashed or with which it is associated.

Nehanda and Shona Origins

Traditions of Shona origins tell of migrations from a place called Guruuswa in the grasslands of the African Great Lakes region. Some scholars think the term "Guruuswa" is a generic reference to the savanna. Others hold the view that the mythical reference is to the place of origin of all humanity, the vagina.[6] Whatever the referent, the traditions say Mutota, identified as Nehanda's father, left Guruuswa in the time of the beginning and went to Dande in the northern part of Zimbabwe. There he established himself by conquering the indigenous Tande and Tavara people. However, a division of labor evolved whereby the conquerors—Mutota and his Korekore followers—held and exercised political power over Dande, while the vanquished Tande and Tavara (especially the latter) presided over the spiritual realm, managing the bringing and regulation of rain while promoting fertility.

While Mutota was the mythical, if not divine, founding ancestor of the Korekore, according to the founding myth he remained a transitional figure who lived and died in the liminal space between Guruuswa, the home of the ancestors, and Dande, the abode of the latter's descendants. It was one of Mutota's sons, Matope Nebedza, Nehanda's brother, who became the first Korekore chief in Dande.[7]

The role of Nehanda in all this seems to be that of a mbonga, which is the name given to the sister of a founding male ancestor of a clan.[8] It was the responsibility of the mbonga to keep, sometimes on or in her body, the charms of chiefship in which legitimate political power was vested. She was also charged with training the girls of the clan in the moral system of the clan and to prepare them for womanhood. With the passage of time Nehanda grew in stature as an ancestress. Together with her father, Mutota, she was credited with rain-making capability (although strictly speaking it was the ancestors of the indigenous Tavara who had powers over rain). Today she is ranked among the top national ancestors of Zimbabwe both as a historical and spiritual figure. However, her ascendance to national prominence was not an event; it was a gradual and meandering process.

It is clear that despite the centrality of the Mutota figure in them, the Guruuswa traditions cannot be linked exclusively with Korekore identity, as there are many Shona clans that identify with the Guruuswa traditions but lay no claim to being Korekore. The Korekore are simply one of the "tribes" together with the Zezuru, Manyika, Karanga, Ndau, and Kalanga that make up the Shona people of Zimbabwe. Apart from this mythical link with Mutota, Korekore identity might be of little attraction to many Shona people, due in no small measure to the nature of the formation of Korekore ethnic identity under colonial rule. History shows that although the Korekore homeland of Dande in the northern region of Zimbabwe came into contact with the outside world in precolonial days, through trade with the Portuguese, for instance, and was for a long period the seat of the great Mutapa empire, its fortunes declined considerably under British colonialism. It was as if benign political and administrative neglect conspired with the semiarid physical conditions to relegate the region to the rear of the modernization process. Plagued by a general paucity of schools, health facilities, services, and commerce, the region until recently proved to be an attraction for anthropologists looking to study small-scale societies that were relatively free of contamination by modernizing influences. Korekore and its territory of Dande, especially the poor dry plateau, has come to be associated with backwardness.[9] Even in far-flung South Africa, the xenophobic and derogatory designation of foreign Africans is "Kwerekwere"—an obvious corruption of Korekore, which originally may have been derived from *kurekure* (people from afar)[10]—attests to this.

The forces of missionary education and modernization did much not only to carve out a Korekore identity, but to erect cultural boundaries between the Korekore and some other Shona groups who, though claiming origin in Guruuswa, were now espousing Zezuru, Manyika, or Karanga identity. These regional identities, as well as the emerging national Shona identity, were being forged on the anvil of old chiefdoms with the twin hammers of the colonial administration on the one side, and missionary enterprise on the other. It is important to note here that all this time the name and memory of Nehanda, through the myth of Mutota and the migration from Guruuswa, remained confined to the northern escarpment and the Zambezi Valley as the trademark of spirit mediums who were possessed by this great Korekore *mhondoro* (lion spirit). But as we shall see later, this parochial status would change dramatically and become transformed into a national force.

The Rise of Regional Ethnic Identities

While in precolonial days there were clusters of people who, usually under the political organization of a chiefdom but having different *mutupo* (totem) and *chidao* (praise name), were known or regarded themselves as Karanga, Zezuru, Manyika, Ndau, or Korekore, these identities were neither ideologically grounded nor socially fixed. Very often they were loose descriptive designations. But in the maelstrom of colonization and evangelization these identities underwent a process of renegotiation, redefinition, and strategic positioning in terms of their geographic, linguistic, and political boundaries. Thanks to a conducive confluence of interests, these developments gained an ever-increasing impetus. While the colonial administration desired resources and strategies to facilitate their indirect rule, the various missionary denominations wanted to promote literacy for purposes of evangelization. Both intentions required not only a system of classification for the "tribes" and their dialects, but also called for standardization of names, dialects, and orthography (the regulation of written language). Carving artificial and arbitrary boundaries where there had been none before and shifting extant ones, this process shunted unrelated "tribes" and dialects together, thereby inventing new identities, suppressing some, and completely destroying others.[11]

This was especially the case with the forging (in every sense of the word) of a universal Manyika identity in tandem with a Chimanyika dialect in eastern Zimbabwe. It has become very clear from the work of historians and other scholars that some "tribes" who were made to carry the Manyika ethnic label deeply resented it. A case in point is chief Makoni and his Vaungwe people. It was the people of Makoni's perennial enemy, Chief Mutasa, who were originally called Manyika. In the past only the vanquished were sometimes expected to shed their identities in order to adopt the identity of the victors. But throughout the troubled history of internecine warfare with Mutasa, Makoni had never been vanquished. Therefore, to call Makoni a Manyika was not only inaccurate; it was an unforgivable insult, one that suggested military conquest or political subjugation. The insult went even deeper than the military and political levels to touch on spiritual mainsprings of identity. Fixing the Manyika label on the Makoni people transgressed the mystical basis of clan identity with its roots embedded as it was in the tripartite mechanism of *mutupo* (totem), *chidao* (praise name), and *dzinza* (clan name). In the totem system, a clan associates itself with an animal or vegetable species which clan members then taboo. They show deep knowledge and admiration of its qualities or, in the case of an animal, its behaviors or habits. Makoni's people had the *Shonga* (buffalo) for their totem, while the totem of Mutasa's Manyika is *Tembo* (zebra).

As the missionaries and early converts of the American Methodist Episcopal Church were creating a Chimanyika dialect and a Manyika "tribe" to speak, read, and write it, their efforts were sometimes supplemented and in other respects contested by those of their rivals, the Anglicans who established a base in Makoni's territory. The Dutch Reformed Church was inventing the Chikaranga language in the south, and the Roman Catholics were cobbling together the Chizezuru dialect at Chishawasha near Harare.[12] No sooner had schoolbooks and Bible portions come off the missionary presses than the process to standardize all those regional dialects into a national Shona language and a unified orthography began. With this, a politicized Shona ethnic identity was emerging, being defined on the one hand by its transregional status and, on the other, in contradistinction from the conqueror Ndebele identity in the west.

One of the unintended outcomes of the missionary language projects was the popularization and nationalization of some religious cults. For instance, the cult of Mwari which, though spreading rapidly, had been confined to the center and south of the country, received a boost when the missionaries translated the Christian name for God as "Mwari."[13] This had the double effect of more clearly defining Shona cosmology by placing a high God or Supreme Being at its apex, and generalizing Mwari to areas the cult had not touched so far. At the same time, it further redefined the cosmology by bringing into sharp relief a category of divinities (super-*mhondoro*) that were higher in status than clan spirits and were ensconced immediately below the high God. These included Mukwati, Chaminuka, Kaguvi, and Nehanda. Because it was hard to directly associate these spirits with any specific dynasty, they came to be regarded as *majukwa*—spirits that were emanations of the high God. Their importance as super-*mhondoro* was greatly enhanced through the courageous activities of the mediums they possessed at the turn of the twentieth century who interpreted colonization to their people and organized and led *chimurenga* (resistance, rebellion) against colonial subjugation. Charwe, the medium of Nehanda, and Gumboreshumba, the medium of Kaguvi, were arrested and executed by the British colonists at the end of Chimurenga I.

If up to this point Nehanda had only been a mythical or spiritual figure, in the death of Charwe the *mhondoro* became a historical fact. Ironically, this historicity gave birth to further mythologization of the Nehanda spirit. In intervening years between Chimurenga I in 1896–1897 and Chimurenga II of 1966–1980, it was mostly the memory of Nehanda that galvanized nationalist politics. But it was especially in Chimurenga II that Nehanda, about whom there are two traditions of mediums—a Korekore tradition based in Dande, and a Zezuru tradition with its home in the Mazowe Valley near the capital, Harare—rose to national prominence. Charwe, the martyred and immortalized heroine of Chimurenga I, belonged to the Mazowe Valley tradition.[14] Guerrillas on the battlefield, or in the all-night conscientization sessions they regularly held with villagers everywhere in Chimurenga II, celebrated Nehanda and drew inspiration from her memory. This was all incapsulated in the song:

> Mbuya Nehanda kufa vachitaura shuwa
> Kuti tinotora sei nyika ino
> Shoko rimwe ravakatiudza
> Tora gidi uzvitonge
>
> Grandmother Nehanda died talking
> About how to take back the land
> In but one word she said it all
> Pick up the gun and free your self.

This shooting to national elevation of the Mazowe Valley Nehanda effectively suppressed and silenced the Dande Nehanda in a manner that shows the internal contours and fissures of Zimbabwean nationalist politics. For one thing, it highlights the dominance of the Zezuru strand of Shona identity over the Korekore and the resistance to it that may be expected from the other regional tributaries of Shona identity, such as Manyika, Karanga, Ndau, and Kalanga. If one major goal of the conscientization of the masses during the liberation struggle was the demolition of regional and ethnic chauvinism, if not identities, and paving the way to a unified nation on the basis of a broad Shona identity, the Nehanda myth-history supplied an ideal symbol for the task. People who could claim descent from neither the Nehanda of myth nor the Charwe of history confidently adopted Nehanda as their stamp of freedom and hope for the future. Branches of the ruling ZANU(PF) party were named Nehanda all over the country. In an age when women's rights were being recognized, contested, legislated, and litigated, women found a fitting role model, precedent and inspiration in the multilayered memory and intimate reality of Nehanda.

However, while being used as a symbol of national solidarity in the struggle against colonial rule, Nehanda, both as ancestral memory and contemporary inspiration, has been harnessed to party political agendas that have the potential to divide the nation along the much condemned ethnic or "tribal" lines. In other words, to the extent that Nehanda's memory is used in post-independence Zimbabwean politics as if it were owned by the dominant Zezuru faction of the ruling ZANU(PF) party, it ceases to be a unifying symbol in the task of nation building. However, as is usually the case with religious symbols, Nehanda's memory is too powerful at the moment for it to simply be abandoned by other sections of the Zimbabwean population who might feel alienated by its ZANU(PF) captivity.

What is more likely to happen is contestation of ownership of the symbol. If the Korekore were up to it (commendably they do not seem to be), they might want to revive the Dande tradition of Nehanda mediums and forge for it a link with the powerful more recent history of resistance to colonization and colonial overlordship. Or the Karanga might want to exploit their history as the oldest indigenes of Zimbabwe and find ways of linking this history to the powerful mythology and history of Nehanda. But such regional options would be just as opportunistic and detrimental to national unity as de facto ownership of the Nehanda symbol by any single political party or faction.

Breaching Structural Boundaries

Whether it was fighting for ownership of powerful symbols, or a share of the national cake in the form of education, health services, or jobs, the reality of regional and ethnic identities always lurked in the background as a latent threat to national unity. As we have seen, ethnic identities were deeply rooted in the totem (*mutupo*) system, which was further delimited by the praise name (*chidao*) as markers within a clan (*dzinza*). In a strict exogamous society (one that requires marriage outside of the clan), these identity beacons served to enclose kin within boundaries that kept out non-kin or outsiders. No entrenched anti-outsider sentiments should be read into this arrangement, however. As a redeeming factor, we find that the distinctive feature of an outsider was not systematic earmarking for bad treatment, as some observers allege. The outsider represented a reservoir of potentialities as friend, neighbor, or above all, in-law. This last potential is very important, for it highlights the importance of "alien blood" in the perpetuation of any lineage. Without outsiders, legitimate biological and social reproduction would be impossible, since incest is detested by most Shona. This means that among the Shona the totem system contains both the seeds of ethnic chauvinism and the potential for creative breaching of boundaries in the construction of new relationships based on choice and mutual agreement.

This principle is important in an attempt to understand the role of religious myth in the formation of Shona identity. It is instructive at this point to see Nehanda from two different points: as an insider and an outsider. As the former she was at the epicenter of political power as a *mbonga* (designated sister of the founding ancestor). But her role as a *mhondoro* (lion spirit) had to be performed by her possessing a medium from an outside lineage.[15] The services of the medium had to be secured by a process akin to marriage proceedings, so that the medium became the symbolic "wife" of the possessing spirit (mhondoro), irrespective of the gender of the latter. Political pragmatism reaches high levels of sophistication here. Otherness is embraced in a manner that opens opportunities for creative work in community or nation building.

To go back to the two Nehanda traditions, one in the north and the other in the central region, this division of labor may be at the center of a possible explanation. It may well be that while the Korekore or Zambezi Valley Nehanda could legitimately function as a mbonga among her people, within the founding lineage, as mhondoro she could only possess outsiders. This may explain the existence of the Mazowe Valley Nehanda tradition; it arose out of the activities of Nehanda outside of the insider Korekore royal circle of Mutota and Matope Nebedza. Thus, well before Nehanda was popularized through the acts of valor of the medium Charwe at the turn of the twentieth century, it seems, there was already rapprochement between Korekore and Zezuru through the primordial division of labor that assigned political work to the Korekore and spiritual work to the outsider Zezuru.

Another version of this paradigm is played out in the suggestion that the Nehanda of Chimurenga I was the wife of Kaguvi (a powerful Zezuru mhondoro). Or that Nehanda was Chaminuka's sister. What all these formulations point to is the lack of links between this class of spirit and any local political dynasties. If Zimbabweans were looking for a supraethnic spiritual structure to provide them with a theoretical foundation for a national identity, this cosmology has the perfect answer. All that may be needed is ingenuity in crafting supraethnic political mythologies to go with this religious mythology and history. However, this may be easier said than done, given the competitive and divisive nature of party politics. At the time of this writing, Zimbabweans are standing in long lines as they wait to cast their votes in a closely contested presidential election. It may be too early to attempt an analysis of the ways in which the Nehanda and other national religious and political symbols are being used both to win the election and to continue to mold the diverse ethnic and regional identities of Zimbabwe into one politically stable and economically viable and prosperous nation.

Any discussion of Shona identity as part of a broader Zimbabwean identity must include something on relations with the Ndebele in the western part of the country. The Ndebele arrived in Zimbabwe in the early part of the nineteenth century as conquerors from the south led by Mzilikazi. They effectively established a kingdom that was destroyed by the British not until the turn of the century. However, their cultural and religious power did not match their military prowess. So pervasive was the influence of Shona religious ideas and practices on them that historian Ngwabi Bhebe refers to the situation as "A religious conquest of the victors by the vanquished."[16] Today, Ndebele heroes of Chimurenga II, such as Jason Ziyapapa Moyo, are celebrated in the new Zimbabwean state and proudly take their place of honor at Heroes Acre, the burial shrine of Zimbabwe's fallen heroes. How the Ndebele may affect and be affected by the new religious mythology of Nehanda and Kaguvi is yet to be seen. After all, Nehanda is no stranger to Ndebele history, as the powerful medium of Chaminuka—Nehanda's brother, according to some traditions—who was killed by an act of treachery in the late nineteenth century, is said to have died at the instigation of the Ndebele.

Another interesting relation to comment on is the one between Nehanda and Christianity. Perhaps the majority of those among the Shona who today celebrate Mbuya Nehanda for political and other reasons profess one or another form of Christianity. This is truly interesting since ancestral spirits were condemned as evil by missionaries who imposed severe penalties for noncompliance and their prohibitions against revering them. So infatuated with the Nehanda myth are contemporary Zimbabwean Christians that liberation theologian Canaan Banana once named Nehanda among those ancestral heroes of the past that he argued must be included in a new Bible he proposes should be written.[17] The irony of it all is that Mbuya Nehanda herself refused baptism when it was offered to her as a last rite before execution. Thus, Mbuya Nehanda continues to inspire the present generation in politics, religion, social movements, ethics, and the arts, to name just a few. Where once in the deepest past she was at the core of Korekore identity, in time she insinuated herself into the formation of a Zezuru identity in the form of the Mazowe Valley Nehanda tradition. With the transformations that came with missionary work and literacy, as well as the two resistance wars against British overlordship, Mbuya Nehanda, more so in death than in life, became a major inspiration in the search for a truly national Zimbabwean identity, and continues to be so.

NOTES

The author is grateful to the University of Cape Town for funding toward research for this chapter through the services of the Vacation Training Program.

1. *Chimurenga* means rebellion in Shona. Historically, it refers to the wars of resistance against British overlordship in Zimbabwe. The Ndebel equivalent of *chimurenga* is *ndunduma*.

2. See, among others, David Lan, *Guns and Rain: Guerrillas and Spirit Mediums in Zimbabwe* (Harare: Zimbabwe Publishing House, 1985), 31–43.

3. Searching the Internet will yield many informative websites on Mbuya Nehanda. The information in some of these may need to be cross-checked against standard historical sources on Zimbabwe for accuracy.

4. Anthony Gubbay, the former chief justice of Zimbabwe, in an article titled "Decline and Fall of the Sanctity of the Law," writes: "Let me stress that today it is the human rights performance of a government—which implies observance of the rule of law—that provides the most material criterion of its legitimacy." *Sunday Times* (London), November 11, 2001, 19.

5. Lan, *Guns and Rain*, 228.

6. Ibid., 77–78.

7. Ibid., 81.

8. A. C. Hodza and G. Fortune, *Shona Praise Poetry* (Oxford: Clarendon Press, 1979), 15.

9. Lan, *Guns and Rain*, 10–13.

10. Ibid., 14; Aeneas Chigwedere, *The Karanga Empire* (Harare: Books for Africa, 1986), 10–13.

11. Chigwedere, *The Karanga Empire*, 10–13.

12. Terence Ranger, "Missionaries, Migrants and the Manyika: The Invention of Ethnicity in Zimbabwe," in Leroy Vail, ed., *The Creation of Tribalism in Southern Africa* (London: J. Currey; Berkeley: University of California Press, 1989), 127.

13. M. F. C. Bourdillon, *The Shona Peoples: An Ethnography of the Contemporary Shona, with Special Reference to Their Religion* (Gweru: Mambo Press, 1976), 321.

14. Lan, *Guns and Rain*, 6.

15. Hodza and Fortune, *Shona Praise Poetry*, 14.

16. Ngwabi Bhebe, "The Ndebele and Mwari: A Religious Conquest of the Conquerors by the Vanguished," in J. M. Schoffeleers, ed., *Guardians of the Land* (Gweru: Mambo Press, 1978), 287.

17. Canaan Banana, "The Case for a New Bible," in I. Mukonyora, J. L. Cox, and F. J. Versttraelen. eds., *Rewriting the Bible: The Real Issues* (Gweru: Mambo Press, 1993), 29.

SUGGESTIONS FOR FURTHER READING

Bourdillon, M. F. C. *The Shona Peoples: An Ethnography of the Contemporary Shona, with Special Reference to Their Religion.* Gweru: Mambo Press, 1976.

Chigwedere, Aeneas. *The Karanga Empire.* Harare: Books for Africa, 1986.

Lan, David. *Guns and Rain: Guerrillas and Spirit Mediums in Zimbabwe.* Harare: Zimbabwe Publishing House, 1985.

Schoffeleers, J. M. ed., *Guardians of the Land.* Gweru: Mambo Press, 1978.

Chapter 14

Sacral Ruins in Bosnia-Herzegovina
Mapping Ethnoreligious Nationalism

Michael A. Sells

The genocide and "ethnic cleansing" that took place in Bosnia-Herzegovina (hereafter referred to as BiH) from 1992 to 1995 employed religious persecution and religious markers to construct homogeneous, mutually exclusive block "ethnicities" of Serbs, Croats, and Muslims. During the campaign, the consensus in the press, in the popular literature, and in much of the scholarly literature was that religion was not an important factor in the violence, and that it was, at most, a screen for political, economic, and social agendas. There were several reasons for this denial: disciplinary prejudices that led some to posit only one valid area of inquiry (social, historical, economic, or political); the popular assumption that religion was no longer a major factor in modern and postindustrial civilization; and the apologetic belief that religion is a matter of private beliefs or behavior and that, therefore, it could never be a factor in mass killing and genocide. There is no single causal factor in any historical transformation; such events are conditioned and guided by a variety of forces that form a power more than the sum of their parts. This chapter will examine the role of religion in motivating, justifying, and disguising genocidal and potentially genocidal violence in BiH.

The role played in the tragedy by Serbian Orthodoxy offers the clearest and most obvious example of how religious myth and ritual were exploited to achieve the breakdown of differences and to construct artificial mutually exclusive ethnicities through violence based on an assumed and/or imposed religious difference. Catholic religious nationalism was

less blatant (in fact, I will argue it follows a reverse code), but no less to-
talizing in its instigation of religious "cleansing" operations. The Muslims
of the Balkans, lacking any single nationalist state to speak for them and
being themselves under siege, never achieved (or resorted to) a religious
nationalist identity of any widespread acceptance (despite the allegation
of an Islamic plot to form an Islamic state in the Balkans). But in the aftermath of the tragedy, outside groups have attempted to turn the Bosnian Muslims (*Bosjnaks*) into the kind of militants that their enemies had
long and inaccurately accused them of being. Each of the three religious
nationalisms is embodied most tangibly in the destruction, transformation, and rewriting of sacral architecture, and it is with such tangible
signs that I open discussion of each.[1] It should be emphasized from the
outset that the equal attention given to the three religious nationalisms is
in no way meant to suggest a moral equivalency among them. In the case
of Bosnia, Serbian religious nationalism was genocidal, in both intent
and in on-the-ground reality. Catholic nationalism was reactively genocidal; when the Catholic nationalists in Zagreb and Herzegovina saw the
opportunity, they modeled their program of "ethnic cleansing" on that of
the larger Serb nationalist program, with equal brutality. Islamic nationalism is largely imposed on Bosnia from outside. Although there were
some Bosnjak religious nationalists, the vast majority of Bosnjaks were
opposed to religious nationalism. The large majority of victims of "ethnic
cleansing" were Muslim.

Serb Orthodox Nationalism

Foča was an ancient center of culture in southeastern Bosnia. The town
on the Drina River had thrived as a trade station between Ragusa and
Constantinople. In the fifteenth and sixteenth centuries, it was graced
with major south Slavic architectural monuments, including the Aladza
(Colored) Mosque (Aladza dzamija), constructed in 1551, one of the
masterworks of south Slavic architecture, and dozens of other Islamic
sacral sites. For generations the town had a roughly equal division between Serb Orthodox and Muslim populations.

In the spring of 1992 the Serb army overran Foča. As was the case
throughout areas occupied by the Serb forces, the Muslim population in
Foča was largely defenseless and offered no organized armed resistance.
Bosnian Muslims in the town and surrounding villages were subjected to

mass killings, organized rape, and expulsion. All Islamic monuments, including the sixteenth-century masterwork, the Aladza (Colored) Mosque, were destroyed. The monuments were dynamited and bulldozed. A rape-camp network was established through which Muslim women and girls were enslaved, tortured, gang raped, then killed or sold. After the town was certified as 100 percent Muslim-free, its name was changed from Foča to Srbinje, amid religious and civic ceremonies. A new Serbian Orthodox seminary was established, and some of the novitiates were veterans of "ethnic cleansing" operations.[2] Serb Orthodox bishops led ceremonies commemorating the newly named town and new seminary. A university professor from Sarajevo, Vojislav Maksimovic, explained that "the [Serb] fighters from Foča and the region were worthy defenders of Serbdom and of Orthodoxy."[3] When asked why all the mosques had been dynamited, the new Serbian nationalist mayor responded that "there never were any mosques in Foča."[4]

The fate of Foča, emblematic of what occurred throughout the 70 percent of BiH that fell to Serb nationalists, becomes explicable, in part, through consideration of an event that occurred three years earlier: the June 11, 1989, commemoration of the 600th anniversary of the death of Prince Lazar in the battle of Kosovo.[5] During the period of revolutionary nationalism in the mid-nineteenth century, Prince Lazar was elevated above other figures from the heroic tradition, and his death was figured—in Serb art, literature, theater, and popular and religious writings—as the "Serbian Golgotha." The knights who accompanied him to the battle of Kosovo became the apostles, one of whom, Vuk Brankovic, was a traitor. Painters modeled Lazar's supper on the eve of the battle on Italian representations of the Last Supper of Jesus. The maiden of Kosovo, a Mary Magdalene figure, ministered to the fallen.

The power of the remembrance of the passion and death of Lazar was harnessed and militarized in the literature of revolutionary nationalism that culminated in the writing of *The Mountain Wreath* (*Gorski Vijenac*) by the Montenegrin Orthodox Bishop Petar Petrovic II, better known as Njegoš. *The Mountain Wreath* is a poetic reenactment of the "Extermination of the Turkifiers," the liquidation of Slavic Muslims in Montenegro believed to have taken place in the eighteenth century. In Njegoš's version, the Serb knight-bishop (Vladika) Danilo calls a meeting of Serb leaders to discuss the problem of the "Turkifiers." The Muslim leaders suggest a reconciliation based upon the ancient south Slavic Kum (godfather) ceremony, in which the two leaders of warring tribes each take the child of the other as godson. The Orthodox clerics object saying that in order to have a Kum ceremony, both children need to be baptized. The Muslim leaders counter that Christian and Muslims Slavs are all one people (*narod*) and suggest an interreligious ceremony in which the Christian child is baptized and the Muslim child undergoes a ritual tonsure, the Islamic analog to baptism. The proposal is rejected and the Muslims are sent away with curses on Muhammad, their religion, and their souls. *The Mountain Wreath* ends with a graphic depiction of the extermination of the Slavic Muslims and the burning of their settlements, acts presented not only as justified, but as sanctifying.[6]

By transforming themselves into Turks, Njegoš implies, the Slavic Muslims transform themselves into the people held responsible for the Serbian Golgotha and the death of the Christ-Prince Lazar. The Serbian *narod* must be "cleansed" of such "Turkifiers" before it can be resurrected along with Lazar. Nobel laureate Ivo Andrić wrote that Njegoš's judgment against the Slavic Muslims was the timeless voice of "the people," thus placing Slavic Muslims at a double remove from the people: it is the timeless voice of the people that rejects them as being part of the people. Njegoš and Andrić espoused the ideology that I have labeled "Christoslavism": the assumption that Slavs are Christian by nature; to convert to another religion is to transform oneself ethnically or racially, and in so doing, betray one's Slavic identity.

Andrić and other twentieth-century writers portray Slavic Muslims as agents of an Ottoman Empire of absolute evil—an empire that, through the *devshirme* system of forced conscription into the Janissary corps (an elite corps of Ottoman soldiers made up of Christian converts to Islam), systematically drained Serbian blood.[7] The depiction of Turks and "Turkifiers" as parasites living on the blood drained from the Serbian people added another layer of emotive symbolism to the charge that Slavic Muslims were responsible for the Serbian Golgotha. At the same time, Vidovdan (St. Vitus Day) was developing from a relatively circumscribed place in religious calendars to a dominant role in religious and national ideology. The centrality and symbolic power of Vidovdan increased in stages, from the time of Njegoš, through the assassination of the Archduke Ferdinand by a Serb who had memorized Njegoš, to the Vidovdan constitution of Yugoslavia in 1931, to the momentous events of the 1989 600th anniversary commemoration. As the 1989 Vidovdan commemoration approached, Serbian Orthodox clergy and University of Belgrade academics repeated the charge that Slavic Muslims had the blood on their hands of the Serbian martyrs who fell before the Turks, martyrs embodied in the fallen Lazar.[8]

Another layer of Christoslavic symbolism is found in the conception of the entire region of Kosovo as the "Serb Jerusalem." The region is the site not only of the famous battle but many of the monasteries, churches, and artistic treasures of medieval Serbia as well.[9] In the decade of the 1980s, after the death of Yugoslav President Marshal Tito, tensions grew as the majority Albanian population (most of whom were nominally, at least, Muslim and Catholic) began demanding fuller autonomy. As the Yugoslav government repressed the Kosovar Albanians, hostility rose between the Albanian and Serb residents of Kosovo. In 1986 the Serbian Orthodox Church published an official, though false, claim that Kosovo Serbs were being subjected to an Albanian program of "genocide."[10] While human-rights groups and Serbian police reports disproved the claims of mass murder, organized rape, and systematic annihilation of Serbian cultural heritage,[11] those claims were nevertheless taken up by Serbian intellectuals and academics and incorporated into the *Serbian Memorandum* of 1986, the document that heralded the end of Yugoslavia.[12]

As the 1989 Vidovdan commemoration approached, the generational memory of World War II atrocities returned with the power of the repressed. During the era of Marshal Tito, serious discussion of these atrocities had been suppressed. As Tito's Yugoslavia crumbled, Serbs began to formally disinter the remains of Serb victims of Nazi and Ustashe atrocities (the Ustashe was a fascist Croatian movement during World War II that aligned itself with the Nazis).[13] Militant religious and political leaders took control of the ceremonies of disinterment and used them to portray the Croatian people as genocidal by nature, and to brand all Muslims, generically, as collaborators with the Ustashe (despite the facts that many Muslims and Croats fought against the Ustashe in the Partisan army and most contemporary Muslims and Croats had not yet been born during the terrible years of World War II). The accusation that Croats and Muslims were a genocidal people and were plotting a new genocide was repeated throughout Serbian Orthodox Church publications combined with the inflammatory allegation that Serbs were already undergoing genocide at the hands of Albanians in Kosovo province.

All of the streams of ethnoreligious mythology came together on June 11, 1989. In the reenactments of the death of Lazar, the primordial time of 1389 collapsed into the present. The power of the classical passion play to affect such a collapse is best illustrated by the advice given to actors charged with portraying the killers of Lazar: kill the martyr swiftly (before the crowd can rush the stage and stop you) and exit the stage immediately after the act (before the crowd can rush the stage and beat you). At this moment of rushing the stage, the boundary between then and now, audience and actor, representation and reality breaks down.

The momentous nature of the 600th anniversary commemoration was compounded by the factors mentioned above: more than ten years of increasing Christoslavic rhetoric, demonization of Ottomans and Slavic Muslims, fabricated charges of ongoing genocide against Serbs in the Serb Jerusalem of Kosovo, and the release of pent-up memories of World War II atrocities by Nazis and Ustashe against Serbs. At times, the conjunction of these factors took on particularly graphic expression. As the relics of Lazar were paraded around the greater Serbia to arrive at the battlefield in Kosovo on June 11 and be shown for the first time in history, the remains of Serb victims of World War II were being unearthed from the taboo on discussing the atrocities that had existed under Tito and, in ceremonies charged with religious hate, were literally disinterred and given ritual reburial. The Vidovdan event was harnessed and manipulated by extremist bishops, Serbian intellectuals, and political leaders to create a mass psychology and to sever all ties, all bonds of humanity, between Serbs and the other nationalities of the former Yugoslavia, especially Muslims.[14]

The religious mythology was necessary for motivating and justifying genocide, but it was not sufficient. To be effective, it needed to be instrumentalized through the actions of the army, secret police, religious-nationalist militias, Serbian Orthodox bishops, networks of organized crime, and the media; and through the coordination of the provocations and propaganda among these various sectors.[15] Religious nationalist militias carried out a campaign of atrocity and provocation against non-Serbs, especially Muslims, and a simultaneous campaign of intimidation and, if necessary, liquidation of Serbs who refused to participate in the attack on the non-Serb population. By forcing as many Serbs as possible to engage in the atrocities, the organizers guaranteed that complicity would be spread throughout a wide section of the population who would, thereafter, have a vested interest in denying what happened and in obstructing investigations into the atrocities.[16] As the property of non-Serbs was distributed to the local Serb population, the circle of complicity and solidarity was further strengthened. The lines between military, political, and organized crime leaders became blurred, with figures such as Arkan (Željko Raznjatović) and Vojislav Šešelj exercising all three roles simultaneously.[17] Serbian Orthodox priests and bishops played central roles in demonizing Muslims, urging ever more extreme actions, condemning any dissidents as traitors, and blessing the perpetrators.[18]

> A final twist was added when Serbian religious nationalists wrote that Slavic Muslims suffered from a "defective gene."[19] This theory was embraced by Biljana Plavšić, the former dean of the Faculty of Natural Science and Mathematics in Sarajevo and a member of the Bosnia-Herzegovina Academy of Arts and Sciences. Plavšić explained that it was useless to reason with Bosnian Muslims because it was "genetically deformed material" that embraced Islam and became further deformed through the centuries of Islamic behavior.[20]

Plavšić is representative of those former members of the urban intelligentsia who, within the period of a few months, had converted to a racialist ideology that breaks with every aspect of the academic ideals and standards of reason they had spent their lives professing.[21] The sudden conversion and subsequent acts of such people indicate the fragility of reason in the face of a resurgent and militant religious mythology. That Plavšić and her audience, many of whom were highly educated, could adopt such ideas cannot be explained, I would wager, without taking seriously the power of religio-mythic ideology (in this case Christoslavism) to offer a counterlogic that would justify the abandonment of lifelong commitments to science, human rights, and community in favor of a mass psychology of fear, hate, and domination.

Catholic Nationalism

The town of Stolac in Herzegovina was the site of pre-Roman and Roman ruins, one of the most impressive collections of medieval grave monuments from the period of the independent Bosnian church, and historical jewels of the Ottoman period. In 1993, after a combined force of Croat and Bosnian government forces had repelled the Serb army, the Croat nationalists turned on their Muslim allies and neighbors. Then members of the Catholic nationalist militia (the Croat Defense League or HVO) arrested the Muslims of Stolac, deported many of them, interned others in concentration camps, and killed those who resisted or who were thought to have leadership potential. HVO units annihilated the town's historical heritage, its four major mosques (including the Careva mosque, dating from 1519, the third oldest surviving mosque in BiH), and many smaller, local mosques. Even after the Dayton accords (a framework for peace in BiH initialed by the rival parties in Dayton, Ohio, in 1995), Catholic nationalists were destroying the Muslim graveyard, and the diocesan and Franciscan leaders of Herzegovina were blocking efforts to reconstruct the Careva mosque.

The Catholic Church in BiH includes both supporters of interreligious tolerance as well as ethnoreligious extremists. Among those who support a multireligious BiH are the leaders of the archdiocese of Sarajevo as well as many Franciscan friars from central Bosnia.[22] Franciscan and diocesan support for violent religious nationalism is centered in Herzegovina. Ratko Perić, the bishop of Mostar, has distinguished himself, in particular, for consistent policies and statements of violent religious intolerance. The Franciscans of Herzegovina have found a base of power in the lucrative pilgrimage center of Medjugorje, and they have been competing with Bishop Perić in efforts to show the most zealous Catholic nationalism and to support the illegal state of Catholic "Herceg-Bosna" cleansed of Muslims and Serbs.

The Medjugorje pilgrimage industry supplies the Catholic nationalists with economic and social support as well as a reverse-code ideology that contrasts radically with the more overt ideology of Serb Orthodox nationalism.[23] Since the 1981 announcement by six young Croatians that they had seen the Virgin Mary, more than 20 million pilgrims have journeyed from around the world to view the site of the vision. The pilgrims seek and sometimes claim visionary experiences. They meet either the visionaries or at least the Franciscan friars who manage the site and frame the religious experience of the pilgrims. And with overseas pilgrims paying as much as $2,500 for a tour package, they provide an enormous reservoir of capital.[24]

The message from the Virgin of Medjugorje focuses upon prayer and fasting. The Medjugorje publicity literature claims that the town was the only place in BiH to escape ethnoreligious strife during the 1992–1995 nightmare of "ethnic cleansing," having been preserved as a haven of love and tolerance by the Virgin of Peace herself. In the name of charity and compassion, Medjugorje-based charities have collected millions of dollars for orphans and other good causes. Many pilgrims (largely from the

United States, Ireland, Australia, and Northern Europe) return home from their experience with glowing tales of the profound and transformative spiritual peace they have encountered.

Yet the same Medjugorje of peace and brotherhood, allegedly preserved by the Virgin from war, served as an epicenter of ethnoreligious aggression in Herzegovina, and as the headquarters of particularly violent units of the Croat Defense Union (HDS) and their militias (HVO). At least five HDS-run concentration camps were set within only miles of the apparitions of Medjugorje, camps in which Muslim prisoners were starved, tortured, and murdered. In 1993 the HDS-controlled leadership decreed the expulsion of any Serb or Muslim still in the town (most had already been driven out of the area) and the dynamiting of the home of any Catholic shielding a Serb or Muslim. In the same year, an HVO expedition was launched from Medjugorje itself to attack the ancient Serb monastery of Zitomišlići. The monastery, which had no military protection or value, was seized, the priests and nuns were killed or driven out, and the ancient complex was burned to the ground.[25] Goods purchased with money donated for Medjugorje were funneled directly into HVO militia operations. The Franciscan friars running the Medjugorje pilgrimage center, which had become the beacon of peace and brotherhood for millions of Catholic pilgrims, operated, in effect, a major garrison and supply network for the HVO.

The diocesan leaders of Mostar have been no less militant, despite their feud with the Franciscans and their opposition to the Franciscan claims concerning Medjugorje.[26] Bishop Perić and his diocesan authority have disrupted efforts at interreligious reconciliation and have thwarted efforts to rebuild the historic Careva mosque in Stolac. Their opposition is based in part on the claim that the Careva mosque rests on the foundations of an ancient church. Claims of a prior religious site to oppose reconstruction of a destroyed site of worship are a common tactic of religious nationalists; militant Hindus have used the same logic first to burn down the sixteenth-century Ayodhya mosque in India and then to thwart all efforts to reconstruct it. Perić also supports the presence of the massive cross above Pocitelj erected by Catholic nationalists after they had cleansed the town of its non-Catholic population and destroyed the historic complex of Ottoman-era buildings that included a mosque, madrasah, baths, and other buildings.[27] A similar cross was placed on the tower of the ruins of the historic Žitomislići Serb monastery complex destroyed by the HVO in 1993. The diocese has snubbed international efforts at remembering the monastery's victims and reconstructing the site.[28] Yet another massive Latin cross stands on the hillside over Mostar, the formerly magnificent capital of Herzegovina that was subjected to a ruthless campaign of Catholic nationalist violence, ethnic cleansing, and systematic annihilation of the historical, sacral, and artistic, including the famous Old Bridge destroyed on November 9, 1993.[29] The cross was erected ostensibly as part of the "Jubilee Year" of 2000, but the consistent pattern shown by Herzegovinan Catholic nationalists above towns recently cleansed of non-Catholics suggests a deeper motive.[30]

The support of militant Catholic nationalism has turned up in other areas of BiH and Croatia. The *Iustitia et Pax* (Justice and Peace) commission of the Croatian Bishops charged that the International Criminal Tribunal in the Hague Tribunal was part of a plot against Croats, a charge that parallels perfectly the accusations by Serb Orthodox bishops that the tribunal is seeking to destroy Serbs.[31] During the violence that occurred from 1992 to 1995, the Vatican issued formal statements supporting a multireligious BiH, yet the Vatican's persistent refusal to demand that the Mostar clergy respect the papal pronouncements further heightens the contradiction between the Catholic rhetoric of peace and tolerance and the words and actions of the Catholic church leadership in Herzegovina.[32] Some would excuse the Vatican on the grounds that it cannot control the bishopric of Mostar. Yet the same Vatican leadership that had vigorously shut down liberation theologians and the bishops who supported them is hardly helpless in the face of specific systematic crimes against humanity and continued ethnoreligious extremism carried out in the name of Catholicism in direct contradiction to Vatican pronouncements, all occurring only forty minutes across the Adriatic in Mostar.

Islamic Nationalism

By the time the bloodshed was stopped in 1995, the vast majority of mosques in Bosnia-Herzegovina had been destroyed, as had Catholic churches in areas controlled by Serb Orthodox forces and Serbian Orthodox churches and monasteries in areas controlled by Catholic forces. Although the Bosnian army was guilty of war crimes, those crimes were not part of a systematic policy. Nor was there any Bosnian government policy to destroy Catholic or Serb Orthodox sites of worship; most churches remained intact throughout the war in areas controlled by the Bosnian army.

Long after the Dayton accords ending the fighting, Sarajevans woke up to find that the magnificent interior of sixteenth-century Begova Džamija (the mosque of Ghazi Husrev Beg), one of the few remaining historic and architectural treasures to survive the attacks by religious nationalists, had been gutted. The vandals in this case were not the Serb and Croat militiamen who had destroyed Islamic heritage in areas under their control, although the Serb army had inflicted damage to the exterior of the great mosque through carefully targeted shelling. Those who damaged the masterwork of Bosnian national and Islamic religious heritage were themselves Muslim, acting with the advice and financial support of the Saudi High Commission for aid to BiH.[33]

This last wave of religious and cultural violence epitomizes the topsyturvy version of Islamic nationalism now confronting Bosnia, a "nationalism" directed and imposed from outside the country. Although Serb and Croat nationalists and their supporters in Europe and the United States had depicted Bosnian Muslims (the Bosnjaks) as militant Islamists, their assault on Bosnia, allegedly to save Bosnia from Islamic fundamentalism, made the Bosnjak community more vulnerable to pressures to adopt fundamentalism than they had been before.

Years earlier, as the repression of religion under the Tito regime had weakened, Catholic, Serb Orthodox, and Muslim communities began to assert themselves. Alija Izetbegović, who later became president of the independent BiH, issued an Islamic Manifesto that praised Islamic *shari'a* (law) as an alternative to the Cold War ideologies of capitalism and communism, especially the communism that had repressed religion in Yugoslavia for the past fifty years. Decades later, the Manifesto became the principle pretext for violent opposition to the Bosnian government led by Izetbegović, despite the very limited readership and influence of the document and despite Izetbegović's later writings advocating multireligious civic democracy. Izetbegović's stubborn refusal to renounce the Manifesto encouraged and emboldened the attacks on Bosnia and on Bosnjaks.

Bosnjak attainment of the status of "nationality" within the Yugoslav system offered a second pretext for the assault on BiH. Within Tito's Yugoslavia, rights and privileges had been distributed in part according to group population totals. In the census, citizens had to declare themselves as one of the recognized nationalities (Serb, Croat, Albanian, Slovene, and Macedonian) or choose the option of declaring themselves as "Yugoslavs." The Muslims of Bosnia had been left with a choice of swelling either the Serb or the Croat political block or declaring themselves Yugoslavs and, in effect, losing all distributive rights within the system. Croat and Serb nationalists claimed the Slavic Muslims as deviant Croats or deviant Serbs, respectively, and worked to bolster their block power with Muslims declaring Croat or Serb nationality. By 1986 the Bosnjaks achieved recognition as a "nationality," leading to charges that they were seeking an independent, Islamic state. The Bosnjaks had been caught in a dilemma: continued status as second-class citizens within a system based upon ethnoreligious nationalities or recognition as a nationality that would make it all the easier for Croat and Serb nationalists to declare them an alien element.

Allegations that Bosnjaks were allied with radical Arab and Islamic regimes offered a third pretext. During the Cold War, when Marshal Tito and Libya's Muammar Qaddafi were championing the Third World or nonaligned movement, many Yugoslavs, including Bosnian intellectuals such as Haris Silajdžic, who in 1994 would become prime minister of BiH, had studied in nonaligned nations such as Libya. Despite Silajdžic's unequivocal position in support of a multireligious, civic democracy in BiH, past stays in Libya offered Catholic and Orthodox nationalists the opportunity to stoke fears of radical, Qaddafi-style Bosnjaks. Ironically, Libya and Iraq not only did not support Bosnia during the genocide from 1992 to 1995; they were, in fact, the world's most faithful allies of Serbian President Slobodan Milošević. The Yugoslav government-dominated press bristled with indictments of Bosnjaks, Libyan agents, and Iraqi-sponsored terrorists; at the same time, the official Yugoslavia news agency Tanjug was publishing effusive reports on the close brotherhood and co-operation between such rogue states and Milošević's Yugoslavia.[34]

Although the fall of communism had led to some revival of piety and a religious sense of identity among a minority of Bosnjaks, there was almost no ethnoreligious nationalism among either the majority of largely secularized Muslims or the religiously observant minority. With powerful Croat and Serb states as neighbors, Bosnjaks were caught in a trap. After Croatia seceded, Croat nationalists demanded that Bosnjaks side with Croatia and support the secession of BiH from Yugoslavia. Many Bosnian Serbs feared that an independent BiH in alignment would bring back the Ustashe horrors of World War II. As these fears were inflamed by both Croat extremists and Serb nationalist manipulation of World War II history, many Serbs demanded that Bosnjaks work to keep Bosnia a part of Yugoslavia and fight with Serb-dominated rump Yugoslavia against Croatia. European and American negotiators and columnists blamed the Bosnjaks for voting for an independent BiH and held them responsible for the genocide they suffered after independence. Yet those making the accusation offer no viable vision to the quandary in which the Bosnian Muslims found themselves. Voting to secede led to a genocidal assault by Serb nationalists. Voting to remain part of Yugoslavia would have triggered an attack by Croat nationalists and, for those in areas not taken by Croat armies, a fragile existence as a hated minority in a Yugoslavia controlled by virulently Islamophobic Orthodox nationalists.

Shortly after Bosnia's independence in April 1992, the Bosnian Muslim population found itself under assault from Orthodox nationalists and, within months, from Catholic nationalists who had tacitly allied themselves with Serbia. In 1992, Croatia and Serbia agreed to partition Bosnia between them, leaving Muslims concentrated in a few urban ghettos. By 1993 the Bosnian Muslim population was on the edge of extinction; indeed, had Sarajevo or Tuzla fallen, the mass killing that occurred in Srebrenica would have occurred with far greater numbers killed.

The refusal of the world community to lift the arms embargo to allow the Bosnian Muslims to defend themselves or to come to their aid came as a stunning betrayal to the Bosnjaks and to the Serbs and Croats who joined them in supporting a multireligious independent state. This state of shock was exploited by well-funded, outside missionary groups from the Arabian Gulf who provided desperate Bosnians with humanitarian aid and, in the case of Iran, desperately needed arms. In some cases, Bosnjaks were denied food and medicine if they did not dress in accordance with the taste of Saudi or Kuwait aid groups. By 1994 some factions within the Bosnian government and ruling party (the SDA) had abandoned hope of a multireligious state and were ready to accept United Nations and Western pressure for religious-based partition that would result in an Islamic state confined to a small portion of the BiH territory.

After the bloodshed ended, the attempt by outside groups to radicalize Bosnjaks had caused a backlash. But Saudi and other Gulf aid groups were able, even so, to exploit the desperation of a shattered Bosnia with promises of financial aid for hospitals, schools, water, and infrastructure. The precondition was that the local Islamic community cede control to aid groups such as the Saudi High Commission. These groups, dominated by a Saudi Wahhabi Islam that holds in contempt Ottoman and

Bosnian cultural heritage (in part because it is accepting of non-Muslims), began their program. Mosques, libraries, religious schools, tombs, and other monuments that had managed to survive the Catholic and Orthodox programs of annihilation were suddenly threatened by Islamic aid groups from outside BiH and a small group of their Bosnian supporters.[35]

Epilogue: Sacred Architecture, Desecration, and Domination

The same Saudi commission that financed the lamented work on Sarajevo's Begova Mosque also backed the construction of the massive King Fahd mosque complex. The King Fahd mosque is everything the Begova is not: cold, artistically sterile, and massively out-of-scale in relation to the rest of the city, both its civic architecture and its churches, synagogues, and other mosques. It is meant to project power. Similarly, the Saudi-financed mosque the commission constructed in the Kosovo town of Rahovec (Orahovac)—after a Saudi-financed group dynamited the town's historic central mosque—towers above the Sufi *tekkes* (lodges) across the street as a symbol of domination over the local Islamic community.

In the heart of west Mostar, a similarly massive Franciscan priory church has risen, grotesquely out of scale with the rest of the city. Its towering campanile is visible from each street, alleyway, and vista of a west Mostar still largely cleansed of its former Muslim and Serb population and in a state of economic despair. The church is financed by the Medjugorje pilgrimage trade, the spoils of ethnic cleansing, and the same Croat nationalist expatriates—in Australia and the Americas—who financed the original program of ethnoreligious violence carried out by former Croat president Franjo Tudjman and his allies in Mostar.[36]

The mother of all these projects of religious nationalism is the massive cathedral of St. Sava in Belgrade, built in imitation of the Hagia Sophia in Istanbul that was lost to Christianity in 1453. The cathedral was financed by nationalist Serb expatriates from the same countries as the Croat expatriate communities. The project and the fund drive were tied to the emotionally charged preparations for the 1989 600th anniversary of the death of Lazar. The same Serbian religious publications that pleaded for more contributions stoked Orthodox nationalism with false charges of genocide against Serbs in Kosovo and manipulation of World War II history and the Lazar story. The cathedral is named for the patron saint of the ideology of "Saint-Savaism" that is based upon the call for a greater Serbia, purified of non-Serbs and dominated by the Serb Orthodox religious establishment.

This chapter has traced the interplay of ethnic cleansing with annihilation of religious monuments. Another essay could be written tracing the construction of a very different kind of religious monument. This new monument is the out-of-scale church or mosque towering over the city and over its impoverished inhabitants as a symbol of power and exclusivity. It also towers over the ruins of the small, in-scale, sacral sites that encouraged diversity within traditions, communication among traditions, a shared visual landscape, and a shared sense of civilizational identity. The building of the power-church or the power-mosque also becomes the pretext for an international campaign that finances, motivates, and justifies attacks on local Bosnian expressions of religion and upon any empathetic interaction among peoples of differing religious affiliations. The attack on Bosnia was and is based upon the pretext that Bosnia is a country of "age-old hatreds," of a "clash of civilizations." In fact, Bosnia was, despite the very real conflicts and hatreds of the past, a civilization distinctive in its subtle textures of multireligious and interreligious life.

Yet forces acting toward a clash of civilizations, what we might call forces of globalized nationalism, were central to the effort to annihilate Bosnia and replace it with the world of religious apartheid and conflict that the cliché of age-old hatreds implied had been there all along. In all three cases, major religious leaders were complicit in the violence. Those same leaders have yet to be held morally accountable by their own flocks or by the larger international community.

NOTES

1. See András Riedlmayer, "Killing Memory: The Targeting of Libraries and Archives in Bosnia-Herzegovina," *MELA Notes: Newsletter of the Middle East Librarians Association* 61 (Fall 1994): 3; András Riedlmayer, *Killing Memory: Bosnia's Cultural Heritage and Its Destruction* (Haverford: Community of Bosnia Foundation, 1994), videocassette; Amir Pašić, *Islamic Architecture in Bosnia and Hercegovina* (Istanbul: Research Centre for Islamic History, Art, and Culture, 1994); and Michael Sells, Balkan Human Rights and War Crimes Page at: http://www.haverford.edu/relg/sells/reports.html.

2. For an illustrated history of the "ethnic cleansing" of Foča see the Foča page at http://www.haverford.edu/relg/sells/reports.html (hereafter referred to as

"reports.html". The page includes the historic International Tribunal indictment for torture, rape, and sexual enslavement of Bosnian Muslim women, the "Gagovic indictment," the first indictment for rape as a crime against humanity ever issued by an international tribunal, and other documentation.

3. Vojislav Maksimović, "Podseca na robovanje" (It is Remindful of Slavery), *Evropske Novosti*, 27 January 1994, 18, cited and translated by Norman Cigar, *Genocide in Bosnia: The Policy of "Ethnic Cleansing"* (College Station: Texas A&M Press, 1995), 61. For the role of Maksimović at Foča, see Roy Gutman, *A Witness to Genocide: The 1993 Pulitzer-Prize Winning Dispatches on the "Ethnic Cleansing" of Bosnia* (New York: Macmillan, 1993), 157–63; cf. BBC broadcast, 7 January 1994, from the Belgrade Newspaper *Borba*, 5 January 1994, "Foča Becomes Srebinje"; BBC, 3 October 1994, "Serbian Orthodox Patriarch Meets Karadzicon Tour of Bosnian Serb Republic," based on the Yugolsav Telegraph Service news agency, Belgrade, 30 September 1994; Inter Press Service, 13 January 1995; for the term "Srbinje" during expulsions, see the *Cleveland Plain Dealer*, 2 April 1995.

4. See the account in the *Cleveland Plain Dealer*, 2 April 1995. Similarly, when asked about the mosques of the town of Zvornik, all dynamited by Serb nationalists in 1992, the town's new Serb mayor denied that they had ever existed. Carol Williams, *New York Times*, 28 March 1993; and Roger Cohen, "In a Town 'Cleansed' of Muslims, Serb Church Will Crown the Deed," *New York Times*, 7 March 1994.

5. Below, I offer basic documentation for the sections below on Serb and Catholic nationalism. For fuller documentation, see Michael Sells, *The Bridge Betrayed: Religion and Genocide in Bosnia* (Berkeley: University of California Press, 1998), and Michael Sells, Balkan Human Rights and War Crimes Page (cited above, n. 1).

6. After the slaughter, the Orthodox bishop insists that the warriors take the eucharist without going to confession. In traditional Montenegrin Christianity, confession was mandatory after any killing, even if the killing was considered justified. By insisting on communion without confession, the bishop marks the inherently sanctifying quality of these particular acts of extermination.

7. See Ivo Andrić, *The Bridge on the Drina*, translated from the Serbo-Croatian by Lovett F. Edwards (New York: Macmillan, 1959; Chicago: University of Chicago Press, 1977), from *Na Drini cuprija*. See also Ivo Andrić, *The Development of Spiritual Life*, cited above, passim. For specific examples of how Andric builds the theme of the "stealing of Serb" blood into *The Bridge on the Drina*, see Sells, *The Bridge Betrayed*, 45–50.

8. Professor Miroljub Jevtić, for example, a specialist on Middle Eastern studies at the University of Belgrade, propounded the theory that contemporary Slavic Muslims still have on their hands the blood of the Serbian martyrs who died five hundred years ago. See H. T. Norris, *Islam in the Balkans* (Columbia: University of South Carolina Press, 1993), 295–98; and Cigar, *Genocide in Bosnia*,

29. Of *The Mountain Wreath* itself, one enthusiast stated the poem was "resurrected" on Vidovdan 1989. See Pavle Zorić in *Kosovo 1989*, 79. *The Mountain Wreath* was memorized by many of the militia members committing atrocities, militiamen who decorated themselves with medals named after heroes from the Kosovo story and the Njegoš tradition.

9. See Sava Peić, *Medieval Serbian Culture* (London: Alpine Fine Arts Collection, UK, 1994). See also the collection of essays, sumptuously illustrated: *Kosovo*, compiled and produced by William Dorich, edited by Basil Jenkins (Alhambra, CA; Kosovo Charity Fund '92 of the Serbian Orthodox Diocese of Western America, 1992).

10. "It is no exaggeration to say that planned GENOCIDE [emphasis in original] is being perpetrated against the Serbian people in Kosovo! What otherwise would be the meaning of 'ethnically pure Kosovo' which is being relentlessly put into effect through ceaseless and never-ending migrations." Appeal by the Clergy in Gordana Filipović, *Kosovo: Past and Present* (Belgrade: Review of International Affairs, 1989), 355–60. The Serbian Church claims of genocide in Kosovo continued in 1987 and 1988; see ibid., 360–63, and the *American Srbobran*, 2 November 1988.

11. Amnesty International, *Yugoslavia: Ethnic Albanian Victims of Torture and Ill-treatment by Police* (New York: Amnesty International, 1992). Cf. Helsinki Watch reports on Kosovo for the years *Helsinki Watch* 1986, 1989, and 1990; and see Branka Magaš, *The Destruction of Yugoslavia: Tracking the Break-up, 1980–92* (London: Verso, 1993), 49–73.

12. "Memorandum on the Position of Serbia in Yugoslavia" (Belgrade, 1986). The document was authored by members of the Serbian Academy of Sciences and Arts, but the names were not made public. The Manifesto was never published, but leaked to the nationalists in the media.

13. Muharem Durić and Mirko Carić, "Kako srpski nacionalisti odmazu srpskom narodu i sta prati kosti kneza Lazara" (How Serbian Nationalists Are Avenging the Serbian People and What Accompanies the Relics of Prince Lazar), *Politika*, 17 September 1988, 7. Cited and translated by Cigar, *Genocide in Bosnia*, 35. Cf. Milan Milošević and Velizar Brajovićc in *Vreme* 145 4 July 1994: "At about the same time the Serbian Orthodox Church carried the relics of Grand Duke Lazar (the leader of the Kosovo battle) around the Serb lands and religious services were held over the remains of the victims of genocide of a half a century ago that were retrieved from mass graves for that purpose."

14. For a thorough discussion of the role of Serbian intellectuals in developing a mass psychology of hate and fear in the years leading up to 1989, see Norman Cigar, "The Nationalist Serbian Intellectuals and Islam: Defining and Eliminating a Muslim Community," in Emran Qureshi and Michael Sells, eds., *The New Crusades? Constructing the Muslim Enemy* (New York: Columbia University Press, 2003).

15. The groups behind the program of "ethnic cleansing" had developed and refined its techniques during the war with Croatia that preceded the genocide in Bosnia, particularly in and around the city of Vukovar. For a good account of the Bosnian tragedy in the wider context of the Yugoslav wars, see the video series *Yugoslavia, Death of a Nation* (BBC/Discovery, 1995) and the accompanying book, Laura Silber and Allan Little, *Yugoslavia: Death of a Nation* (New York: TV Books, 1995). For a discussion of the use of the media to stir up fear and hatred, see Mark Thompson, *Forging War: The Media in Serbia, Croatia, and Bosnia-Hercegovina* (Avon, UK: Bath Press and Article 19 International Centre Against Censorship, 1994). According to the Serbian dissident magazine *Vreme,* more than forty major militia groups were operating from Serbia. None of this could have occurred without the cooperation of the Yugoslav secret police and the Yugoslav army.

16. See U.S. Department of State, "War Crimes in the Former Yugoslavia: Submission of Information to the United States Security Council in Accordance with Paragraph 5 of Resolution 771 (1992)," *U.S. Department of State Dispatch,* 4th report, 9 May 1992 (incident no. 12). For other examples, see Cigar, *Genocide in Bosnia,* 84.

17. The standard tactic, as observed by UN observers who were on the spot but not allowed to intervene, was to broadcast to the Serb villagers that Muslims were preparing a massacre. The villagers would then be told to leave the village before it was surrounded, shelled, and overtaken by the Serbian army and militias, after which the organized atrocities would begin. Among the major militia figures, several had three bases of support: organized crime, the Serbian bishops, and the Milošević controlled secret police. Arkan, who claims credit for beginning the "ethnic cleansing" of Bosnia with his attack on Muslim civilians in the eastern town of Bijeljina in March 1992, was a clear beneficiary of this threefold support. In 1994, Arkan was married to a Serbian folk-pop singer in one of the most extraordinary public events in Serbia since the 1989 Vidovdan celebration. Serbian Orthodox bishops journeyed from Croatia and Bosnia (including areas where Arkan's men had carried out organized atrocities) to preside over a fully mythologized wedding, with Arkan dressed up as a Serbian hero from the Lazar and post-Lazar revolutionary tradition, and his bride dressed up as the Maiden of Kosovo, the Mary Magdalene figure who in legend had ministered to the fallen and dying Serb soldiers.

One of the most fervent supporters of Arkan was Orthodox bishop Vasilije of the Tuzla-Zvornik region, just as one of the areas of the most widespread killings, organized rape, and torture had been the town of Zvornik. See the three articles in *Vreme* 178 (27 February 1995): Alexander Cirić, "Turbo Land: Machine Gun Wedding (with Singing)"; Dejan Anastasijević, "Zeljko Raznjatović Arkan: The Groom," and idem, "Ceca Veliković: The Bride." See also Roger Cohen, "Serbia

Dazzles Itself: Terror Suspect Weds Singer," *New York Times,* 20 February 1995; and John Kifner, "An Outlaw in the Balkans Is Basking in the Spotlight," *New York Times,* 23 November 1993. For the most thorough war-crimes report on the "ethnic cleansing" of Zvornik, see Hannes Tretter et al., "Ethnic Cleansing Operations in the North-east Bosnian City of Zvornik from April through June 1992," 1994. This report was carried out at the suggestion of the commission of experts established pursuant to Security Council Resolution 780 (1992). In the Final Report of the Commission (UN Doc. S/1994/674) the report of Tretter et al. was cited as an exemplary study on "ethnic cleansing" and published as an annex (UN Doc. S/1994/674/add.2 [vol.I], December 1994), available on-line at www.haverford .edu/relg/sells/reports.html.

This was a near-term extension of the longer-term pattern seen in Kosovo in the 1980s where Serbian religious nationalist charges of "ethnic cleansing" led to actual ethnic cleansing in Bosnia three years later. See the eyewitness testimony of UNHCR official José María Mendiluce, *Vreme,* 26 December 1994. A particularly grim example of such reality reversal was the charges by Bosnian Serb newspapers and radio stations that Muslims were planning a fourfold crime against the Serbian woman: to remove her from her own family, impregnate her by undesirable [Islamic] seeds, to make her bear a stranger and then take him away from her." Roy Gutman, *Witness to Genocide* (New York: Macmillan, 1993), x. Cf. Vamik Volkan, *Blood Lines: From Ethnic Pride to Ethnic Terrorism* (New York: Farrar, Straus and Giroux, 1997), 75–80. These claims, which played upon the Serbian nationalist preoccupation with the Ottoman *devshirme* system as a "stealing of Serb blood," were followed by the commission of this precise program by Serb militiamen against Bosnian Muslim women.

18. As was the case in Brčko, a center of some of the worst genocidal campaigns of 1992, which included killing centers, makeshift body disposal operations, and a concentration camp run by Goran Jelišić, who has been indicted for genocide by the International Tribunal in The Hague and who proudly calls himself the "Serb Adolf." During and after the atrocities, Serbian Orthodox clergy, such as Episkop Slavko Maksimović of Brčko, denied any campaign against the non-Serb population and actually maintained (despite overwhelming evidence to the contrary) that it was the Muslims who attacked the Serbs. For the details of the genocide indictment against Goran Jelišić for crimes at Brčko, see http://www.haverford.edu/relg/sells/reports.html. For a recent account of the "ethnic cleansing" of Brčko, based on evidence from excavations of mass graves, see Scott Peterson, "The Town Where Truth Is a Victim of Ethnic Hatred," *Daily Telegraph,* 23 January 1996), 11. Peterson writes:

The "cleansing" of Brčko began in the town's Serb Orthodox Church, several weeks before the Serb onslaught. Witnesses say meetings were held at night and street lights were turned out to protect identities. Serb paramilitary groups also began forming. A Muslim refugee said: "We all knew that Serb guys were going to Serb villages for training."

In the same article, Serb Orthodox Episkop Maksimović is quoted as claiming that "the Muslims started leaving, destroying everything they were leaving behind. The Serbs didn't leave this town because they felt they were here in their homeland, in the land of their fathers. So many people were killed here because the Muslims withdrew to the suburbs from where they shelled the town." Cf. Sonia Bakarić, "NATO Troops Arrest Bosnia's Self-styled 'Serb Adolf,'" AAP Information Services Pty. Ltd., 22 January 1998. Serbian Orthodox bishop Atanasije wrote that Slavic Muslims were part of a chain of primitivism. See Atanasije Jevtić, in the Serbian Orthodox Church publication *Glas Crkve,* cited by Cigar, *Genocide in Bosnia,* 31–32.

19. Serbian religious nationalist Dragoš Kalajić was one of the proponents of this theory. Kalajić was a mentor for the militia known as the "White Eagles" *(beli orlovi)* associated with some of the most inhuman atrocities in Bosnia. See Dragoš Kalajić, "Kvazi Arapi protiv Evropljana" (Semi-Arabs versus Europeans), *Duga,* 13–19 September 1987, 14–15, translated and cited by Cigar in *Genocide in Bosnia,* 26. For the genetically caused flaws supposedly resulting from this "special gene" of Ottoman soldiery, see Cigar, *Genocide in Bosnia,* 26–27.

20. Biljana Plavšić, *Svet* (Novi Sad), September 1993, cited and translated by Slobodan Inić, "Biljana Plavšić: Geneticist in the Service of a Great Crime," *Bosnia Report: Newsletter of the Alliance to Defend Bosnia-Herzegovina* 19 (June/August 1997), translated from *Helsinska povelja* (Helsinki Charter), Belgrade, November 1996. After leaving her position in Sarajevo and joining the Serb Democratic Party (SDS) of Radovan Karadñć, which had embraced the program of "ethnic cleansing," Plavšić began writing about the "genetically deformed" element in Bosnian Muslims.

21. This was the group that led the deliberate attack on the cultural infrastructure of Sarajevo and directed the Serbian army in its burning of the National and University Library in Sarajevo (with more than a million books and 100,000 rare books and manuscripts destroyed); in its annihilation of the Oriental Institute of Sarajevo, with its priceless collection of manuscripts in Ottoman, Persian, Arabic, Bosnian Slavic, and Bosnian Aljamiado (Slavic in Arabic script) and other languages; and in its shelling of the National Museum of Sarajevo. A number of their own former students were killed as they retrieved cultural treasures during the midst of these attacks by the Serbian army. Other members of the academic elite in Bosnia who joined the Serbian Christoslavic movement include Nikola Koljević, former professor of English and noted Shakespeare scholar; Aleksa Buha, former professor of philosophy; Radovan Karadžić, psychi-

atrist and poet; and Vojislav Maksimović, former professor of Marxism and a major suspect in the annihilation of the Muslim community in Foča and the "ethnic cleansing" of the University of Banja Luka. All these academicians lived and practiced in Sarajevo. The psychoanalytic parallel to Plavsić's theory of genetic deformation was the theory held by Jovan Rašković, the mentor of Dr. Radovan Karadžić, who maintained that Muslim use of ablutions before prayer indicated the "anal analytic" nature of Muslims as a people. See C. Bennett, *Yugoslavia's Bloody Collapse: Causes, Course, and Consequences* (New York: New York University Press, 1995), 126–29.

22. The bishop of Sarajevo, Vinko Cardinal Puljić, was distinguished by a persistent refusal to support the religious wars advocated by former Croatian president Franjo Tudjman and his HDZ party. Puljić has formed a series of internationally compelling statements and symbolic gestures in support of interreligious understanding. Franciscans in Sarajevo and in the central town of Fojnica showed special courage in resisting calls for religious war and apartheid.

23. The pilgrimage center grew up in the midst of feuds between the Franciscans and the bishopric of Mostar over several disputed, Franciscan-controlled parishes. The appearance of the Virgin has been neither affirmed nor denied by the Vatican, despite the efforts of one bishop of Mostar to have it denounced as a fraud. Among the early statements from the Blessed Virgin was an expression of the Madonna's support for two Franciscans in the dispute with the bishop. Soon thereafter, the overt political messages ended.

24. By conservative estimate, the international pilgrim spends a thousand dollars or more for the pilgrimage. The Franciscans in Medjugorje have refused to publish financial accountings of their lucrative pilgrimage industry. Nor did Bishop Ratko Perić's predecessor fare much better when he defied the Herzegovina Franciscans and their supporters. At one point during his quarrel with the Franciscans, he was picked up by some Franciscan-sympathetic HVO units, held captive, and ritually defrocked, having the buttons of his cassock ripped off one by one like a military uniform being stripped of its medals.

25. The expedition consultant was a historian of art from the Herzegovinan town of Stolac who was able to guide the militias to the artistically and historically priceless objects and monuments and make sure they were thoroughly destroyed.

26. For the controversy over efforts to reconstruct the mosque, see http://www.ohr.int/roundup/bih010827.htm. BiH Media Round-up, 27 August 2001, "Disputable Commencement of the Reconstruction of Stolac Mosque—Archeology in the Service of Reconciliation or New Tensions."

27. The complex was masterfully designed and placed in striking relationship one to another in a kind of vertiginous descent toward the river. During the Tito years, Počitelj had become home to an artist colony and a center of interreligious culture. In 1993, units of the HVO (Croat defense union), the militia of

the governing HDS party in Croatia, descended upon the town (which was unde-fended and without military significance).

28. See the 9 April 2002 Radio Doboj News report, as transmitted in *Tuzla Night Owl* on 10 April 2002. The report describes the visit of Wolfgang Petritsch to Žitomislići and the regret expressed by Orthodox bishop Grigorje that "no high dignitaries or priests of the Catholic Church were at the ruins of the Zito-mislici Monastery." See http://www.tfeagle.army.mil/tfeno/Feature_Story.asp?Ar-ticle=28900.

29. See Mirsad Behram, "Giant Cross Dominating the City Is Perceived as Provocation by non-Catholics," AP, 4 July 2000. According to the Behram article, Bishop Ratko Perić has refused to respond to inquiries about the cross or make himself available to reporters.

30. See Mile Stogie's editorial, "Cross and Rage," in the Croat newspaper *Feral Tribune* (Split), 15 January 2002, translated in OHR (Office of the High Commis-sioner), BiH Media Round-up, 15 January 2002.

31. See the report "ICTY Spokeswoman Criticizes Croatia's Catholic Church," Zagreb, 26 July 2001 (Agence France-Presse), for an account of the con-troversy. She said the church's "political declaration" was jeopardizing Croatia's political reputation.

32. See the Catholic Church, *Assisi 1993: Giovanni Paolo II per la pace in Bosnia ed Erzegovina* (Citta del Vaticano: Libreria Editrice Vaticana, 1993). Earlier Vatican documents did focus on the death and destruction suffered by Catholic Croats, especially in Dubrovnik, while still wishing peace for all parties. See *La Crisi Jugoslava: Posizione e azione della Santa Sede* (1991–1992) (Libreria Editrice Vaticana: Libreria Editrice Vaticana, 1992).

33. See Michael A. Sells, "The Begova Džamija Restoration: An Illustrated Re-port," posted at http://www.haverford.edu/relg/sells/reports.html; and Omar Denison, "The New Idolatry," in *Q-News*, no. 30 (April 2001): 33.

34. Libya, Iraq, and Serbia were all considered pariah nations and subjected to embargoes, giving them a sense of solidarity, and all three had major interests in criminal arms and oil-smuggling enterprises.

35. See Mone Slingerland, "Fight over Ruins: The Struggle for the Heritage of Kosovo," *Het Parool* (Amsterdam), 24 December 2001, English translation by Kate Kruize-O'Neill, published on "Domovina Net," 14 February 2002 at http://www.domovina.net/fightoverruins.html.

36. Croats opposed to the religious nationalism dominating Herzegovina have taken some satisfaction in the fact that the hubristic size of the campanile, combined with crude engineering, led to a leaning of the tower and the inability to complete its construction.

SUGGESTIONS FOR FURTHER READING

Buturovic, Amila and Francis Jones. *Stone Speaker: Medieval Tombs, Landscape, and Bosnian Identity in the Poetry Of Mak Dizdar.* New York: Palgrave, 2002.

Cigar, Norman. *Genocide in Bosnia: The Policy of Ethnic Cleansing.* College Station: Texas A&M University Press, 1995.

Lovrenovic, Ivan. *Bosnia: A Cultural History.* New York: New York University Press, 2001.

Rohde, David. *Endgame: The Betrayal and Fall of Srebrenica, Europe's Worst Massacre since World War II.* New York: Farrar, Straus and Giroux, 1997.

Sells, Michael. *The Bridge Betrayed: Religion and Genocide in Bosnia.* Berkeley: University of California Press, 1996.

Vulliamy, Ed. *Seasons in Hell.* New York: St. Martin's Press, 1994.

Silber, Laura. *Yugoslavia: Death of a Nation.* New York: Penguin, 1995.

About the Contributors

DOUGLAS E. COWAN is Assistant Professor of Religious Studies and Sociology at the University of Missouri—Kansas City. Among other works, he is the author of *Bearing False Witness? An Introduction to the Christian Countercult* and *The Remnant Spirit: Conservative Reform Movements in Mainline Protestantism*, both published by Praeger Publishers.

EDDIE S. GLAUDE, JR., is Associate Professor of Religion at Princeton University. He is author of *Exodus! Religion, Race, and Nation in Early 19th Century Black American* (University of Chicago Press, 2000); editor of *Is It Nation Time! Contemporary Essays on Black Power and Black Nationalism* (University of Chicago Press, 2002); and co-editor with Cornel West of *African American Religious Studies: An Anthology* (Westminster/John Knox, 2003).

ROBERTO S. GOIZUETA is Professor of Theology at Boston College. His book, *Caminemos con Jesús: Toward a Hispanic/Latino Theology of Accompaniment* (Orbis, 1995), received a Catholic Press Association Book Award. He has served as president of the Academy of Catholic Hispanic Theologians of the United States, and as associate editor of the *Journal of Hispanic/Latino Theology*.

PAUL HARVEY is Associate Professor of History at the University of Colorado at Colorado Springs, and author of *Redeeming the South: Religious Cultures and Racial Identities among Southern Baptists, 1865–1925* (University of North Carolina Press, 1997).

NimacHIa HERNANDEZ is Assistant Professor of Native American Studies at the University of California at Berkeley. Her dissertation, "Mokakssini: A Blackfoot Theory of Knowledge," investigates the intersection of cosmology and the practice of knowledge. She is the recipient of numerous fellowships, including a Fulbright and a Smithsonian, and is finishing a book on gender, the sacred, and Native cosmology.

CHIREVO V. KWENDA is Chair of the Department of Religious Studies and Senior Lecturer at the University of Cape Town, South Africa. He has co-authored *African Traditional Religion in South Africa: An Annotated Bibliography* (Greenwood, 1997) and *African Religion and Culture Alive* (Collegium, 1997), as well as articles in scholarly journals and chapters in edited books.

JOEL MARTIN is the first permanent holder of the Rupert Costo Endowed Chair in American Indian History at the University of California, Riverside, and author of *Sacred Revolt: The Muskogees' Struggle for a New World* (Beacon, 1991), *The Land Looks After Us: A History of Native American Religion* (Oxford University Press, 2001), and other publications.

AMINAH BEVERLY McCLOUD is Associate Professor of Islamic Studies in the Department of Religious Studies at DePaul University. She is the author of *African American Islam* (Routledge, 1995) and is currently working on *The Religion and Philosophy of the Nation of Islam* and *American Muslim Women*. She is the managing editor of *The Journal of Islamic Law and Culture* and has received grants for her work from the Ford Foundation, Illinois Humanities Council, Graham Architectural Foundation, and the Lilly Foundation.

JOHN K. NELSON is an Assistant Professor of East Asian religions in the Department of Theology and Religious Studies, University of San Francisco. He is the author of *A Year in the Life of a Shinto Shrine* (University of Washington, 1996) and *Enduring Identities: The Guise of Shinto in Contemporary Japan* (University of Hawaii, 2000), numerous articles, and has produced two short documentary videos, "Japan's Rituals of Renewal" (1988) and "Japan's Rituals of Remembrance: 50 Years after the Pacific War" (1997).

JACOB NEUSNER is Research Professor of Religion and Theology and Senior Fellow of the Institute of Advanced Theology at Bard College. He is also a Member of the Institute for Advanced Study, Princeton, N.J., and a Life Member of Clare Hall, Cambridge University, in England. He has published more than 850 books and unnumbered articles, both scholarly and academic and popular and journalistic, and is the most published humanities scholar in the world. In addition to numerous awards, fellowships, and honorary degrees, he is editor of *Academic Studies in the History of Judaism, Academic Studies on Religion and the Social Order,* and *International Studies in Formative Christianity and Judaism,* all at Global Publications, and is editor of the *Encyclopaedia of Judaism* (Brill, 1999, I–III) and its supplements.

LAURIE L. PATTON is Associate Professor and Chair of the Department of Religion at Emory University. She has recently edited *Jewels of Authority: Women and Text in the Hindu Tradition* (Oxford University Press) and is co-editing with Edwin Bryant, *The Indo-Aryan Controversy: Evidence and Evocation* (Curzon Press). She is presently completing her second authored book on the use of poetry in Vedic ritual, *Bringing the Gods to Mind* (University of California Press), and her book of poetry, *Fire's Goal: Poems from a Hindu Year,* is forthcoming from White Clouds Press.

CRAIG R. PRENTISS is Assistant Professor of Religious Studies at Rockhurst University in Kansas City, Missouri. He is a historian of American religion and received his doctorate from the University of Chicago in 1997. His research and publications have focused on the role of myth in economic thought as well as myth's role in racial imagination.

MICHAEL A. SELLS is Professor of Religion at Haverford College. His 1996 book, *The Bridge Betrayed: Religion and Genocide in Bosnia* (University of California Press), received the American Academy of Religion award for excellence in historical studies. He is also co-editor and contributor to the forthcoming *The New Crusades: Constructing the Muslim Enemy.* He is also a founder and director of the nonprofit "Community of Bosnia," which supports an interreligious and democratic Bosnia-Herzegovina and resists "ethnic cleansing" and religious apartheid in the Balkans.

AZZAM TAMIMI is Senior Lecturer at the Markfield Institute of Higher Education in Leicestershire, U.K., and director of the Institute of Islamic Political Thought, London. His most recent English publications include *Rachid Ghannouchi, a Democrat within Islamism* (Oxford University Press, 2001), and *Islam and Secularism in the Middle East,* co-edited with John Esposito (Hurst and New York University Press, 2000).

Index